EMBASSIES
IN
CRISIS

•

Diplomats
and Demagogues
Behind the Six-Day War

BY MICHAEL BAR-ZOHAR

Translated from the French by Monroe Stearns

PRENTICE-HALL, INC.
ENGLEWOOD CLIFFS, NEW JERSEY

Books by Michael Bar-Zohar

Suez Top Secret
The Hunt for German Scientists
Ben-Gurion: The Armed Prophet
The Avengers
Embassies in Crisis

*Embassies in Crisis: Diplomats and Demagogues Behind the
Six-Day War* by Michael Bar-Zohar

© 1970 by Michael Bar-Zohar

ISBN 0-13-274506-2

Library of Congress Catalog Card Number: 71-102278

Printed in the United States of America *T*

Prentice-Hall International, Inc., London
Prentice-Hall of Australia, Pty. Ltd., Sydney
Prentice-Hall of Canada, Ltd., Toronto
Prentice-Hall of India Private Ltd., New Delhi
Prentice-Hall of Japan, Inc., Tokyo

FOREWORD

THE SIX-DAY War has been called the "Lightning War" and the "Miracle War." It is supposed to have begun on June 5, but there have been endless arguments over when the first shot was fired. Dozens of books have been written about it, each giving plenty of details and many anecdotes on the start and the progress of the military operations.

It is sometimes forgotten that the six days of actual war were preceded by three tedious weeks of anxiety during which the whole world believed that Israel was doomed. There were secret diplomatic conferences; confidential dispatches; special envoys to Cairo, Paris, and Washington; and top-secret meetings in Cairo, in the Kremlin, in the White House, and in Tel Aviv, at which the crisis was truly created. Works about the war itself have totally disregarded this submerged part of the iceberg. Both before and during the war almost unbelievable events occurred in the "hot spots" of the crisis—seats of government throughout the world, Arab palaces, and political centers in Israel itself.

It has been overlooked—or perhaps it was never known—that at one moment World War III was much closer at hand than anyone could have believed: the most dramatic of the frequently mentioned calls over the hot line have been thickly shrouded in silence. It is not even known that at one point the White House thought World War III had actually begun.

I believe that no one can understand the Six-Day War with-

iii

out a thorough knowledge of the period that immediately preceded it and that no one can trace the progress of its military operations without an understanding of certain phases of the worldwide political crisis that formed their context.

A three-week nightmare preceded the one week of triumph for the people of Israel. For the Arab nations that one week of disaster came at the end of three weeks of intoxicating success.

This book is a day-by-day account of that month, which began on the eve of the nineteenth birthday of the State of Israel and lasted until the night of June 10, when the guns in the Middle East fell silent.

CONTENTS

EMBASSIES
IN
CRISIS

•

THE SPARK

EARLY IN THE evening of May 12, 1967, the highly sensitive receiving apparatus of an information service somewhere in western Europe picked up a coded message. The bureau was a highly respected one, and despite a few blunders and some never-to-be-forgotten false reports, it still has its reputation.

The entire text of the message was immediately decoded, and before midnight it was on the desk of the chief executive of the bureau. It was a report from the Soviet embassy in Cairo, signed by Ambassador Dimitri Podyedyeev and intended for the Ministry of Foreign Affairs in Moscow. For the information service its interception was a common enough occurrence. Several months previously its cryptographers had broken the code of Moscow-Cairo communications. When first read, the telegram seemed merely another daily report from the Ambassador to his Moscow headquarters. No one attached any great importance to it.

It proved, however, to be a kind of time bomb. The next-to-last sentences of the report read: "Today we passed on to the Egyptian authorities information concerning the massing of Israeli troops on the northern frontier for a surprise attack on Syria. We have advised the U.A.R. government to take the necessary steps."*

No one on that spring evening had the faintest suspicion that

---

* This text was obtained from an American whom I interviewed in New York on November 8, 1967. See "Bibliography" at the end of this book.

those sentences were the spark that would explode the huge powder barrel that geographers call the Middle East.

The information in the telegram was completely false. Israel had not concentrated its troops on the Syrian border and had no intention of attacking Syria. No matter. By spreading this false information in Cairo, the Soviets were pursuing their own ends. Frequent incidents between the Israelis and the Syrians had made the Russians fearful for the future of the Syrian government, which they strongly supported. The warning of an imminent attack on Syria, they hoped, would induce Cairo to rush openly to the defense of its sister nation. Furthermore, it was part of the Soviet global policy to counteract American intervention in Vietnam by creating several areas of tension in which the East might take a strong position against the West. On that day the Russians' choice was the Middle East. The Soviets would probably never have dared such intrigue had they been able to foresee its disastrous results.

PART ONE

•

Confusion

•

NASSER HOLDS A SECRET CONFERENCE

ISRAEL WAS IN a holiday mood. In Haifa, Tel Aviv, and Jerusalem there were fireworks displays in which the set piece was frequently a seven-branched candlestick. On top of Jerusalem's Mount Herzl the torches of the Twelve Tribes burned. The streets and the squares swarmed with merrymakers in summer dresses or open-necked shirts with rolled-up sleeves. The Jewish state was celebrating its nineteenth birthday.

Bandstands had been erected in all the city squares. The enormous stadium at Ramat Gan was jammed for an international all-star concert featuring French Enrico Macias, American Pete Seeger, Greek Nana Mouskouri, and the British Shadows.

In the Jerusalem stadium another crowd was cheering a full-dress night parade of units of the defense army, the Zahal. On the reviewing stand, which was decorated with the national crest, President Zalman Shazar was delivering the customary long inspirational address. All through the country tens of thousands of Israelis were, as usual, out in the streets, where children were dancing. Happy little gangs ran about, hitting their friends over the head with the traditional plastic mallets and screaming shrilly.

It was a perfectly normal Independence eve.

In this gala crowd of rejoicing Israelis, one might have caught a glimpse of Captain Amos Katz, a strapping little career officer with an armored division, who was walking in Tel

5

Aviv with his fiancée, Jenny. In other years he would have
been passing this holiday eve supervising his men in camp as
they polished the tanks for the following day's parade. But this
year those steel giants would not be in the small parade in
Jerusalem. The terms of the armistice with the Arab countries
permitted no heavy armaments inside Jerusalem, and the Israeli government was keeping to the letter of those terms. The
army would march through Jerusalem's streets, but in order to
conciliate the United Nations and the great powers there
would be only a mild little show with no tanks or planes and a
mere handful of infantrymen.

For the same reason Mirage pilot Arie Ben Or, who had
recently been promoted to squadron leader, was on leave. In
previous years he would have been in the air show that accompanied the parade. Now he and his wife, Yonina, were
spending a pleasant evening in conversation with an engineer
friend. The talk turned to a delicate subject—the emigration of
Israel's intellectuals. Ben Or declared that he would rather be a
street cleaner than leave his country. He was a tall, sinewy,
well-set-up man whose rough exterior concealed considerable
sensitivity, and he made no secret of his fervent Zionist sentiments. A few months before he had been offered a cushy job as
flight pilot for El Al Airlines, but after seriously considering the
offer for a long time he had decided to stick with the air force
until he retired.

In a small apartment on Jerusalem's Founders Street, Esther
Arditi was putting her ten-year-old Ilan and seven-year-old
Noorit to bed. She was a small, dark-haired woman with a
turned-up nose, and she spoke Hebrew with a soft and beguil-
ing Italian accent. Every time a national holiday occurred she
celebrated it with a wonderful party for her children. The
family of three, which had become especially close since her
divorce, had spent the entire day decorating the apartment and
its balcony with flags and flowers and ribbons in preparation
for the party.

Ilan looked at the flag holders, and after thinking a moment asked his mother, "Is there going to be a war?" It was a question many people were asking that evening. If not an actual war, might there not be at least a serious military confrontation with Syria, Israel's neighbor to the north, which kept sending terrorists from the organization al-Fatah into Israeli territory in ever-increasing numbers? They blew up bridges, mined roads, and murdered farmers in the kibbutzim on the frontier. On several occasions the Israeli army had retaliated with raids limited to reprisals beyond the frontier, but they had not put an end to the incursions. During the preceding month fourteen serious incidents had occurred, the most desperate of which had been the sabotage of the highway between Tiberias and Safad. The Israelis were worried. The government and the army high command had been sending more and more explicit warnings to Damascus.

On that eve of Independence Day, I returned to Israel after a long stay abroad. At the night parade in the Jerusalem stadium I met the military reporter of a prominent daily newspaper. "Did you come home for the war?" he asked me in a tone that was only half joking.

Would there be war with Syria? It was hardly a subject for argument in the middle of a surprise party, but that is what some young folk were earnestly discussing at a party in Ramat Gan at the house of Ido Dissentshik, whose father was editor of Israel's biggest evening paper. One of young Dissentshik's best friends, Guy Jacobson, a brilliant and serious young man from a well-to-do family and an economist with a chemical company in Arad, was insisting that imminent military action in the north was quite possible. As he was a reserve artillery officer, he was sure to be recalled to duty immediately if the situation there grew much worse.

In Jerusalem several old friends had gathered at Miles Shirover's for a quiet, cozy evening: General Uzzi Narkiss, commander of the central district; General Yitzhak Rabin, Chief of the General Staff; General Yigal Yadin, former Chief of the General Staff, who had since become a celebrated archaeologist; and Admiral Mordechai ("Moka") Limon of the Defense Ministry Commission in Europe. They were indeed talking about war but not about the one everyone dreaded; rather they were discussing the one that had begun nineteen years earlier that very day, the War of Independence. They were reminiscing about those already distant days while they awaited the arrival of Mayor Teddy Killek of Jerusalem, who had promised to honor Shirover's party with his presence.

Just then the telephone rang.

"Yitzhak, it's for you."

Over the receiver came the voice of Colonel Rafi Ephrat of Rabin's private staff: "Yitzhak, 'Arale' Yariv [Aaron Yariv, head of intelligence] has asked me to tell you that some Egyptian units are moving toward Sinai."

Rabin was surprised. "Very interesting! We're going to have to keep our eyes open." After a moment he added: "Where is Arale? I'd like a word with him."

"I'll put him on right away." Rafi spoke loudly with a trace of a German accent.

Rabin waited by the telephone. He was not unduly worried, but he kept wondering about the reason for this military move of the Egyptians.

The heavy rains that had been drenching Damascus stopped during the evening. For three days an unseasonable storm had been raging in Syria. The Euphrates had overflowed, drowning thousands of cattle in the muddy waters that spread over the countryside. Night and day, army helicopters had hummed over stricken villages to evacuate the inhabitants. Finally, that same night of May 14, the clouds broke and the wind fell.

The waiting room of the Damascus airport was full of high-ranking officers, whom General Ahmed Suedani, Chief of the General Staff, presently joined. In a few minutes an Egyptian military plane would be bringing Mohammed Fawzi, Commander in Chief of the U.A.R.'s Armed Forces, and an impressive delegation of other generals. Defense Minister Hafez Assad was waiting for these visitors in his office, where an urgent telegram from Cairo had advised him of their imminent arrival. Apparently the reason for the unexpected visit was the tension of the Israeli frontier.

Paradoxically, that tension had been damaging the relations between Damascus and Cairo, which had not been very cordial since the union of Syria and Egypt had been dissolved in 1961. Mutual distrust had grown into an open quarrel after February 1965, when al-Fatah commandos had begun their terrorist activities in Israeli territory. Repeated coups d'état in Syria had not changed its policy toward Israel, which was one of fanatical violence designed to draw Israel into total war through a succession of provocations, outrages, and murders. By itself the Syrian army was no match for the Zionist forces; in the event of total war, therefore, the Syrians aimed for a crusade against Israel in which all the Arab armies would participate under the leadership of the U.A.R. army.

It would be an exaggeration to say that this Syrian dream had aroused much enthusiasm in the heart of Gamal Abdel Nasser, who was up to his neck in war with Yemen. The President of Egypt was convinced that his army was still inferior to that of Israel and so had turned a deaf ear to Damascus' repeated summons to holy war. Broadcasts on Radio Damascus and Radio Cairo, conferences of the Arab League, summit meetings among the heads of Arab states—all far too often reflected a vigorous argument between the Syrians, who wanted a war that others would fight for them, and the Egyptians, who did not think they were ready for it.

The quarrel had reached a peak in November 1966 as a result of the Samu incident. In reprisal for acts of sabotage committed by al-Fatah commandos from the Jordanian village of Samu, the Israeli army had raided the village. Military units had blown up the police station and dozens of houses and had annihilated the reinforcements hastily supplied by the Arab Legion. Israeli planes, armored cars, and infantry had participated in this operation, the most important ever to have been launched in enemy territory.

Thereafter a wave of unrest and demonstrations had swept over Jordan. The Syrians had blamed King Hussein of Jordan for his poor showing against the Israelis and had loudly demanded that Nasser take punitive action against Israel. But the Egyptian army had not budged. Nasser had been willing only to sign a mutual-defense treaty with Syria. This treaty had become a dead letter on the afternoon of April 7, 1967, when an incident on the Israeli-Syrian frontier developed into a major air battle. Dozens of Israeli Mirages had penetrated enemy air space and downed six Syrian MIGs before circling freely over the minarets of Damascus. That evening all the world had learned of the sad end of one-third of Syria's air power. And still the Egyptian army had not budged.

A few days later Marshal Mohammed Sidki Mahmoud, commandant of the Egyptian air force, had come to Damascus with a proposal—and a warning. His proposal was to send Syria some air squadrons to be based at its airfields, but to remain under Egyptian command. The Syrians had turned it down. Then Mahmoud proceeded to his warning. "Understand," he had said to his counterparts in Damascus, "that if you stubbornly persist in provoking incidents, you will get no aid whatever from us. We are not going to let ourselves be dragged into a war."

In order to make things perfectly clear, Nasser had sent his prime minister to Damascus on May 5. The prime minister had been no less explicit: "Our agreement for mutual defense will apply only in the event of a general attack on Syria by Israel. No merely local incident will cause us to intervene."

But then what new development was bringing Fawzi on an unexpected visit to Damascus? Recently frontier tensions had increased after al-Fatah had attacked Israeli villages with mortar fire and had committed a series of acts of sabotage in Galilee.

On May 13 the Foreign Ministry in Damascus had issued a statement denouncing Israel's preparations as acts of aggression and had sent an urgent letter to the U.N. Security Council. The Syrian Ministry of Information had sent Egypt top-secret information from an impeccable source—Israel was planning to attack Syria on May 17.

The Syrian leaders were anxiously wondering whether or not Fawzi would shake a threatening finger under their noses also and would demand that they put an end to al-Fatah raids. Fawzi, however, reassured them as soon as he alighted from his plane. "President Nasser," he said, "is convinced that Israel does indeed intend to attack Syria on May 17. This morning the high command of Egypt decided to send me to Damascus in order to coordinate with Syria plans for a campaign against Israel."

For more than twelve years Nasser, like a modern pharaoh, had been the absolute and omnipotent ruler of the Nile valley. His dreams of grandeur and his political ambitions were, however, in strange contrast to the simplicity of his way of life. He still lived in the same house in the Manshiet al Bakri suburb of Cairo that had been his when he had been only an obscure lieutenant colonel. True enough, as the years had gone by he had added a second story to his house, a tennis court, and a swimming pool, and he had commissioned professional gardeners to make him a park. But the house itself was no gorgeous palace. The drawing room, where so many major decisions had been taken after important conferences, was furnished in imitation Régence and Louis XV armchairs, a cushioned sofa, and a low marble table on which there were always a gigantic ash tray, a package of American cigarettes, and a heavy silver cigarette lighter.

On the morning of May 14, a small meeting was going on in Nasser's drawing room. Among the conferees was Nasser's right arm, Field-Marshal Abdel Hakim Amer, and intelligence chief Salah Nasser. The latter had in his briefcase reports that all pointed to one conclusion: Israel intended to attack Syria.

These documents seemed very convincing. On the previous morning Nasser had been informed by the Soviet embassy in Cairo that Israel was concentrating eleven to fifteen brigades of infantry and artillery on the Syrian frontier. On May 17, these troops would attack Syria between 4:00 and 5:00 A.M.

This was precise intelligence which confirmed the general hints the Soviets had already whispered into the ears of some Egyptian members of Parliament who had visited Moscow for the May 1 celebrations.

Salah Nasser took into account several other reports corroborating the information, which had already been confirmed by Lebanese, as well as by Syrian, intelligence. Besides, it was enough merely to glance at the Israeli newspapers—containing nothing but warnings and threats from the Zionist statesmen. On May 11 Rabin had declared:

> The reprisals against Jordan and Lebanon were directed at nations that do not encourage terrorism, but whose territory, against their will, serves as a base for terrorists. In Syria the situation is different, for the government of that state actually directs the work of the saboteurs. Consequently, our aims in regard to Syria are different from our aims in respect to Jordan and Lebanon.

Could there not be detected in that statement a clear reference to an intention to overthrow the government of Syria? Furthermore, Prime Minister Levi Eshkol had remarked in a recent conversation that in the event of war the American 6th Fleet would certainly intervene on the Israeli side. On May 12 he had declared, "As a result of the fourteen incidents that occurred last month, we may be obliged to take measures no less strong than those of April 7" (the day on which Israel had shot down six Syrian MIGs). On that same Friday several Israeli ministers had taken the floor to utter grave warnings to Syria.

Nasser was convinced that Israel was about to initiate some military activity. At the end of the conference he instructed Amer to start an immediate mobilization, which might persuade the Israelis to change their plans. Armored vehicles, airplanes, and infantry units were to be massed in the Sinai peninsula. They would be such a clear threat to Israel's southern frontier that the Israelis would find it hazardous to launch an offensive in the north.

While Amer and his colleagues were hurrying back to headquarters, Nasser brooded alone. Everything seemed very clear to him, yet he was wrong. He was unaware that all the "confidential" information about Israel's contemplated attack on Syria came from a single source: Soviet agents who had given the same information to the Syrians, the Lebanese, and the Egyptians simultaneously. Nor did he realize that it had long been a kind of national pastime for Israeli leaders to make flag-waving speeches of an aggressive nature as their Independence Day approached. And he was also completely ignorant of the fact that, regardless of what was said in those overheated orations, it had been definitely decided in Tel Aviv that no action was to be undertaken against Syria in order not to aggravate the tension. According to that line, the Israeli security services had even played down news of their reports of terrorist actions and counteractions, such as the arrest of Samir Shafik Darvish, a blue-eyed Syrian who had been sent into Israel disguised as a British tourist. With the bombs and other explosives he brought with him, Darvish had intended to perpetrate a series of sabotages in the very heart of Jerusalem on Independence eve before being arrested. But the Israeli authorities wanted to keep his arrest a secret. Even more careful was Prime Minister Levi Eshkol in his attempts to avoid any incident that could raise the tension in the area.

During the night parade in Jerusalem an actor was to recite Nathan Altermann's poem, "At Break of Day," a poignant reminder to his countrymen of their triumph and of the ruin of the seven Arab states that had sworn to exterminate the State of Israel. Listening to the actor rehearse his rendition, a professor in Jerusalem took alarm at the effect that the last stanza of the poem might have:

> *Think, oh Araby, of where thou art going before it*
>   *is too late.*
> *Only in thy dreams do thy chains fetter my hands*
> *And thy ruler condemns me to eternal exile.*
> *Wake from these senseless dreams.*
> *Before the last hour has struck!*

The professor went to the Presidency of the Cabinet and recommended that, in view of the highly emotional response Altermann's eloquence was likely to produce, the passage in question should be toned down. After a last minute conference with the Prime Minister, it was decided that Altermann should be asked to temper his sentiments slightly. And so, when tens of thousands heard the poem recited over the loudspeakers on the eve of the national holiday, the final stanza had been changed:

> *Oh, Araby, before the die is cast*
> *And the sun goes down for both of us,*
> *Withdraw thy hand from the gates of war.*
> *Consider the difference between the curse of war*
> *Too terrible to think on, and the fruits of peace—*
> *A peace such as the children of Shem have never*
> *known.*

As the resonant voice of the actor echoed through the night air of Jerusalem, the camps of the Egyptian army seethed with feverish activity. The commanding officer of every tactical unit had received battle order no. 1, which Amer had signed a few hours earlier:

> A state of emergency is decreed as from 2:30 P.M., on May 15.
> All divisions and units disposed according to the plan of operations will leave their present positions and proceed to the zones of concentration and regroupment that have been assigned to them.
> The armed forces will prepare for combat on the Israeli frontier, according to the development of the situation.

In the streets of Cairo, on the roads between the capital and Port Said, Ismailia, and Suez, and at the bridges over the Suez canal, the cars and motorcycles of the military police whizzed along at top speed. Roadblocks went up, and all civilian traffic was strictly banned from the main highways. Tanks, lorries, and half-trucks refueled by the light of torches. Brand-new guns were brought out of storerooms. Thousands of soldiers made their gear ready for the order to march, which was to come at dawn the following day.

On the other side of the frontier, an entire nation was dancing in carefree, confident enjoyment of its holiday.

•

TANKS IN THE DESERT

A LITTLE AFTER 9:00 A.M. on May 15, Eshkol, who was serving as both Prime Minister and Defense Minister, passed through the lobby of the King David Hotel in Jerusalem. The huge hall was already full of people. A group of American tourists was focusing cameras on the Israeli VIPs who were arriving in unprecedented numbers, for the King David was the point of assembly and departure for the high government officials who would proceed in groups from there to the municipal stadium. An audience of 18,000 had already arrived at the stadium and was waiting in the early sunlight for the military parade to begin. Along the route 200,000 people had been waiting since dawn.

The first to leave the hotel was General Narkiss, a short man with the energy of a coiled spring. Following him went Kadish Luz, Speaker of the Knesset; Mrs. Itzhak Ben Zvi, widow of a former president of Israel; and Nahum Goldmann, president of the Jewish Agency. On the dot of 9:30 three automobiles were to take Eshkol, his bodyguard, and Rabin to the stadium.

Rabin, in an olive-green uniform, beckoned Eshkol to a secluded corner of the lobby to brief him on the state of alert that Egypt had decreed. The Prime Minister had already been told by his military secretary, Colonel Israel ("Red") Lior, who had learned of it during the night. Since then nothing new had been reported.

Shortly after 9:30, President and Mrs. Eshkol took their

places on the official platform. The next half-hour was devoted to reading greetings in French, English, Hebrew, and Spanish over the loudspeakers to distinguished guests from the four corners of the earth. As a matter of fact, only a few of the guests were indeed distinguished: the Vice-President of the Malagasy Republic, two generals from developing countries, French General Pierre Koenig, and several representatives of the French aviation industry.

The masters of ceremonies, however, studiously ignored the presence in the stadium of the French former minister Jacques Soustelle, whose anti-Gaullist sentiments were embarrassing to the extremely pro-Gaullist State of Israel. Soustelle was a loyal friend of Israel nevertheless, and it was in recognition of his assistance to the state that he had been invited to be present on this occasion. In Israel he still continued to make violent pronouncements against President Charles de Gaulle. Just the day before he had told a reporter that De Gaulle and Maurice Couve de Murville were pro-Arab. "There is no doubt," he had said, "that French foreign policy is going to change radically in the very near future, and Israel will suffer accordingly." No one took him seriously; everyone knew that De Gaulle was an outspokenly loyal friend of the State of Israel.

The parade began at exactly 10 A.M. Sixteen hundred soldiers marched past the reviewing stand, but there was no heavy war matériel—only a handful of jeeps, some command cars, and a few antiaircraft guns. Yet, although the composition of the parade was in exact conformity with the terms of the 1949 armistice, which allowed no heavy arms to be shifted to Jerusalem, the ambassadors of the great powers had refused to attend. For the same reason, another distinguished guest had declined: David Ben-Gurion, former Prime Minister and former Defense Minister was conspicuously absent. Nine years earlier, on the tenth birthday of the State of Israel, he had presided from the same platform over a different parade. What a parade it had been! It had seemed as if all the heavy matériel available in the entire territory of Israel had been gathered together for the occasion.

At the stadium entrance policemen broke up two small gangs of young Israelis who were waving cardboard tanks in protest against the prohibition of tanks in the parade. Twenty-six minutes after the order to march had been given, the last soldier passed the reviewing stand in Jerusalem.

On the opposite side of the border, in the ancient Philistine city of Gaza, now the principal town of the famous Gaza Strip, there was an even less elaborate parade. For more than an hour tens of thousands of Arab refugees from Palestine watched the long procession of civil and military marchers with bitterness. To these unhappy people it was a mournful occasion, for the parade commemorated the anniversary of the loss of Palestine to the Zionists, who had conquered it. The whole spectacle awakened in them a fanatical yearning for revenge and retribution.

In the army marching through Gaza were units of refugees from Palestine. Leading them was the mascot of the army, a ten-year-old boy wearing a helmet, carrying a "Port Said" machine gun, and sporting lieutenant's stripes.

Ahmed Shukairy, head of the Palestine Liberation Organization, reviewed his troops from the top of a small wooden platform. His guest of honor was the ambassador to Egypt from the People's Republic of China. A large part of the light armament of the Palestinian army had come from Mainland China. In a few moments Shukairy began to speak and to promise his entranced audience, for the thousandth time, the coming annihilation of all Zionists.

The most important parade that morning, however, was in Cairo. Since daybreak vast numbers of tanks, half-tracks, guns, and trucks had been flooding the main highways of the capital as if from the Nile itself. Before leaving the city the armored column made a deliberate detour in order to pass through the foreign-embassy section of Cairo. Traffic in the center of the city was hopelessly snarled. Foreign journalists estimated the force at no less than an entire army division.

From Cairo the column headed for Ismailia and crossed the Suez canal by the great revolving El Firdan bridge. At the same time MIG-19 and MIG-21 fighter planes took off from the air bases along the canal toward the airfields at El Thamad and Bîr Gifgâfa in the heart of the Sinai desert. MIG-17s landed on the Gebel Libni and El ʿArîsh runways. About noon Amer himself landed at Bîr el Thamâda and, in order to keep in close touch with the troop movements, set up headquarters in the underground command post that Egyptian engineers had built near Gebel Yi ʿAllaq.

While the seemingly endless lines of soldiers were marching through Cairo, sirens sounded an air alert, and fighter planes flew in formation above the city. The semiofficial *al-Ahram* announced that, "in accordance with the Syrian-Egyptian mutual defense pact," steps had been taken to deal with the concentration of Israeli troops on the Syrian frontier. If Nasser was intending to make a show of force, he could not have succeeded better.

The tramp of soldiers' boots was hardly the ideal accompaniment for the announcement by Hervé Alphand, Secretary General of the French Foreign Office, as he boarded his plane at the Cairo airport: "I will recommend that my government tighten its ties with Egypt."

At 9:45 A.M. the Israeli embassy on Twenty-second Street in Washington, D.C., was preparing a small reception in honor of the Israeli national holiday; the only guests were to be members of the Israeli colony in the District of Columbia. Bald, round-shouldered, colorless Ambassador Avraham ("Abe") Harman was studying some documents that he wished to introduce at the press conference that was about to begin. As the tension between his country and Syria was increasing, he wished to explain his government's position to the fifteen or so prominent reporters whom he had invited. His telephone rang.

"Who is it? Battle? Yes indeed, put him on."

Lucius D. ("Luke") Battle, a blond giant, had been U.S. Ambassador to Cairo before becoming Assistant Secretary of State for Middle Eastern and South Asian Affairs. After the usual exchange of diplomatic civilities, Battle began to talk at length. One of the embassy officials who happened to come into the Ambassador's office just then noticed how deathly white Harman's face became. Battle was informing him that at that moment the Egyptian army was passing under the balcony of the U.S. embassy in Cairo on its way to the Sinai desert. Battle, however, was not too worried. "It's probably only a show of strength," he said, "a reply to the parade in Jerusalem. You're shifting your troops; they're shifting theirs."

After this telephone conversation Ambassador Harman briefly considered canceling the press conference, but his Counselor, Dan Patir, persuaded him instead to add to his remarks a short report of the troop movements in Egypt. While Harman was telling the astonished journalists about this unexpected event, an urgent cable was sent off to Jerusalem.

That afternoon it arrived in the office of Moshe Raviv, diplomatic secretary to the Minister of Foreign Affairs. It was the Ministry's first notification of the Egyptian army units' penetration of Sinai.

The two great rivals on the Israeli political scene, Eshkol and Ben-Gurion, were attending the Junior Bible Contest at the Jerusalem city hall. Eshkol presented the winner with a prize of £1,000 Israeli and a deluxe edition of the Bible. It was 4:00 P.M. when Rabin asked permission to leave: "I must go back to my office in Tel Aviv."

There Rabin heard a brief report on the developments, then picked up the telephone: "Get me Talik."

"Talik" was General Israel Tal, commander of the armored corps and a close friend of Rabin's A small, squat, taciturn man, he looked rather like Anthony Quinn. For years he had been an infantry officer. Then Moshe Dayan had called him in and told him: "I am going to appoint you deputy commander of the armored corps. When can you get started?"

The astonished Talik had replied, "In two or three weeks, I think."

"No," Dayan said. "I want to know at what hour."

Once with the "black berets," Talik applied himself to learning all about the training of tank fighters by going through it himself as if he were a new recruit. After a few months he had everything at his fingertips. A few years later, in 1961, he was awarded the Israel Defense prize for his improvements and inventions in the field of defensive weapons. Now he was so closely identified with this field that he was often called "Mister Armor."

While Rabin waited for his call to go through, he recalled the days in 1960 when he was chief of operations, and Talik was the commander of the "S" armored brigade. Following an Israeli reprisal raid on Syrian Tawafik, Egypt had moved several army units into Sinai and had massed them on the Israeli frontier. In contrast to the troop movements of this morning of May 15, however, the 1960 operations had been conducted in the utmost secrecy. Before the Israelis had been aware of what was happening, 400 tanks had been lined up on the frontier.

Rabin also recalled the code name of the operation he had ordered at that time, when he had had to rush the Israeli tanks to the opposite side of the frontier: "Rotem." Rabin had telephoned Talik then, instructing him to take his brigade south at top speed.

Rabin heard the telephone ring at the other end.

"Where are you, Talik?"

"At Moussik's* in Neve Maguen."

"Talik, do you remember Rotem?"

After a fraction of a second, Tal replied, "Certainly."

"Well, we're going to play Rotem again. You're It."

"Can you give me any details?"

"You get over to my house PDQ, and I'll give them to you."

Half an hour later Talik arrived at Rabin's house in Zahala.† He had already phoned Colonel Kalman, his chief of operations, in order to give him some preliminary instructions. After being briefed on the Egyptian troop movements he called Kalman again. In a few hours the tanks of S Brigade were moving south.

At the Israeli embassy in Moscow the reception in honor of the national holiday was especially brilliant that year. Among

---

* Colonel Moshe Gidron, chief of communications in the Israeli army.
† A residential suburb of Tel Aviv popular with the military.

the guests was one of particular distinction from Israel: Yigal
Allon, Minister of Labor. The tall, handsome, and highly intel-
ligent Allon had achieved fame before his thirtieth birthday as
commander of the Palmach shock brigade in the War of Independence. He had become one of the youngest leaders of the
left-socialist Achdut Ha'avoda-Poalei Zion Party, and many
people thought him the most likely candidate for Prime Minister when the new generation took over. For some time already he had been the government's official spokesman on
political and defensive measures.

There was no particular reason for his being in the U.S.S.R.
at that time. He had come for three weeks in order to attend a
conference on social questions at which many specialists were
assembled. But his political opponents maintained that he had
gone to Russia in order to strengthen his own position in Israeli
politics, and his supporters claimed that his visit was intended
to strengthen understanding between Jerusalem and Moscow.

Russian Jews had welcomed Allon to the U.S.S.R., calling
out his name whenever they saw him in the street. At the
embassy reception he was surrounded by an impressive group
of Jews and non-Jews—men of letters, intellectuals, politicians,
and Soviet leaders. Among the other guests at the embassy was
Assistant Foreign Minister Vladimir Semyonov.

Despite the formal though cordial atmosphere of the reception, however, Israeli Ambassador Katriel Katz was worried.

Relations between the U.S.S.R. and Israel were tense. In
1955 the U.S.S.R. had begun to stake out claims on the map of
the Arab countries of the Middle East and had given Egypt
access to its arsenals. Into the Arab ports had come a steady
stream of trucks, fighter planes, bombers, submarines, and
warships. In subsequent years Ben-Gurion had become convinced that all Israel's efforts to bring a change in that unilateral policy would come to nothing and that only a new
direction in Soviet policy would put an end to it. Ben-Gurion's
successor, Eshkol, with the support of Foreign Minister Abba
Eban, had nevertheless undertaken to improve Israel's relations
with the Kremlin. Every time even a third-rate Russian circus

or company of folk artists came to Israel, the official government spokesmen never failed to label its visit an example of the increasing friendship between the two countries.

The U.S.S.R. sent no circuses to the Arab countries; rather it sent the First Deputy Chairman of the Council of Ministers, the Chairman of the Presidium of the Supreme Soviet, ministers, generals, and army commanders. In 1965 Marshal Andrei Gretchko headed a military mission to the Middle East under the auspices of the Soviet Defense Ministry, which later prepared a plan for a strategic Soviet infiltration into Egyptian administration. Fearing that the "neocolonial and imperialist" powers were preparing to overthrow the progressive regime in the U.A.R., Moscow put pressure on Egypt to become even more socialist than it was.

In 1966 a pro-Soviet government took office in Damascus, and Russia began to envisage creating another Cuba in the Middle East. The Soviets paid more and more attention to the frequent clashes between the Israelis and the Syrians, for such incidents provided a perfect excuse for the "forces of evil"— notably the C.I.A. and American money—to overthrow the Syrian government with the help of their Israeli "toadies."

In May and again in October 1966, when al-Fatah sabotage was producing tension on the frontiers, the Kremlin immediately took pains to send firm warnings to the Israeli government. Just before the Twenty-third Congress of the Communist Party, its leaders decided to gamble on the Arab countries. The intensification of Soviet infiltration was in accordance with the global strategy of the U.S.S.R., which at that time was being weakened by the collapse of several important socialist programs throughout the world.

Ahmed Ben Bella's fall was followed by those of Sukarno and Kwame Nkrumah. In the Congo the reactionaries had taken over. In Greece the ultraconservative military was stamping out democratic freedoms. In Syria the fever was mounting. In Egypt a conspiracy of the Moslem Brotherhood was uncovered. Saudi Arabia was mobilizing the faithful in a conservative Islamic alliance.

To the Soviets it appeared that Washington was pulling strings behind the scenes. On the other hand, a considerable number of representatives of Communist China were descending upon Arab capitals with offers of arms and specialists and making no secret of their belief that Israel should be exterminated. Caught between these two fires, the Russians saw only one escape—to become more deeply involved with the Arabs.

Various departments of the Israeli government issued warnings in the spring of 1966. During a dinner party for Israeli and American officials in Tel Aviv, a representative of the Israeli government put the question bluntly: "Haven't you noticed that the Soviets are trying right now to infiltrate this whole area?" The guests from Washington were content to smile condescendingly.

October 1966 saw the beginning of a dangerous escalation all along the frontier between Israel and Syria. The Soviets, much concerned with maintaining the existing regime in Damascus, increased their warnings and threats to Israel. After every incident the Soviet Ambassador in Tel Aviv, Dimitri Chuvakin, would say to anyone who would listen to him: "Do that again, and you'll be punished! You are pawns in the hands of the imperialists and the big oil companies."

A better way to reduce the tension, the Israelis replied, would be for the U.S.S.R. to advise its Syrian friends to put a stop to al-Fatah terrorism. The Russians said nothing, however. They could hardly admit to the Israelis that Soviet relations with Syria were, at that moment, not so close, and they did not want those relations to deteriorate because of ill-timed interference. When the Israelis kept bringing up the subject of terrorism, the only notice the Soviet Ambassador took of their complaints was to make rather awkward attempts to shift the blame for the raids from the Syrians to the C.I.A., which, he implied, was secretly encouraging the terrorists.

By the spring of 1967 the Soviets were convinced that Israel was preparing an extremely subtle campaign of aggression against Syria. From that point of view the reprisal raid on the Jordanian village of Samu in November 1966 was clearly a diversionary tactic to blind the Soviets to an imminent all-out offensive against Syria. The destruction of the Syrian MIGs in April 1967 confirmed Moscow's suspicion that an invasion was in the works.

The Russians had, therefore, informed the Syrians, the Lebanese, and the Egyptians that Israel was preparing an attack— to be launched on May 17. Subsequently, the U.N. observers, who had been scrutinizing the situation in northern Israel, officially reported absolutely no concentration of troops on the Syrian border on that date. It has now been established that the rumors about the fifteen brigades supposedly massed in that area were completely groundless. Some have advanced the theory that the Russians deliberately lied in order to persuade Egypt to take a more clear-cut position in support of Syria. Perhaps the Kremlin wanted to create a new area of tension in order to counterbalance American pressure in Vietnam.

On that May 15 Semyonov drew Allon aside. "I am happy to make your acquaintance, General Allon," he said.

Allon smiled. "I am only a general of the reserves, and in my capacity as Minister I even omit my training periods."

"We know that you are the strong man of your government."

"You underestimate the Israeli government."

Semyonov avoided any mention of the message that his government had just sent to Egypt.

The Assissistant Foreign Minister directed the conversation to Israel's warnings to Syria. An intense young Russian translated Allon's replies, although it was unnecessary, as Semyonov could speak English fluently.

Allon was particularly interested in the topic, for it was a matter close to his heart. "In not condemning Syrian terrorism, you encourage it," he said. "My kibbutz of Ginnosar is in the north. Our fishermen frequently come under the fire of Syrian positions. A mine that al-Fatah planted exploded on the road that my wife and I take regularly four times a week."

"We want only one thing—peace."

"Don't preach to me about peace!" Allon interrupted. "We are constantly ready to apply the principle of peaceful coexistence. And what is the meaning of your reports that we intend to overthrow the Syrian government? It is a matter of total indifference to us what kind of government is in Damascus or Amman or Cairo."

"The Syrian government has nothing to do with the terrorists."

Allon smiled. "How would you like to listen to the broadcasts from Radio Damascus? You do nothing, you say nothing to the Syrians. Kindly notice that the Egyptian frontier is quiet because the Egyptians are quiet."

Semyonov did not answer. He knew that the Egyptian frontier was no longer so quiet. Before sending their troops into Sinai, the Egyptians had conferred with the Soviet embassy in Cairo, which had openly encouraged them.

The Assistant Minister offered his hand to Allon, saying: "Good-bye, General. You must understand that the peace will not be broken."

"I quite agree with you, Mr. Semyonov. But there is still the right of self-defense."

It was a futile conversation. Nevertheless, on the following day Eban stated in a Tel Aviv press conference on Israel's relations with the Soviet bloc: "There is no longer any iron curtain so far as we are concerned. The curtain is rising."

A young, dark-haired woman stood on the huge stage. The orchestra was silent as the girl plucked a white guitar on her knees. Her voice rose, liquid and pure as crystal, in a song that seemed a kind of incantation. The last notes of her guitar were drowned in the ovation that greeted "Jerusalem the Golden" as interpreted by Shuli Natan. Applause filled the huge auditorium of the National Building in Jerusalem.

No one could have foreseen that three weeks later this poignant song would become the national hymn of Israel because of the prophetic tone of its second stanza:

> *How dry are the deep wells,*
> *How empty the marketplace!*

No one climbs the hill of the Temple
In the Old City.
The wind howls through the rocky caves.
No one goes down to the Dead Sea
Any more over the Road to Jericho.

Events were to give a new dimension to the song, one of nostalgia for the Old City, the hill of the Temple, the Wailing Wall, and all the rest of that holy world that lay on the far side of the frontier almost within reach yet inaccessible. It was a world that no Israeli believed, on that May 15, 1967, he would ever enter.

A large helicopter put down at an airfield in the center of the country, and Eshkol climbed down to attend the air force's Independence ball. For the first time the pleasures of the evening were to be preceded by a ceremony: the awarding of diplomas to pilots who had downed enemy aircraft in battle.

Arie Ben Or was not among them, and he regretted it. Since he had first sat at the controls of a Mirage, his fondest dream had been to shoot down a MIG. He had even been in a fight with two Egyptian MIGs in the south, but they had escaped before he could fire at them. Now, as the commander of a Fouga squadron and an instructor at the air-force academy, he figured that he would never have the chance again.

Nevertheless, he mounted the platform to take part—along with his students and his faculty colleagues—in a humorous sketch on life at the academy. After the skit the dancing began. The pilots started a chain dance, into which they dragged generals, ministers, and foreign guests, including some directors of the French aviation industry.

Yitzak Rabin, who had remained on the sidelines, leaped onto a table in order to catch Eshkol's attention. In the best of humor, Eshkol himself jumped onto the same table. "Anything you can do, I can do also," he said to Rabin. It was on that long wooden table that Rabin, against a background of boisterous folk songs, told Eshkol of the Egyptian troop movements and that he had ordered his tanks to the south.

At midnight Captain Amos Katz reached the house of his parents in Rehovot and, turning on his transistor radio, learned that Egyptian troops were massing in Sinai. The young officer realized immediately that there would be no bed for him that night. He was commander of a platoon of Patton tanks at the school for tank officers and also of a company of reserve combat soldiers.

All the same he began to undress for bed. As he had expected, there was a knock on his door. A soldier told him to report at once to camp. By 2:00 A.M. Katz was at his base.

•

U THANT'S FATAL ERROR

THE MORNING OF May 16 there were many people who tried to telephone Rabin in his Tel Aviv office. His pretty secretary, Captain Ruhama, gave the same answer to all of them: "Yitzhak is on a tour of inspection."

A few weeks earlier the seventh Chief of the General Staff of the Israeli army had invited his six predecessors to accompany him on such a tour. Nothing that had happened made it necessary for him to cancel it. All his guests had arrived: Yaakov Dori, the general of the War of Independence; Yigal Yadin, the archaeologist who had excavated Masada, a tall man with a mustache who always had a pipe in his mouth; Mordecai Macleff, director of the Dead Sea explorations; Dayan, a Rafi; deputy in the Knesset; Chaim Laskov, the supervisor of harbor installations, a strong, taciturn man; Zvi Zur, an excellent administrator, director of the Mekorot water supply and irrigation company. Near a French AML half-track the former Chiefs of the General Staff were quizzing Yitzhak Rabin about the Egyptian action.

"They are continuing to concentrate troops in Sinai," Rabin said. "Usually the Egyptians keep about 1 division and 250 tanks in that area, but now they are sending 100 supplemental tanks. There's no doubt that it's a show of strength. But what will they do next?"

Dayan interrupted him. "I can tell you what they'll do next. They'll demand the withdrawal of the U.N. forces, which will

29

be obliged to obey because they are on Egyptian soil. Then, if
Nasser wants to go further, he will be able to seal the strait of
Tiran."

No one shared this opinion. When Dayan repeated it some
time later at a secret meeting of several Knesset members, he
was greeted with a similar skepticism. On that morning of May
16, however, no one could imagine that the situation would
grow more desperate. In Washington qualified observers told
reporters that the crisis had already reached its peak. The Israeli
ministers, meeting in Jerusalem, concluded that the Egyptian
movements were nothing more than a propaganda ploy. Then
they went on to the agenda for the day, which was to consider a
report from Minister of Social Welfare Joseph Burg, on the
unveiling ceremony for the monument at Auschwitz, at which
he had represented the State of Israel.

Israeli newspaper editorials expressed the same conclusion,
as did the foreign press. May 16 was a day like any other in
Israel and throughout the world. In Vietnam there was nothing
new. During a press conference in Paris De Gaulle announced
(as usual) that he would keep Great Britain out of the Common Market. In Geneva there was continued discussion of the
Kennedy Round. From Guatemala came a report that a man
supposed to be Martin Bormann had been released after he
had furnished proof of his true identity, the seventh pseudo-
Bormann to have been arrested since the beginning of the year.

Nor did Amos Katz believe that a real crisis would materialize as a result of the Egyptian tank movements. As soon as he
reached camp he mustered his company, took the reserve
equipment out of storage, and lined up his tanks for the order
to leave. By 10:00 A.M. his company was ready. "Now," Katz
reflected, "they're going to order us back to the barracks, and
that will be the end of it." But, to his astonishment, that order
did not come. Instead he received an order to head for the
Negev and to take up a position south of Beersheba. He always
kept his kit ready for a sudden move. He stowed it in his jeep
and headed southward in advance of his tanks, who were being
transported on giant tank carriers.

At 2:00 P.M. the unit was fanned out on the sandy terrain of the Negev. Camouflage nets were spread, and the commissary, the repair shop, and the cook stoves had been set up. Katz gathered his men by a clump of bushes and explained the situation to them—or to be more exact, told them what he had gleaned from the newspapers: "Egyptian tanks are in Sinai. If anything can stop them, we can. Tomorrow we will start practice in order to get familiar with the area, but for now, you can go to sleep."

At that very moment at the advance headquarters of the Egyptian troops in Sinai, an interminable top-level conference was going on. Amer was there, as well as the commander of the ground forces, General Murtaghi, who had been put in charge of the Sinai sector. Commander in Chief Fawzi had flown back from Damascus in a special plane. The commanders of the air and naval forces were also present at the conference. The troop deployment had proceeded according to schedule; in a few hours the first-line tanks would reach the Israeli frontier, where they could be a real threat to the southern part of "Occupied Palestine."

The first item on the agenda was the problem of what to do about the U.N. force. Since the Sinai campaign had ended in 1957, 3,400 men of the U.N. Emergency Force had been stationed along the Israeli-Egyptian frontier and at the mouth of the strait of Tiran. From a military point of view, the force was, of course, negligible, but its presence on the frontier was a distinct hindrance to the Egyptians' project. As long as the United Nations soldiers were stationed between the Egyptian and the Israeli armies, nobody would take seriously Egypt's warning to attack Israel if fighting broke out on the Syrian border. That very morning Amer had discussed the matter with Nasser, who had instructed him to demand that the U.N. forces evacuate their positions along the border and regroup in isolated bases, in order not to impede the Egyptians' strategy.

It was not the first time such a demand had been made. In 1960, when Egyptian troops had been extended along the Israeli frontier, the Commander in Chief had also demanded that U.N. forces abandon their positions and fall back to their bases. Dag Hammarskjöld, at that time Secretary-General of the United Nations, had agreed, with the result that the U.N. troops had had a month's vacation—and a month's boredom—in their encampments. When the tensions had eased, Egyptian tanks had withdrawn to the western side of the canal, and the U.N. soldiers had resumed their watch along the frontier. There was, therefore, no reason not to repeat the same maneuver again.

But the United Nations was no longer under the direction of Hammarskjöld, a man who could wink at distortions of the rules he was bound to respect. U Thant was a passive but stubborn Oriental, who respected the letter rather than the spirit of the law.

Night had fallen before the conference of the Egyptian army high command had ended. Night comes swiftly in the East. That night was colder than usual, bringing rain and here and there hail. In Gaza about 10:00 P.M. an envoy from the Egyptian General Staff presented himself in a great hurry to Major General Indar Jit Rikhye, the round-faced Indian who commanded the U.N. force, and delivered to him a message signed by General Fawzi:

> I wish to inform you that I gave my instructions to all UAR armed forces to be ready for action against Israel the moment it might carry out any aggressive action against any Arab country. Due to these instructions, our troops are already concentrated in Sinai on our eastern borders. For the sake of complete security for all UN troops in observations posts along our borders, I request that you issue orders to withdraw all these troops immediately. . . . The troops should be concentrated inside the Gaza Strip.

Every word of that letter had been carefully weighed and considered. It did not ask for withdrawal of the U.N. force but merely its redeployment in encampments, and it did not mention the U.N. troops at Sharm el Sheikh, the strategic point of land controlling the entrance to the strait of Tiran. The letter had a double aim: to restore government prestige at home by proving to the masses that Nasser would not hesitate to engage the U.N. forces in order to deal freely with Israel, and to let the big powers know that Egypt had no intention of making war on Israel or of closing the strait of Tiran.

All the astonished Rikhye could think of was what U Thant would do. He immediately cabled the text of the message to New York, where the Secretary-General received it in the early afternoon of May 16. U Thant instructed his assistants to call an emergency meeting with the U.A.R. delegate to the United Nations, Mohamed Awad El Kony and Ralph Bunche. Bunche had been an expert on Middle Eastern affairs since 1948 and had inspected the U.N. Emergency Force installations only three months previously. During that trip he had had an opportunity to talk with the heads of the Egyptian government.

Bunche appeared in Thant's office a few minutes later. He read Rikhye's cable and shook his head. When he had been in Egypt in February, the Egyptians had assured him that they definitely wanted the U.N. force on their frontier. Bunche informed Thant that the present demand was illegal and that it looked very much like a device for feeling out the situation.

"Egypt must be told," Bunche said, "that we will accept no half-measures like this. Either the U.N. forces accomplish their mission without reservation, or they will be withdrawn from Egypt once and for all. As Nasser does not want them withdrawn, he will have to go into reverse."

U Thant accepted Bunche's opinion. At 6:00 P.M. the gaunt, bald, strong-chinned El Kony entered the Secretary-General's large office on the thirty-eighth floor of the U.N. Secretariat on New York's First Avenue. The inscrutable U Thant spoke calmly and at considerable length as usual, expressing to the Egyptian his astonishment at the demands of his government, emphasizing that the function of the U.N. force was to safeguard peace in the area, and calling attention to the tranquillity that the Israeli-Egyptian frontier had enjoyed for the past ten years. The demand made on General Rikhye was inadmissible in both form and substance, said U Thant. He maintained that the Egyptian Commander in Chief had no right to give orders to the commander of the U.N. force, who took orders only from the Secretary-General of the United Nations. It would have been advisable to submit the question to the U.N. Secretariat. As for the content of the letter, U Thant declared, the presence of the U.N. force in the area was inseparably linked to its freedom of action and movement. Egypt would have to choose between two alternatives: Either to restore the status quo or to have all U.N. forces in the region withdrawn.

El Kony promised to send this answer to his government at once and left U Thant's office. It was already 12:30 A.M. on May 17 in Israel.

Although he did not know it, U Thant had just dislodged the stone that heralded an avalanche.

•

LYNDON JOHNSON INTERVENES

AT 5:00 A.M. the Syrians were waiting for the expected attack from Israel. They were prepared to repel it. Almost no one had slept that night in the trenches and defense works that had been dug deep into the rock of the Syrian plateau. That hilly terrain overlooking the Jordan valley and the Sea of Galilee had for a long time been transformed into a menacing fortress —the Maginot Line of the Middle East—consisting of half a million mines, two-level underground bases of operations, miles of trenches and communication tunnels, and thick concrete walls on which machine guns and batteries of antiaircraft guns had been mounted and concealed under camouflage nets. It was intended as a fatal trap for anyone who dared to scale it, and it also hung like a sword of Damocles over the Israeli villages scattered on the plain below.

The line of fortifications was jam-packed with soldiers on May 17. For two days the roads leading to the frontier had been choked with trucks and tanks proceeding south. When the first rays of sun lit the brightly colored checkerboard of the Israeli plain, hundreds of army field glasses were nervously trained on it. Every stone, every house, and every bush were scrutinized. But nothing seemed irregular, and no suspicious activity could be seen.

But such a normal scene could not be depended upon. Perhaps the Israelis were afraid of an immediate reaction from the Syrian and Egyptian forces and would attack on the following

day or the day after. The Russian warning had said only that
the offensive would be mounted between May 17 and 21. That
was why Syrian reserves had been moved up on foot while the
coordination with the Egyptian forces was still being worked
out. On May 16 Syrian Deputy Prime Minister and Foreign
Minister Ibrahim Makhous had gone to Cairo to arrange this
coordination.

In Sinai also, long Egyptian armored columns were moving
continuously toward the eastern frontier. Two additional divisions were to cross the canal that day and the next. At El 'Arîsh
airfield in Sinai, Egyptian air-force headquarters for the region,
stenographers were typing out General Jalal Ibrahim Zaid's
instructions, encompassing the entire strategy of the Egyptians. In the event of an Israeli attack on Syria, the air force
would have to strike a decisive blow on vital targets in Israel.
If the Israelis replied with a land attack on Egypt, the tanks in
Sinai could withstand the first wave before mounting a counteroffensive. Order no. 122/1967/3/35, signed by General Zaid
on May 17, listed the objectives of the Egyptian air force in the
event of a clash:

> Brigades 2, 12, 15 (fighters and bombers) and Brigade
> 61 (light bombers) will strike together at targets in the
> central and southern sectors under an aerial umbrella pro-
> vided by Brigade 9.
> Brigade 2 is to attack Akir airfield and destroy the planes
> on it. (Alternative plan: Attack the principal targets on the
> airfield, the radar station in the south, and the "Hawk"
> missile base in the northwest, near the coast, so that each
> target will be destroyed.) Ceiling: above the target, 50
> meters. Direction of attack: from south to north, banking
> to the right after flying over the target and rising to no more
> than 1,000 meters.

The first airborne expedition of the day met with success. A
MIG-21 equipped with Russian cameras made a surprise raid

into Israeli territory and photographed the region around Dimona. The Israeli Mirages that pursued it were unable to catch it before it returned to its base.

About 10:00 A.M. the Egyptians' first armored units reached the frontier. The tanks were spread out near the positions of the U.N. soldiers, who were still occupying them. Very early that morning U.N. headquarters in Gaza had received a message for General Rikhye. U Thant's directive could be summed up in the single sentence: "Don't budge until I order you to."

The Egyptian government met in Cairo with Mohammed Sidki Soliman presiding. U Thant had put Egypt in a difficult position: It had either to retract the demand made on the U.N. Emergency Force and lose face or to demand the immediate and final withdrawal of the "blue helmets" from its territory.

While the council of ministers was in session, new information kept flooding in to aggravate the situation further. In New York the official spokesman of the U.N. Secretary-General, Ramses Nassif, had made public the exchanges between the U.N. Secretariat and the Egyptian government. Some foreign ministries, and especially the State Department in Washington, had expressed their opposition to any policy that would remove the U.N. forces from the frontier. The radio stations in Jordan, where Nasser's regime was not popular, had expressed the opinion that Egypt ought to oust the U.N. forces and close the strait of Tiran to Israeli shipping.

During their meeting the ministers kept in touch with the President of the U.A.R. They decided to ignore U Thant's formal notice and to go straight to Rikhye again. At 2:00 P.M. Fawzi once more demanded the withdrawal of the forces within twenty-four hours. Rikhye refused to comply.

U Thant had hoped that his immediate action would drive Nasser into a corner and oblige him to back down. But he did not know Gamal Abdel Nasser. Consequently, when the meeting adjourned after five hours of deliberation, Mahmoud Riad returned to his office on Nile Street and composed the following letter:

Dear U Thant:

The government of the United Arab Republic has the honor to inform you that it has decided to end the presence of the U.N. Emergency Force in the U.A.R. territory and in the Gaza Strip. Please take the necessary measures to evacuate these troops as soon as possible.

I take this opportunity to express to you my profound gratitude and respect.

Mahmoud Riad
Minister of Foreign Affairs

That letter did not reach U Thant until the following day, May 18, but the Secretary-General was already aware that his little army was being threatened with ejection. He had just invited to a conference in his New York office the representatives of the seven countries whose soldiers served on the U.N. Emergency Force: Brazil, Canada, Denmark, India, Norway, Sweden, and Yugoslavia. At the beginning of the conference the representatives of India and Yugoslavia took the floor, saying that, if the U.A.R. demanded withdrawal of the U.N. force, then they would recall their soldiers with or without the official consent of the U.N. Secretariat. U Thant saw that discussion would be futile. The Belgrade-New Delhi-Cairo bloc had long dominated the neutrals, and two of its members had no intention of disagreeing with the third on so minor a point.

From then on, nothing made any difference—not pressure from the U.S. State Department; not the immediate approach by Gideon Rafael, Israel's delegate to the United Nations, to U Thant with a demand that he not give in to the Egyptian order; not the top-secret document kept in the U.N. files that Hammarskjöld had drawn up in 1957 after a seven-hour conference with Nasser in which it had definitely been agreed that the U.N. forces stationed in Sinai could not be withdrawn without the consent of the U.N. General Assembly.

In Tel Aviv, Foreign Minister Eban again tried to explain that, according to the decision of the United Nations, Egypt could not force the U.N. troops to leave its territory. He seemed to forget that the most solemn treaty becomes only a scrap of paper as soon as one of its signatories decides to disregard it.

The afternoon of May 17 was the turning point of the drama. Up until that time retreat had been possible. Nasser could have satisfied himself with his show of strength and ordered his troops back to Cairo, leaving the impression that they had forestalled an attack by the Zionists. All the melodrama of warnings, threats, and accusations on each side would have been as swiftly forgotten as had many of the flurries that were so frequent in the Middle East. But that brief letter from Egypt to the Secretary-General of the United Nations represented the point of no return.

In Jerusalem a few optimists in the Foreign Ministry advised reporters that from now on, an easing of the tension was to be expected. Life went on as usual in Israel, and a new committee met to study electoral reform. Some extremist religious groups made a show of protest against autopsies performed on corpses, and the leaders of the Alignment* applied themselves to ironing out internal difficulties.

But one luncheon conference between Eshkol and Rabin lasted well into the afternoon, and for the first time the question whether or not Nasser would undertake war with Israel while a large part of his army was tied up in Yemen was given serious consideration. Rabin informed Eshkol that the armored forces had been sent south and were prepared for any eventuality that might bring them into conflict with the Egyptian tanks. On the previous evening, a reserve brigade of tank operators had been mobilized, and others would soon be called to duty.

It seemed necessary to inform the nation, though in a restrained way, so as not to overcharge the atmosphere. Toward evening, after a long exchange of opinions between the Ministry of Foreign Affairs and the Army Headquarters, a military

* The united front of the two labor parties, Mapai and A'hdut Ha'avoda.

spokesman made the official announcement that "the Israeli army had taken appropriate measures against the increasing concentration of Egyptian troops in the Sinai peninsula."

For several days Guy Jacobson, the young economist, had been expecting to be called up. On the evening of May 17 he did not even lock his garden gate. At 11:30 he laid his book aside and went to bed. At 6:00 the following morning he was to meet an American engineer at the Tel Aviv Sheraton Hotel and take him to Arad. At 12:30 Jacobson was awakened by a knock on his door from a sergeant in his unit who was bringing him orders to report. A tidy and systematic fellow, Jacobson calmly packed his bag. As he said good-bye to his wife, he recalled that a month earlier General Tal, with whom he had gone to the movies and later to dinner at the Alibi, had said, "You can pay this time if you like, but it'll be my turn next time."

"Next time," Jacobson had answered, "you'll be Governor of Damascus, and you can give me an Oriental banquet such as I've always dreamed of."

He too had thought war would begin in the north.

At that very moment in Tel Aviv the radio receiver of U.S. Ambassador Walworth Barbour buzzed. The Ambassador was requested to transmit a cable from the White House to Eshkol, expressing the anxiety of the United States over the recent developments in the Middle Eastern situation. The message mentioned the steps the American government had taken toward appeasement of Syrian and Egyptian leaders and its endeavors for peace. Its conclusion was as follows:

> I know that you and your people are having your patience tried to the limit by continuing incidents along your border. In this situation, I would like to emphasize in the strongest terms the need to avoid any action on your side, which would add further to the violence and tension in your area. I urge the closest consultation between you and your principal friends. I am sure that you will understand

that I cannot accept any responsibilities on behalf of the United States for situations which arise as the results of actions on which we are not consulted.

With personal regards,

Sincerely,
Lyndon Johnson

•

THE LAST OF THE "BLUE HELMETS"

ON THE MORNING of May 18, Eshkol shut himself up in his office in Tel Aviv with Rabin, the officers in charge of defense, and the heads of the intelligence services. Eban and the high officials of the Foreign Ministry were also at the meeting.

While the meeting was in progress the message from the President of the United States was delivered. A few moments later another piece of information arrived: Egypt was demanding the evacuation of the U.N. forces, and the Secretary-General had decided to accede to that demand.

Eban immediately summoned the Ambassadors of the United States, France, and Great Britain. U Thant's unexpected decision to withdraw the U.N. forces without the authorization of the General Assembly or the Security Council disturbed him deeply: In 1957, when he had still been Ambassador from Israel to the United States and also Israel's representative in the United Nations, Eban had participated in the discussions that had led to the establishment of the U.N. force. He had not forgotten Egypt's oft-repeated promises and its assurances to Hammarskjöld that the "blue helmets" were desired and welcome. Now, as he talked with the representatives of the great powers in his office, he could not conceal his indignation. He reminded them of Egypt's pledge in connection with the U.N. troops and declared his apprehension that Nasser would close the strait of Tiran to Israeli shipping. He

42

ended with a sentence that later gravely offended U Thant: "Thant's attitude makes me think of an umbrella which folds up as soon as the rain begins."

In New York U Thant announced his decision to the Security Council. Arthur Goldberg, the U.S. representative, tried to persuade him to change it but to no avail. Israel's representative, Rafael, asked the Secretary-General to at least leave the U.N. unit in the Sharm el Sheikh area, so that its presence there might deter the Egyptians from closing the strait. U Thant refused. In the final cable that Rafael dispatched to the Israeli government, he said, "We'd better stop the useless struggle for the maintenance of the U.N. force. It's a dead horse, and nothing can bring it back to life."

Meanwhile, the Egyptian troops had already moved right up to the positions occupied by the "blue helmets" at El Kuntilla and Gebel el Hamra. The Egyptian officers gave the half-company of thirty-two Yugoslav infantrymen at Sharm el Sheikh five minutes to leave. At El Quseima and Gebel el Sabha, the Egyptian guns even fired a couple of rounds at the "blue helmets." The U.N. Emergency Force, which many people had thought the greatest achievement of the United Nations, collapsed like a house of cards.

Near a barricade separating Israel from the Gaza Strip, dozens of Arabs shouted with joy and shook their fists at the Israeli farmers. "Just you wait! We are coming and now you'll see!" Three Egyptian divisions and more than 500 tanks were spread over the Sinai peninsula. Traffic had been halted in the center of Cairo, in order to let the artillery pieces through and to allow the engineering units to load their equipment onto trains for the east. Civil defense, hospitals and first-aid centers were put on the alert. Schools became enlistment centers for young volunteers. The military-communications networks broadcast orders in code to various air bases:

Top secret! Action is expected, designed to cut off the southern part of the Negev and capture Eilat. The air force will bomb the Eilat airfield, radio station, and gasoline reserves during an attack which will be ordered by the Commander in Chief of the Air Force.

Syria mobilized fifty cadet battalions. Iraqi brigades started moving toward the frontier. The governments of Kuwait, Yemen, and Algeria declared their readiness to send soldiers and planes to Syria and Egypt.

Scarcely by lifting his little finger, Nasser had won a brilliant victory. Once more he was the most respected leader in the Arab world, which was losing no time in coming enthusiastically to his support and putting ever-increasing numbers of troops at his disposal. "Nasser has taken the initiative" proclaimed editorials in the Israeli newspapers and reports of the secret services. The number of tourists in Israel had dropped considerably, but the influx of foreign reporters made up for it. These keen-nosed terriers flocked into the Holy Land the minute they smelled powder. The Paris newspapers were the first that morning to predict the beginning of a "third round" in the Arab-Israeli war.

Eshkol's aides tried in vain to cancel his appointments with Jewish contributors from abroad, so that he would have more time for problems of defense. Eshkol was not noted for his ability to make rapid or startling decisions; his custom was to multiply committees to study a matter. In the Red House in Tel Aviv's Kiryah,* where the offices of the Prime Minister and the Defense Minister are located, politicans, military personnel, and representatives of the various political parties trod on one another's heels as they hurried to give their opinions.

By afternoon, however, the Foreign Minister had managed to have a few moments alone in his office with Eshkol. He was preparing a five-point answer to Lyndon Johnson:

1. The serious crisis presently threatening the Middle East originated in the attitude of Syria. Until now Israel has

* The section of the city where the government buildings are located.

shown great patience by not taking reprisals for the fourteen acts of Syrian sabotage during the past month.

2. Egypt has spread out over the Sinai peninsula an offensive force of at least 500 tanks. It is advisable to insist that
that country return its forces immediately to the other side
of the canal.

3. The U.N. force should not abandon its positions. The
Secretary-General of the United Nations ought to inform
Egypt that only the General Assembly can order the
evacuation of the U.N.E.F.

4. Cairo and Damascus seem to believe that the Soviet
Union is on their side in the present crisis. The United
States should publicly reaffirm the guarantees it has given
Israel in the past.

5. On the occasion of Eshkol's visit to the United States
in 1964, President Johnson promised that his country
would act either with the United Nations or independently
to preserve Israel's integrity and independence. The United
States should honor that pledge.

Eshkol approved the substance of the communication. The
same text was used as a basis for letters to the British Prime
Minister and to the President of France. On the evening of
May 18 the messages were delivered to the ambassadors from
the three great powers, who cabled their contents to Paris,
London, and Washington.

The situation was becoming more serious by the hour, but
the Israelis did not yet think that disaster was imminent. That
evening night clubs and discotheques in Tel Aviv were
jammed, as they usually were on Thursdays. The most popular
record in the discotheques was the French singer Adamo's "Insh
Allah," a prayer for peace between Jews and Arabs. That same
evening the popular American singer Pete Seeger, who had
been in Tel Aviv for a convention of the Organization for Judeo-
Arab Cooperation, sang a similar plea. The broadcasts from
Radio Damascus, however, were quite different. There, the
favorite song was "Cut Their Throats!"

Late that night the editors of Israel's daily newspapers met with the head of government. Eshkol, information minister Israel Galili, and Rabin addressed them at length on the subject of the concentration of Egyptian troops in Sinai. Eshkol asked the editorial writers to emphasize that stories about the concentration of Israeli units on the northern frontier in preparation for an attack on Syria had been fabricated out of whole cloth. Rabin described his anxiety over the withdrawal of the U.N. forces.

"What are you worried about that for?" Hanna Zemer, a reporter for *Davar*, asked him. "Let the U.N. get out of Gaza. It hardly matters."

The Chief of Staff replied slowly: "I don't think the U.N. force will leave Gaza without abandoning Sharm el Sheikh. Neither do I think that Nasser will take Sharm el Sheikh without closing the strait."

That night Yonina Ben Or and her two little girls, six-year-old Arza and three-year-old Mikhal, spent the night alone in their apartment near an airfield in the center of the country. Her husband had not returned, having been sent to another airfield to organize the Fouga squadron he was to lead.

Late that night official instructions that U.N. troops were to regroup at their bases before quitting Egyptian territory were sent by the Secretary-General's New York office to the commander in Gaza.

From every direction the U.N. troops returned to their encampments one by one, leaving behind them the graves of seventy soldiers of various nationalities who had died during the previous ten years, mostly in automobile accidents. On each tombstone these words were chiseled: "Fallen for the cause of peace."

•

KOSYGIN RECEIVES A MESSAGE

"THIS IS THE fourth day of the circus," were the ironic words with which one Israeli colonel opened his press conference. His remark was greeted with shouts of laughter. All the hubbub—the hundreds of tanks and guns, the vast numbers of troops in Sinai—how could it all be taken seriously?

That Friday, May 19, there were signs that the tensions were easing. Rabin went to Lydda airport twice, to bid farewell first to his Liberian counterpart, who had been visiting, and then to President Zalman Shazar, who was off to Canada. If the situation on the frontiers were really serious, it seemed, the government would not have permitted the President to leave the country on such a mission of state etiquette. Another sign that the situation could not be all that serious was the Treasury's issue of a commemorative medal reading, "1957–1967, Tenth Anniversary of the Port of Elat," at the very time when the press was intimating that Elat might be blockaded.

But the true situation was something else again: It was indeed serious. As on every other morning, Eshkol found on his desk a summary of events during the night. There were already 70,000 Egyptian soldiers and 600 tanks in the Sinai peninsula. Egyptian troops returning from Yemen had been sent to the Israeli frontier. There were Egyptian units at Sharm el Sheikh. In the Gaza Strip the Palestinian army, composed entirely of refugees, was preparing to seize the frontier positions that had been occupied by the U.N. force.

47

"That was the day," Rabin subsequently remarked, "when I fully understood how serious the situation had become. Nasser had scored a point by achieving the withdrawal of the U.N. troops. What would be his next move? The strait?"

Excitement spread in Washington, where it seemed as if a second Vietnam were about to materialize in the Middle East. Israeli Ambassador Harman and his Minister, Ephraim ("Epi") Evron, descended on the offices of Battle and Undersecretary of State Eugene Rostow. The pro-Israel lobby went into action, and the White House was deluged with calls from political parties, trade unions, industrialists, jurists, and members of Congress demanding that the President issue a warning to Egypt to withdraw.

That morning Johnson dispatched a secret cable to the head of the Soviet government. The latest reports from American diplomats in Cairo and Damascus indicated that the Arab leaders believed that in the event of war with Israel, the U.S.S.R. would support Egypt and Syria. The United States had unilaterally pledged itself to protect the integrity and independence of Israel. It was not difficult to see, therefore, that the two greatest world powers would be in conflict if war broke out in the Middle East. Johnson's cable was designed to avoid just such a confrontation. He proposed to the Soviet leaders a joint program of action to prevent any increase in Arab-Israeli tensions.

That cable was one of the two emergency measures that Secretary of State Dean Rusk recommended. If the Russian response to it was inadequate, then the United States would appeal to Great Britain and France to form a joint political front based on the tripartite agreement of 1950, in which the three powers had pledged themselves to maintain the status quo in the Middle East.

The same alarm sounded that morning in various other parts of the world. In London Foreign Secretary George Brown postponed his departure for Moscow. U Thant told his staff that he intended to fly to Cairo to meet with Nasser. On tens of thousands of Israeli television screens appeared pictures of the mobs in Gaza brandishing rifles and shouting "Death to the Jews!"; pictures of tank columns shrouded in clouds of dust as they penetrated into the Sinai peninsula; and pictures of commandos wearing camouflage uniforms and carrying Soviet rifles as they took up their battle posts.

In contrast, the Israelis had sent only their regular army and two reserve brigades to the south.

In the Ministry of Defense in Tel Aviv, Eshkol asked Rabin: "What are you waiting for? Mobilize the people of Israel."

At noon Colonel Moshe Kashti, Director General of the Defense Ministry, assembled the chiefs of the various service branches: "As of this minute, we are in a state of emergency. From now on, all services will work until 5:00; even on Saturdays and holidays. All shipments of arms from our factories to foreign purchasers have been stopped. Instead, we will do our best to purchase what we can throughout the world. For security reasons, telephone calls to Israeli purchasing agents abroad will be discontinued, and all communications with them will be by telegram round the clock."

Before 1:00 P.M. the Defense Ministry's radio system was humming with messages to Paris, Rome, London, Washington, and Bonn. In the capitals of the three great western European powers, Israel officials were descending upon the Ministries of Foreign Affairs and Defense to request additional guns and ammunition; others were preparing an airlift of both Israeli and foreign planes in order to move these supplies to Israel. But high officials in Paris politely declined the Israeli request for the loan of twenty-five Vautours and Mirages.*

At noon Egyptian time, General Dajidi, commander of the eastern section of the Egyptian air force, signed a paper that had just been brought to him. It had already been signed by the commander of the 2nd Air Brigade and by the leader of the 18th Squadron. The chief of the Egyptian air force had agreed

* Interviews with French officials, November 9–30, 1967.

to it by telephone. It was the plan of attack on Israel's Akir airfield, to be carried out by planes from El 'Arîsh in the Sinai peninsula.

A few moments later Dajidi also signed battle order no. 67/2 for a general raid on the Israeli airfields at Akir, Kastina, Hazzerim, Be'er Menuha, on the principal radio stations throughout the region, and on the launching platforms of Hawk missiles in Tel Aviv and south of that city.

Small groups of U.N. soldiers reported at the three barriers on the roads linking Israel and the Gaza Strip. Two Canadians clambered up the observation tower near Nahal 'Oz, folded the U.N. flag, and disappeared. Not far away four U.N. soldiers took down the U.N. emblem from observation post 25, which they had laboriously constructed out of Carlsberg beer bottles from Denmark. At Erez, near the most important of the barriers, Swedes, Canadians, and Indians stood at attention. It was 3:55 P.M. A red-turbaned Indian band played a march. General Rikhye reviewed his honor guard. At 4:00 P.M. the U.N. flag was lowered and stowed away in a safe spot. Soldiers took down the barrier sign, "King's Gate." Rikhye and his officers walked to the Israeli side to take leave, but the officer they expected to find there did not appear. Instead there was only a party of American tourists made up of elderly women, who focused their Japanese cameras on the group. Rikhye shook the hand of Israeli Corporal Prosper Ben Shitrit, instructed him to give his regards to General Rabin, and stalked away.

The U.N. troops packed up and left.

In Nahal 'Oz, Mefallesim, Nir'am, and Erez, it was a sad evening. After ten peaceful years the pioneers there could think only of how their houses would be used for target practice or looted by saboteurs from the other side of the frontier.

The sun went down. At a tank base somewhere in the south, Guy Jacobson buried in the sand two jam jars filled with gasoline-soaked rags and lit them. The flames scarcely flickered in the hot, dry air.

They were Jacobson's Sabbath candles.

In Jerusalem seven-year-old Ilan said to Esther Arditi: "Mama, did you hear the radio? The Arabs say they're going to cut our throats."

The Sabbath evening fell over Israel. Ritual celebrations were being prepared in the kibbutzim. Everything seemed normal except, perhaps, for the buses lined up in the center of each town; all night long they would be loading reserve soldiers who had been dragged out of bed, pulled off dance floors, or called from dinner to be transported to military camps in the south.

Late that night everything quieted down. The Israeli radio stations signed off. People who could speak Arabic turned their dials to broadcasting stations in neighboring capitals. From time to time they picked up the sarcastic voice of the Jordanian announcer telling Nasser: "Be a man! You chased out the U.N.; now close the strait. Blockade 'Aqaba! Don't let the Zionist ships through! Be a man, Nasser!"

•

DAYAN EXPECTS WAR

IN 1943, WHEN Esther Arditi had been six years old and the Germans occupying northern Italy, she had hidden with her father, mother, and young brother in a bakery in an isolated village. Her older brother belonged to a band of partisans operating out of a nearby forest. In the dead of winter the Germans had learned that a Jewish family was hiding in the village. They had burst into the bakery and dragged off the father to the S.S. barracks in the next town. A storm trooper had killed Esther's mother and young brother before her eyes. In terror she had fled into the street and had succeeded in reaching the forest, where she roamed alone for days, eating roots and sucking from a stray sheep. All she remembered of those days was the morning when two armed men had appeared in front of her. One of them had been her brother.

She stayed with the partisans until the war was over, witnessing bloodshed when most girls her age were playing with dolls. At the end of the war she returned with her brother to their house in Leghorn, where they found their father, who had managed to survive his long imprisonment.

When she was eleven years old, Esther learned that a Jewish state was about to be born in Palestine. One night she broke open her toy bank, jumped on a train for Naples, and climbed aboard the first ship she saw in the harbor. She was found three hours later and taken home, but her frustrated escape only increased her desire to go to Israel. When she was sixteen years old, her dream finally came true. A few months later she enlisted in the army. She was perhaps the smallest soldier in all Israel, because of both her age and her height: fifty inches. After serving as a nurse on the front lines, she was assigned to the air force.

One stormy winter night Esther was on guard when a Mosquito was struck by lightning as it was about to land; it fell in flames on a field not far from the airbase. The plane was loaded with munitions, which began to explode, sending bullets whistling in every direction. The fire trucks and emergency crews stood by helplessly while frail little Esther dashed into the heart of the flaming furnace and, with superhuman effort, pulled out the two unconscious pilots, covering them with her own body to protect them from the fragments of the plane, which exploded immediately.

A week later she stood in the office of Chief of Staff Dayan to receive from his hands the highest award of the Israeli army. Esther was the first woman in Israel to receive the Order of the Army.

During the crisis of May 1967, Esther was living in Jerusalem, bringing up her two children, Ilan and Noorit, alone. As she awoke on May 20 she recalled Ilan's "Mama, they're going to cut our throats!"

Esther knew her duty. She took the children to Yad Vashem Museum, a memorial to the victims of Nazi persecution. There she showed them photographs of children dying of starvation, suffering in concentration camps, being dragged off to gas chambers. Ilan and Noorit burst into tears of fright, but Esther continued her lecture. When they left they went to the military cemetery on Mount Herzl, where she showed them the graves of youths who had fallen, guns in hand, during the War of Independence while defending a Jewish village against Arab attack. Esther told her children the story of that battle, adding as she finished: "The children you saw in the pictures at the museum, as well as those buried here, are all dead. Death is a fact of life, but not a major one. The important fact is *how* you die. Children growing up in our country have the great privilege of being able to fight for their life. Now stop crying."

They did.

On May 20 a hundred thousand happy Israelis, their bodies already tanned, went to the beaches. The bathing season opened officially that day, and no army in the world could prevent a good-looking Israeli girl from showing that she had the smallest bikini in the entire Middle East. For tens of thousands of young people, the beach season ended barely a few hours after it had begun. When they went home at noon, they found a mobilization order, and until evening general mobilization procedures continued.

The telephone rang in the house of Rami Shemer, an El Al pilot who lived near Tel Aviv and who was a reserve pilot in Arie Ben Or's Fouga squadron. Arie was on the other end of the line. "Rami," Arie said, "at 6:45 tomorrow morning a plane will be waiting for you at Dov airfield near Tel Aviv to take you to the base."

"Ah, let me get a few winks of sleep." Rami was not entirely pleased with the prospect. "I just got back from New York. I haven't seen my family for a week."

"Tomorrow at 6:45 A.M.," Arie repeated. "It's not training any more. It's serious."

At that moment a squadron of Egyptian transport planes was flying over one of the world's most extraordinary landscapes: Sharm el Sheikh, the enchanted spot of purple rocks, white sands, and blue water that controls the entrance to the strait of Tiran. On signal the well-oiled bays opened, and the sky was dotted with white parachutes. The Egyptian high command, fearful that after the withdrawal of the U.N. troops the Israelis, in order to preserve their navigation rights, would mount a surprise attack on the gulf, was landing a commando brigade.

"I keep telling you that they will close the strait, and then war will be inevitable!" Once again Dayan was making his prediction to two friends in the course of the Independence Day celebration of the Israel Labor List, or Rafi. Dayan was depressed. The man who had planned and executed the Sinai campaign and who was above all a man of action, was in 1967, thanks to his political isolation, unable either to act or to influence the course of events.

In 1964 he had resigned as Minister of Agriculture in the Cabinet because of disagreements with Eshkol. In 1965 he had reluctantly followed Ben-Gurion after the split in the Mapai Israel Labor Party, in order to become a deputy of the Rafi, a small opposition party with lofty ambitions. Some of his friends were spending their enforced leisure in active opposition in Parliament, but Dayan, who had never been much of a politician, refused to join them and turned to journalism instead. He had published his diary of the Sinai campaign and a series of articles on the war in Vietnam, but such activities scarcely satisfied the man who had been commander in chief. He felt even more useless in this time of crisis, when half the country was being mobilized. The lowliest soldier, gun in hand, was filling the place assigned to him, while Dayan himself, who could contribute so much, had to stand aside.

That same evening he telephoned Colonel Lior, Eshkol's military aide, for permission to inspect the Israeli units massing in the south. After some hesitation Eshkol, who had asked Rabin's opinion, consented.

In London Foreign Minister Brown telephoned twice to Israeli Ambassador Aaron Remez. Brown seemed disturbed, even worried. "Does Mr. Eban think I can leave for Moscow? What do you think? What should we do?"

In Paris Israeli Ambassador Walter Eytan sent a message through devious channels to President de Gaulle requesting him to intervene with Alexei Kosygin to restrain the Egyptians.

In Washington the Israelis tried once more to persuade the United States to announce publicly it would honor its pledge to protect Israel's independence. Israeli diplomats also put pressure on the State Department to renew the declaration of

March 1, 1957, which stated that the United States recognized the international character of the strait of Tiran and the right of "free and innocent" passage to all ships, regardless of the flags they flew. Such a warning at that time would perhaps prevent Egypt from closing the strait rashly.

In the afternoon Harman and Evron went to the eighth floor of the State Department to talk with Undersecretary Eugene Rostow. Evron, short, bald, and perspicacious, seemed more pessimistic than did Harman, who firmly believed that the United States was determined to support Israel.

In talk with his Israeli visitors, Rostow expressed his personal opinion that it would be desirable for the U.N. troops that had been chased out of Egypt to reassemble in Israeli territory. Evron and Harman disagreed and asked instead for American action to demonstrate that the United States would live up to its promises. "An American battleship is leaving the Jordanian port of 'Aqaba today, going through the Strait of Tiran toward the Red Sea. Order it to return through the strait and anchor in Elat harbor. That will show that the United States believes in its policy of maintaining the freedom of the seas."

Rostow demurred and stated: "We advise you not to use force against Egypt unless it does close the strait and even then not to undertake a unilateral action. The agreement on free navigation is the most solemn of all that have been signed by Israel and the United States and the most precise statement of the American government's obligations. Eshkol's letter requests us to make a public statement of our responsibilities to you, and we are considering doing so. But for the time being we prefer to act within the frame of the United Nations. In order not to be overtaken by events, we should not undertake any unilateral action."

Rostow then added an important statement, which was also repeated by Secretary Rusk in other circumstances: "If you want us to be with you at the crash landing, then you had better consult us at the takeoff."

The conference left the Israeli diplomats with the impression that the United States did not know what to do next. Such irresolution was disastrous for Israel. "We must expect," an Israeli diplomat cabled to Jerusalem, "that the United States will put pressure on us to abandon positions that they do not think essential to us."

Late that night a reserve battalion pitched its tents among the dunes in the middle of the Negev. In one tent were a young fellow from a kibbutz and an old reserve soldier. The boy, astonished to see his tentmate take two snow-white, well-ironed sheets from his knapsack, burst out laughing. His companion replied a little sadly: "For years, ever since World War II, I have never parted from my sheets. I used to work in a laundry that worked exclusively for the German army. In the ghetto we had no sheets, and all day long we had to wash theirs. I took an oath then that if I survived the war I would always sleep between sheets."

At 4:00 A.M. in Jerusalem Eban's telephone rang. The caller was Reginald Michael Hadow, Great Britain's Ambassador in Tel Aviv. He apologized for phoning at such an hour: "I am acting on the instructions of the Foreign Minister, who is getting ready to go to Moscow. We would like to know whether you intend to attack now that the Egyptians have seized Sharm el Sheikh or whether you intend to wait until they interfere with freedom of navigation. We would like to advise you to wait, for perhaps the Egyptians don't really want war."*

---

* British sources interviewed in London, January 18–25, 1968.

•

NASSER MAKES UP HIS MIND

A WEEK HAD passed since the beginning of the crisis. Little by little the Sinai desert had filled with soldiers, tanks, guns, and jet airplanes, all of which were menacing the southern part of Israel. The U.N. troops, the guardians of peace, had been chased out of Egyptian territory and away from the strait. The cadis of the Cairo mosques had been ordered to proclaim a "holy war" against the Jews. The Arab armies had been mobilized and made ready for action before being sent to the Israeli frontier. Freedom of navigation in the strait of Tiran was being seriously threatened. And all that time the Israeli government had displayed a distressing paralysis.

At first the government had been surprised. Then it had attached little importance to the concentration of Egyptian troops. Then it had taken a passive, wait-and-see attitude. Except for the mobilization of the reserves, the government had taken no action whatever. The Israeli army had quickly responded to the situation, and the people were alert. Only the authorities remained sluggish.

The Minister of Foreign Affairs and the Prime Minister's staff were exchanging muffled accusations. Why had a meeting of the Security Council not been demanded as soon as U Thant decided to recall the "blue helmets"? Why had the intelligence services not been aware of Nasser's plans? The news of a projected trip by U Thant to Cairo had created a foolish optimism that he could somehow alter the course of history and that

58

everything would turn out for the best. In fact, that very morning Foreign Ministry observers were announcing with typical fatuousness that the situation had considerably improved during the previous twenty-four hours and that the withdrawal of the U.N. force did not necessarily mean the closing of the strait, although the latter was already as good as fact.

Galili feared a surprise attack from Egyptian planes on Israeli airfields. Minister of Education Zalman Aran thought war was not inevitable, even if the Egyptians did bomb Israel and close the gulf of 'Aqaba. The leaders of the National Religious Party headed by Haim Moshe Shapiro, were particularly fearful that the Soviets were preparing an offensive against Western holdings in the area. The leaders of the United Workers' Party (Mapam) had already expressed their opinion, through Yakov Hazan: "It is theoretically incorrect to believe that the mounting danger can be checked by taking the offensive or by large-scale reprisals. Any such action will produce only very serious consequences." Eban confidently called to mind the steps that Israeli diplomats had taken in Washington and restated his opinion that Nasser would not close the strait.

Despite these assurances the government ordered an inventory of its gasoline supplies and reviewed the number of Israeli ships that had used the strait during the past few years. It also examined several forecasts prepared by treasury experts, which might provide an answer to the question of what the price of a barrel of gasoline would be if the strait were closed and it had to go all around the African continent.

Eshkol's shilly-shallying nature kept him from taking direct and concrete action or delivering a stern warning to Egypt. On the following day he was to deliver a speech to the Knesset, and he had granted several ministers permission to inspect his text in advance. It was, therefore, clear in advance that it would be an irresolute address from which every strong statement had been expunged by the "doves" who dominated the government.

No one close to Israeli politics was astonished at this sorry

situation in the Cabinet—in view of political developments
in the country during the previous years. On June 16, 1963,
Ben-Gurion had left power, to be replaced as Prime Minister
and Defense Minister by Eshkol. The elections of November 1965 had confirmed this change by bringing defeat
to Ben-Gurion's partisans. In many respects Eshkol was radically different from his predecessor. Instead of being an activ-
ist, an authority on matters of defense, and a prophet from
morning till night of the danger of a new war with the Arabs,
Eshkol was a peaceful man chiefly interested in economic
matters, which he believed to be the basis of future development. In the period approximately between 1960 and 1965,
Israel seemed to have entered upon an era of tranquillity as far
as its relations with its neighbors were concerned. War did not
seem likely before 1970, and it therefore seemed advisable to
shift from obsessive concern with defensive measures.

After its long spell of well-nigh unbearable tension, rationing,
and financial and personal sacrifice, Israel needed to relax. It
seemed to require no longer the energetic leader who had
saved the country when its survival seemed impossible; rather
it needed a good manager of the problems of daily living.
Hence, Eshkol. He was no expert on military matters, and his
aide Zvi Dinstein had been transferred from the treasury to the
Defense Ministry. This arrangement was fine while everything
remained calm and peaceful. Little by little, Chief of Staff
Rabin had become Defense Minister in fact if not in title. The
government had thus few military experts.

"If you ask Eshkol whether he prefers tea or coffee, he'll
have to think about it before he'll say, 'Half and half.' "

The new U.S. Ambassador to Egypt, Richard Nolte, a dull,
bespectacled man, stepped out of an airplane that had just
landed at Cairo International airport. It had been three months
since his predecessor, Luke Battle, had left the Egyptian capital. Nolte, who looked like a young scholar, was not a career
diplomat but an academician, who had taught for some time at
The American University in Beirut before becoming director of

the Institute of Current World Affairs in New York. When reporters at the airport asked him his opinions about the Middle Eastern crisis, he stared at them blankly and replied, "What crisis?"

His reply infuriated David Nes, deputy chief of the U.S. mission in Cairo, who had come to meet the new Ambassador. Since January 1967 Nes had been convinced that Nasser would be drawn into hostilities with Israel sooner or later. He was an outspoken critic of American policy toward Egypt, which he considered shortsighted and dangerous, and he needed no further proof of it than the deaf ear the United States had turned to Egypt's request for $155 million in aid and U.S. arms shipments to Israel and Saudi Arabia. In his opinion such an attitude only made the Egyptians suspicious and bitter and prevented the United States from having any influence on Egyptian policy. In January Nes had written directly to Senator J. William Fulbright, Chairman of the Senate Foreign Relations Committee, recommending that an experienced career diplomat or a personal friend of President Johnson be appointed Ambassador to Cairo, in order to smooth over Washington's relations with Egypt. But instead there had just arrived an ambassador who said, "What crisis?"

Nes was not the only distressed person at the Cairo airport that morning. Ambassador Nolte himself was also in a quandary. He had received almost completely contradictory instructions on the line he was to take: one from the U.S. delegation to the United Nations, the other from the politicians in Washington. The future looked dark to him.

Still another visitor landed in Cairo that morning: General Amer Hamash, Jordanian Chief of Staff. The Jordanian radio officially announced that the General was visiting Cairo in order to coordinate the military operations of the Arabs under a unified command. But such a command had foundered several years before.

Meanwhile, relations between "revolutionary" Arab countries like Egypt, Iraq, Syria, and Yemen, on one hand, and the conservative states like Jordan and Saudi Arabia, on the other, had declined to the point of hostility. The Syrian government had even authorized terrorist raids on Jordanian territory, in order to topple King Hussein's "reactionary" government. That very morning Ahmed Shukairy had urged the people of Jordan to depose their king. It was precisely that situation that had compelled Hussein to send Hamash to Cairo, for the little King felt the tension mounting in the Arab capitals. The masses were looking only to Nasser, the current champion of the Arab camp, for the liberation of Palestine. In a desperate effort to keep his throne, Hussein was trying a new tack, coming to Nasser's side at the eleventh hour.

His attempt failed. The Egyptians gave Hamash the cold shoulder, and he returned to Amman humiliated.

About noon the Egyptians announced that a battery of heavy artillery had been set up at Sharm el Sheikh. On the other side of the frontier, in the southern part of the Israeli Negev, a sandstorm sprang up. The gravel-laden winds battered the tents and the antennae that had been hastily erected at three spots. Inside the tents, spread out on big wooden tables, were enormous maps of the Sinai peninsula, covered with plastic arrows and sprinkled with coded place names. The three commanders of the Israeli division—Tal, Ariel Sharon, and Abraham Yoffe—had set up their command posts directly opposite the Egyptian installations.

In Washington the Soviet chargé d'affaires was delivering Kosygin's reply to Johnson's cable, a vague reply that did not touch on the essential point: how far the Soviet Union would go in support of the Arabs. Instead the Russians laboriously detailed Israel's aggressive tendencies and demanded that the United States restrain them.

"They're trying to come between us," Ambassador Abe Harman said to Luke Battle.

"They can't. It wouldn't work."

Again the Israelis urged that President Johnson issue a clear and firm statement of United States policy. Again they were told that Johnson did not wish to do anything that might adversely affect U Thant's mission to Egypt. "Just be patient and wait until U Thant gets back from Cairo."

On that calm Sunday morning, Israeli diplomats in Washington were unaware that Eugene Rostow, at the direct request of the White House, would spend his afternoon drafting a statement on the situation in the Middle East for Johnson to issue. The President had decided to grant Eshkol's request and had even fixed the exact time at which his statement would be made: Tuesday, May 23, in the afternoon. In the meantime the American President was in for a few surprises.

In London the Foreign Minister transmitted to the Israeli Ambassador a message from Harold Wilson to Eshkol. In this friendly letter, Wilson praised the close association between the foreign ministries of the two countries and also informed the Israeli leaders that Great Britain would demand that Syria refrain from any rash action against Israel. It also requested that Israel do nothing to aggravate the situation, once again emphasizing that Great Britain would protect free navigation in the Gulf of 'Aqaba and also promising that it would support any international action authorized by the United Nations for the protection of the freedom of the strait of Tiran. Wilson requested the Israeli government to reconsider its refusal to admit the U.N. force to its territory. The presence of U.N. troops on Egyptian soil alone, Wilson wrote, had permitted the government of the U.A.R. to act as the sole arbiter of the fate of those troops.

The Canadian government sent Israel an identical request, and so did Rusk. Pessimistic Israelis had been right in thinking that the passive attitude of their government would bring pressure from the Western powers for concessions from Israel.

In Tel Aviv, directors of the Rafi met in Shimon Peres' office. Among those present were three former chiefs of staff: Dayan, Zur, and Dori. Ben-Gurion was sporting a white shirt open at the collar; he had come from Sede Boqer at the request of the Rafi secretariat, which wished him to remain in Tel Aviv as long as the crisis lasted.

The discussion centered on the possibility that Egypt might

attack Israel. "Will the Egyptians use their missiles?" asked Ben-Gurion.

"A missile is a plane without a pilot," Dayan said. "The question doesn't hinge on that. The Israeli army is superb, and its leadership is excellent. We can stand the test."

Just then an official of the Defense Ministry entered the room with a note for Ben-Gurion. The old leader read the few lines and nodded to the messenger: "Yes." A few minutes later Ben-Gurion excused himself, saying that he had an urgent appointment.

The guest, who had arrived at Ben-Gurion's Tel Aviv house at 7:00 P.M., was Chief of Staff Rabin.

Rabin had a high opinion of Ben-Gurion, but, basing his politics on his experience in the Palmach, he was closer to the Achdut Ha'avoda and had never been one of Ben-Gurion's crowd. Nevertheless, the two had maintained close ties with each other, and in 1963, when Ben-Gurion left power, Rabin had wept in his office.

Now Rabin needed to consult the man who had laid the foundations of the Israeli army and had directed the Sinai campaign. He had come to Ben-Gurion to survey with him the whole political and military situation. Ben-Gurion wanted Rabin's opinion on the military situation. Rabin was cautious; he did not succeed in convincing Ben-Gurion that the Israeli army was strong enough to destroy the Arab forces.

Ben-Gurion was, however, convinced that until May 19 the concentration of Egyptian troops had simply been a play to the gallery. If Israel had not mobilized its reserves, he declared, Nasser would have withdrawn his troops, and the crisis would have ended there. Ben-Gurion was critical of Eshkol's decision to mobilize the reserves.

That evening Eshkol, Eban, and high officials of the Foreign Ministry were at Lydda airport to welcome a distinguished visitor, Raphael Passio, the head of the Finnish government, who was arriving for an official visit. After a long search the Foreign Ministry had at last turned up—in the Israel Museum

—a Jew who could speak Finnish. This man, perhaps the only one of his kind in the country, had been engaged several days before to accompany sixty-four-year-old Passio as interpreter. Eshkol was able to joke about it: "Snap me while I'm talking Finnish," he said to a photographer.

At Nasser's house in Cairo, a summit conference of Egyptian leaders was in progress. Present were the deputy prime ministers, the army commanders, the top officers of the Foreign Ministry, and the heads of the intelligence service. Later came the leaders of the Arab Socialist Union, the only legal party in Egypt.

The situation was reviewed from the political, military, and psychological points of view. Egypt had just won a series of dazzling victories, which had stunned Israel and opened the way for further action. The U.N. troops had been dislodged from Sharm el Sheikh, and Syria and Jordan were demanding the closing of the strait of Tiran to Israeli navigation. Nasser put the question: What would be Israel's reaction to the closing of the strait?

One by one, his advisers gave their opinions. Israel was on the defensive, with its back to the wall, and its government was irresolute. The Israeli government had repeatedly announced that it would consider the closing of the strait a *casus belli*, but would it back up those threats? Even Ben-Gurion, the symbol of Israeli aggressive action, had not gone to war when Egypt had decided to close the strait in September 1955. It was not until a year later that he had begun the Sinai campaign, when he was sure of the support of Great Britain and France. It was hard to believe that Eshkol would risk war, but if he did Egypt was well able to face it. On the other hand, if Egypt did not close the strait, it would be criticized by the entire Arab world. It was no longer possible to back down on the grounds that the U.N. force occupied the shores of the gulf.

Nasser had not yet given his own opinion. A few months earlier, just after the Samu incident, Amer had asked him to close the strait, but he had stubbornly refused, saying: "We are not ready. Israel could declare war, and we are not yet strong enough. I will close the strait only when I am sure of the superiority of Egyptian arms."

Nasser was not yet convinced of that superiority, but that evening he was no longer the moderate and responsible thinker who knew how to appease the frenzy of the Arab masses. From May 13 to May 20 he had appeared, in the eyes of the world, as the supreme leader of the Arabs, rushing to the aid of a sister nation menaced by unprovoked attack. But in his highly emotional state and intoxicated with power, he had become a poker player wildly staking all his winnings.

Late that night, he decided to close the strait. At daybreak two submarines, a destroyer, and four missile-launcher boats left the Suez canal and headed for the Red Sea.

In a Tel Aviv café a comic uttered the latest in Israeli black humor: "With a Chief of Staff like Rabin and a Prime Minister like Nasser, we could go far."

•

THE STRAIT IS CLOSED

ABOUT 10:00 A.M. three big American automobiles, with stocky bodyguards in dark glasses clinging to the doors, stopped at the Cairo West airfield. The guards jumped nimbly to the ground and formed a line around a military transport plane that stood ready to take off. Out of the second car stepped Nasser, tanned and smiling in a dark suit and striped tie, with a neatly folded handkerchief in his breast pocket.

Before leaving his home he had had a chance to chat with his eighteen-year-old son, who had told his father that he was going to enlist in the youth battalion that was being formed as part of the national effort to crush Israel. Nasser had encouraged him to do so. Then he had headed for his office in Koubba Palace in the center of Cairo, where he had an appointment with the Soviet Ambassador Podyedyeev. Their meeting was cordial. The Ambassador informed Nasser of the exchange of messages between Johnson and Kosygin and then emphasized that the Soviet Union had not changed its view. Nasser did not mention the long conference in his office the day before or the serious decision that had been its outcome.

After scanning reports from the intelligence service and the diplomatic cables that had arrived during the night, Nasser left for the airport. The previous evening's decision was still a secret, though there had been a vague allusion to it in *al-Ahram:* "The next few hours will be decisive ones in the Middle Eastern crisis, which has now reached a climax."

As he approached the plane, Nasser was greeted by a group of high officials: his chief officers, Field Marshal Amer and Lieutenant General Zakariah Mohieddin; Ali Sabry, Secretary-General of the Arab Socialist Union; War Minister Shams Badran; Air Force Chief Mohammed Sidky Mahmoud; and Murtaghi, commander of the Sinai forces. They were to accompany President Nasser on his inspection of the military installations in the Sinai peninsula, a day-long excursion.

The plane roared down the runway, while MIG-21s took off from a nearby base to escort it over the peninsula.

In his Jerusalem office, Eshkol was studying the situation with executives of the intelligence service and Director General of his ministry. Afterward Passio paid him a short courtesy visit. A confidential report received that morning ended on an optimistic note: "It seems logical to us, in the light of the diplomatic steps already taken as well as of the coming visit of U Thant to Cairo, that Nasser will refrain from provocation, and so the closing of the strait seems unlikely."

A little later an urgent message was placed on Eshkol's desk—the second cable from President Johnson, which was actually a reply to Eshkol's letter of May 18. Johnson praised Israel's calm and restraint and said that he had approached the head of the Syrian government and the President of the U.A.R. and had asked them to see that war did not break out in the area.

> We have been in touch with the Soviet Union and have received a moderate and encouraging reply. The Soviet leaders have no illusions about the pledge of the United States to prevent, either through the United Nations or independently of that international organization, all aggression in the Middle East. This policy has been defined and confirmed by four American presidents: Truman, Eisenhower, Kennedy, and myself. It is also contained in the three-power agreement of 1950.

Johnson advised Israel to make contact with France and Great Britain, cosigners of the tripartite declaration.

In conclusion the President indicated his disapproval of U Thant's decision to recall the U.N. troops from Egypt, but he expressed the hope that U Thant's trip to Cairo would produce positive results. "I also envisage making a statement in the tone of your letter of May 18, but I prefer to wait until U Thant returns from his visit to Cairo."*

The only one of the three chiefs of state who had not replied to Eshkol was President de Gaulle. Since the crisis had started, France had been strangely silent. True, shipments of arms from France to Israel were still normal and had even increased a little, but why did France make no reply?

As voices were being raised in Israel to protest that silence, the Israeli correspondent of a Paris newspaper noted on the morning of May 22: "It is our duty to state that even now, and now more than ever before, France has not forgotten or abandoned Israel. France remains a true and constant friend. We ask for the confidence of the Israeli public without embarrassing questions.

Barely an hour after that article appeared, France declared that it considered itself no longer bound by the 1950 declaration of the three Western powers.

Eshkol's tardiness in arriving at the Knesset astonished the hundreds of photographers, reporters, deputies, and guests, who did not know that until the last minute half the government had been pondering the speech its chief was about to deliver. Since noon several ministers had read it, and each had crossed out a sentence or two that he had not liked. Minister of the Interior H. M. Shapiro, who was more worried than the rest, begged Eshkol to delete passages that to him seemed likely to offend Nasser.

When Eshkol finally mounted the platform, he therefore made a timid, apologetic speech. He did not even allude to freedom of navigation in the strait of Tiran. The tone was one of appeasement:

* Interview with a high official in Washington, November 1, 1967.

The concentration of Egyptian troops in the Sinai peninsula has reached proportions that have increased tension in
the area and anxiety throughout the world. It seems advisable to return to the *status quo ante* on both sides of the
frontier. . . . I wish to repeat to the Arab countries, especially to Egypt and Syria, that we do not contemplate
any military action. We have no reason to interfere with
their security, their territory, or their legitimate rights. We
have contemplated no intervention in their internal affairs,
whatever may be their government or their mutual and
international relations. We only ask from those states the
application of those same principles toward us as an act of
reciprocity.

Eshkol left to the great powers the task of resolving the
crisis:

It seems advisable to mobilize all the international
forces in order to guarantee the continuation of the tranquillity that has reigned on the Israeli-Egyptian frontier
since March, 1957. . . . We will follow with interest the
progress of the visit of the Secretary-General of the United
Nations to the Middle East, and we will study the results
of it.

In New York U Thant was ending a conference with the
representatives of the great powers before leaving for Cairo. In
the late afternoon he received Goldberg, the U.S. delegate to
the United Nations.

"Secretary of State Dean Rusk," said Goldberg, "asks you to
let Nasser know that the United States is pledged to Israel, as
confirmed by four presidents."

At 7:30 P.M. U Thant took off for Cairo, with plans to stop at
Paris.

At Bîr Gifâfa air base in the heart of the Sinai peninsula, the
MIGs were lined up for takeoff. Inside in the big briefing room,
seated in leather-upholstered armchairs, Marshal Amer and

President Nasser were surrounded by enthusiastic aviators wearing tight-fitting green Soviet flight uniforms in honor of the occasion. The atmosphere was relaxed, and there were jokes and laughter. Nasser's laugh is legendary: It swirls silently through his whole body like a backwash; then he throws back his head and reveals his powerful jaws.

At that moment the Egyptian leader had every reason to be pleased. The ultramodern planes and the confident young aviators produced an impression of solid strength. And the latest news was encouraging. France and Great Britain were flushing the tripartite agreement down the drain; Eshkol had made a pacific speech. The United States did not want to be dragged into another Vietnam. The sooner the previous day's decision was implemented, the better. The Secretary-General of the United Nations, who was expected in Cairo the following morning, would find himself confronted with a *fait accompli* before he could insist on concessions.

Then Nasser's face grew serious, as he launched into an extemporaneous address: "Our troops have been in Sharm el Sheikh since yesterday. The strait of Tiran is part of our territorial waters. No Israeli ship will ever negotiate it again. We also forbid the shipment of strategic materials to Israel on non-Israeli vessels." Silence fell over the huge room. Nasser paused a moment before continuing: "The Jews are threatening us with war. Our answer to them is 'You're welcome! We're ready!' "

In Jerusalem Eshkol went to bed without suspecting a thing. He had just said good-bye to Passio after having honored him with a banquet at the King David Hotel. Afterward Foreign Minister Eban had spoken at length with his political secretary, Moshe Raviv, about the consequences of France's and Great Britain's refusal to honor their 1950 obligations. Raviv had gone home at 1:00 A.M.

At 1:30 A.M. the telephone rang in the office of Aaron Yariv, head of the intelligence service, who had preferred to stay at headquarters that night. The assistant who woke him had just heard Nasser's speech reported over Radio Cairo. Yariv telephoned Rabin at home. "Yitzhak, Nasser has just announced that he is closing the strait."

In Montreal, across the Atlantic, it was early evening. The mayor of the city was giving a banquet in honor of Israeli President Shazar and his wife. It was a thoroughly brilliant affair, with the men in white ties and the women in evening gowns. In the middle of the meal Counselor Patir of the Israeli embassy in Washington, who was accompanying the President on his trip, noticed several Canadian journalists trying excitedly to attract his attention.

He left his seat and went over to them. One handed him a telegram that he had snatched from the teletype machine at the Canadian News Bureau. "The President of the U.A.R. has announced the closing of the gulf of 'Aqaba."

Patir had to wait until the banquet was over before giving the news to President Shazar. Thunderstruck, he nevertheless got control of himself and went quickly back to his hotel. Not being able to sleep, he went to his desk, and during the long silence of the night, began to write at great length. The old man produced a poem addressed to Jews the world over, beseeching them to support Israel in this final test.

In Washington it was again Luke Battle who took the news to Ambassador Harman. Harman took the first plane to New York, where Goldberg was expecting him. "The President phoned to ask me to see you," Goldberg said. "He expressed the devout hope that Israel would not react and would send no ship through the strait for the next forty-eight hours. We are trying to find a solution."

At the same moment State Department experts were preparing an emergency message, which was forwarded at once to the Soviet government: "The United States will regard any impingement on freedom of navigation in the strait of Tiran, whether under the Israeli flag or another, as an act of aggression, against which Israel, in the opinion of the United States, is justified in taking defensive measures."

Late that night U Thant's plane set down at Orly airport in Paris. The United Nations representative in Paris was waiting

for him, breathless. "Nasser has closed the strait!" The Secretary-General was stupefied.

In Washington, Undersecretary Eugene Rostow called
Evron to an emergency conference at 11:30 P.M. The huge
State Department building was utterly deserted, and only a
few lights were on. Evron left the elevator on the eighth floor
and walked down the long blue-carpeted corridors to Rostow's
office. Roger Davies, Battle's assistant, was waiting outside.
With hopelessness written on his face, he grasped Evron's
hand. "This means war!"

In Rome the first editions of the morning newspapers head-
lined Pope Paul VI's pronouncement on the Middle Eastern
crisis: "The only solution is prayer."

•

WAR OVER 'AQABA?

AT 4:30 A.M. on May 23 Rabin telephoned Eshkol in Jerusalem to inform him of the closing of the strait. A few minutes later he woke Eban. At 5:00 Colonel Ephrat, of the Chief of Staff's office, forwarded the news to Kashti.

Eban woke Raviv, who summoned the highest officials of the Foreign Ministry. The officers on guard at General Staff headquarters dragged the generals out of bed. About 6:00 A.M. a wave of telephone calls swept over the country, rousing ministers, officials, diplomats, and reporters. Eban also called British Ambassador Hadow and American Ambassador Barbour.

"You remember our conversation yesterday? You said that no one yet knew whether Nasser would close the strait, and that it could be doubted that he would do so for fear of the consequences. Well, he has gone ahead and done it. I'm just giving you the news now and advising you to look over the speeches that were made by your representatives in the United Nations on March 1, 1957, on the subject of freedom of navigation."

In London the telephone awoke Israeli Ambassador Remez: "George Brown speaking. Were you asleep? I'm astonished to hear it. I'm very worried about your country and its safety. My wife makes life unbearable for me because of it. [Mrs. Brown is Jewish.] I'm leaving for Moscow in a few hours. Have you any proof that the Egyptians have closed the strait?"

74

A telegram marked "Personal, Urgent" had gone to Cairo to be put into U Thant's hands. Signed by President Johnson, its substance was: "Please inform the President of the U.A.R. that any infringement on navigation, including Israeli vessels, in the strait of Tiran, will bring a reaction on the part of the American government."

At 6:00 A.M. the high officials of the Foreign Ministry met at Eban's house in Jerusalem. Most of the diplomats were unshaven and still wearing pajamas under the clothes they had jumped into before dashing out into the deserted streets. Eban's secretary was in the kitchen making coffee.

Eban opened the conference. Around him were seven diplomats, including Director General Arie Levavi of the Foreign Ministry and his deputies Joseph Tekoa and Moshe Bittan. All were in the grip of utter astonishment. What was to be done? One of the aides suggested two related actions: a diplomatic offensive in foreign countries and at the same time a military offensive against Egypt. "Let's take Gaza so we can bargain over it. Diplomacy is fun when one holds all the cards."

His opinion, however, was rejected. Eban wanted to do everything in his power to avoid war. At 8:00 he left with his closest associates for Tel Aviv, in order to attend an emergency meeting in the Defense Minister's office.

On their way they heard an Arab radio station rebroadcast Nasser's speech. Eban translated it for his companions.

Eshkol left for Tel Aviv at 6:30 P.M. On the way he said to his secretary Ady Yoffe, "I'm afraid this is war."

At 7:30 Eshkol entered the War Room to talk with the generals. While he was there Yoffe followed his instructions and telephoned several ministers about the emergency meeting. At 8:30 Chief of the Air Force Mordechai ("Motti") Hod reached Eshkol's office, where his associates were gathered.

Rabin described the situation for the ministers in Eshkol's office, declaring that in the event of a war he was certain of victory. "But it won't be just a route march," he said. "It won't be another Sinai campaign. It won't be easy. We must expect some losses."*

After the meeting one minister said, "I'm not going to war unless the army makes me!" One of his colleagues added, "If the Chief of Staff is so cautious, what do they expect me to be?"

The government came to a decision: "Johnson has asked for forty-eight hours. Let's give it to him." Eban announced that he was going to the United States to talk with President Johnson personally, but one faction of ministers objected, preferring an exchange of diplomatic messages.

At 10:00 members of the opposition came to talk with Eshkol, Eban, and Rabin. Among them were Menachem Begin, Peres, and Dayan, as well as Golda Meir and Ministers H. M. Shapiro, Galili, and Aran.

Eban outlined the political situation and reviewed the pledges that the great powers had made to Israel in 1957 in relation to freedom of navigation. The most explicit of the pledges had been the statement by the French representative in the United Nations, in which he had clearly recognized Israel's right of self-defense in accordance with Article 51 of the U.N. Charter. The British and American statements had claimed only the right of free passage through the strait for their own vessels.

"We should be careful not to make the mistake of 1956 again," Eban said. "We should not lay ourselves open to what happened at the time of the Sinai campaign, when both the United States and the Soviet Union voted against us. At that

---

* Rabin explained his thinking on a later occasion: "In the Sinai campaign, we had airplane coverage. The English bombed the enemy airfields and with the French, were getting ready to land in Egypt. All along the line we could strike where least expected. Our purpose was not to destroy the Egyptian army but simply to compel it to retreat. Now they are waiting for us in the Sinai peninsula, and we have none of the advantages that I just mentioned. We may have to face three Arab armies. I doubt that we can defeat them easily, but I have no doubt that we will defeat them eventually."

time Eisenhower protested strongly that America had not been kept informed of our intentions. We must see that such a situation does not arise again. Those responsible for our defense say that we have time to try every diplomatic means available to us. In this particular case, it seems advisable to concentrate our efforts on the United States."

"What shall we ask them to do for us?" asked a deputy.

"We shall ask that their warships convoy our vessels through the strait," Eban said.

No one thought that would be possible. Golda Meir insisted that President de Gaulle should be consulted. Others were strongly opposed to any approach to Johnson, saying, "If we appeal to him we shall be opening the door to all kinds of pressures."

Dayan took the floor. "If the United States has asked for forty-eight hours, we can give it to them. But I mean forty-eight, not forty-nine. If they open the strait, so much the better. I don't believe that they will do it for us. After that delay we ought to go to war with Egypt and fight a battle that will destroy hundreds of tanks and planes. We shall have very little time—we must try to win in two or three days."

At the end of the meeting Dayan privately told Yoffe not to summon him to any more meetings at which members of both the government and the opposition would be present. "I don't want to have to attend any meeting that doesn't have the power to make a decision," he said. "I'd rather be inspecting the army units and studying the defense problems."

Before leaving for the south Dayan asked his wife to wire their daughter Yaël to come home at once. Father and daughter had made a secret agreement that he would call her home, wherever she was, if war seemed likely. He had done so just before the Sinai campaign, and he was doing so now, for he believed war was inevitable.

About noon the general mobilization became total. Those who had not been called up the previous day and the day before that were being called on May 23 or would be called on May 24. Bus transportation halted, and all available vehicles were commandeered for the transport of men to camps and advance positions. The bus drivers were called up also, and old men on the reserve retired list and even women replaced them on the public-transportation lines. The newspapers devoted whole columns to notices of canceled meetings, postponed weddings, and conventions deferred "because of the situation." On May 22 poets and editorial writers had still been saluting the self-restraint of the city people and their refusal to panic. On May 23 housewives were storming the groceries to stock up on flour, oil, sugar, and canned goods. The government felt obliged to issue several proclamations that there was plenty of reserve food in the country, and it kept warehouses open around the clock in order to allay the general apprehension.

Still people were afraid that food would run out and were preparing for the hardships of a long, bloody war. But no one took the apparently more logical alternative of quitting the country for refuge with relatives in New York, London, or Paris. The very existence of the State of Israel seemed to have dulled the instinct of the Wandering Jew. The people of Israel, few in number though they were and dreading a war that might annihilate them with poison gas, bombs, missiles, and bayonets, would not budge from the country.

Thousands suddenly paid up their taxes, knowing the state needed money. Gifts of all kinds, from cash to wedding rings, flooded the Defense Ministry. Groups formed of their own accord to dig trenches, act as messengers, build bomb shelters, and operate essential services. Soldiers' aid societies received dozens, hundreds, thousands, of cream cakes and chocolate cakes, which were immediately forwarded to the units stationed in the desert opposite the Egyptian army. The Israeli soldiers, exhausted by training in the deep sand of the Negev, stopped to eat their combat rations of canned meat and dry biscuits topped off with big strawberry tarts. Soon the army was drowning in a sea of pastry.

"The first two days," said one soldier, "we managed to eat them. On the third day we stowed them away in boxes. But by the fourth day we didn't know what to do with them and just left them in the sun to decorate the camp."

Civilians appeared in the trenches, handing out cigarettes, soft drinks, books, and magazines to the soldiers from their automobiles. By closing the strait Nasser had accomplished what the Israeli leaders had not been able to bring about: a unity of thought and action such as Israel had not experienced since the War of Independence.

Astonishment and anxiety prevailed in the Kremlin after the closing of the strait. Although the Soviet Union had lit the fire in the Middle East by spreading rumors of Israeli troop concentrations and had induced Nasser to send his army to the frontier, freedom of navigation in the strait was no less important to the Russians than to the Israelis. For years the Dardanelles had been a ticklish problem in Soviet foreign relations. The Russians knew that they could not back Nasser's policies without suffering the consequences. The closing of the strait would doubtless unleash a war that the Russians did not want at any price. To provoke a crisis in the Midddle East, strike a blow at Israel and the West, and hit at American enterprises in the area—all that would have been very desirable. But not a war between East and West.

Kosygin had yielded to the "hawks" who wanted to increase the tension with the West in certain spots throughout the world. But the Soviet leaders did not wish to go too far in that direction. Kosygin had been sincere in telling Johnson that he did not want war. On the morning of May 23, however, the Russians feared that they had dropped the reins and that the Middle Eastern crisis was running away from them.

In Tel Aviv, Ambassador Chuvakin, upon learning of the closing of the strait, reminded Eban, "I warned you that you would pay a penalty for your aggression." But in Moscow no Soviet diplomat mentioned the affair. Tass released a long statement condemning Israeli aggression and its intention to attack Syria "under orders from the imperialists": "Those planning new aggressive action in the Middle East should be under no illusion. They will find themselves confronting the combined strength of the Arab countries and of the Soviet Union and of all other nations dedicated to peace."

A short time later, Israeli Ambassador Katz was called to the Foreign Ministry, where Andrei Gromyko handed him a note strongly condemning the warlike attitude of Israel toward Syria. Neither in that note, in Gromyko's verbal comments on it, nor in the Tass statement was there the slightest mention of Egypt's right to close the strait of Tiran.

At the Soviet Foreign Ministry the specialists were saying: "Nasser's closing of the Strait without consulting us is a personal affront to the Soviet Ambassador in Cairo. Not only was he unable to prevent Nasser from taking this perilous step—he didn't even know about it."

And while the Soviet radio and press were issuing more and more statements about Russian support of the Arab cause and their sympathy with it, the mentors of Soviet foreign policy were busy searching for a replacement for Ambassador Podyedyeev.

Of all the Western powers, Great Britain took the strongest position on the closing of the strait. George Brown had always been a warm admirer of Nasser and had freely stated that the world did not fully appreciate the Egyptian President. But on the morning of May 23 he was saying to anyone who would listen: "This time, Nasser has gone too far. We must restrain him for his own good." The British government reacted instinctively and spontaneously to the Egyptian move. That same morning cables were rushed from London to Washington, proposing immediate international action to reopen the strait.

After leaving the government conference, Brown headed for the airport, from which he was to fly to Moscow and lay his cards on the table before Kosygin. Prime Minister Wilson put the final touches on the address he would make on the following day to the Electrical Trade Unions in Margate and in which he would restate Great Britain's intention to participate in any action necessary to reopen the strait. Under Secretary of State George Thomson flew to the United States to confer with American leaders. Accompanying him was Admiral Henderson, a taciturn man little known to the public, who had a plan for an "international force" designed to open the strait.

The closing of the strait meant a moment of decision for two other nations, France and the United States. Under the Gaullist regime France had officially taken an aloof attitude toward Israel in an attempt to wipe out the memory of France's share in the disastrous Suez expedition of 1956 and to try to regain the friendship of the Arabs. This tactic had been initiated at the end of the Algerian war and was intended to open the way to a gradual understanding with the Arab world, to regain lost influence in the Levant, and to assemble an impressive array of neutral countries whose support would provide France with a new source of strength in international diplomacy. Commentators analyzed France's policy as two chess games played simultaneously yet independently of each other: maintaining friendly relations with the Arab countries and furnishing Israel with arms for defense against them.

This policy might have been successful if the issue had not come to trial. But now France had to choose openly between the Arabs and Israel, and one of the games would have to be sacrificed to the other. When the crisis had begun, the French government had said nothing, as if wishing not to take sides. On May 23, however, when the Israeli representatives called at the French Foreign Office for one of the talks that had become a daily occurrence, they found out that such talks had become little more than intellectual exercises. From the beginning moments of the crisis, the matter had been transferred from the Foreign Office to become the "private property" of the Élysée Palace, which remained the only place in Paris to which the Israelis could appeal. Who could forget President de Gaulle's famous greeting to Ben-Gurion in 1961: "Long live Israel, our friend and our ally"?

For years the United States had tried, even more than had France, to maintain its neutrality in the Middle East. For the

sake of its Arab customers, the United States had determined
not to become the principal supplier of arms to Israel and to
make no deliveries directly. Uncle Sam wanted others to commit themselves and therefore encouraged the Canadians, the
English, the French, and the Germans to sell arms to the
Jewish state while refraining from doing so himself. But for
several years the supply of Soviet arms to the Arabs and the
increasing pressure of the pro-Israel Jewish lobby in the
United States had necessitated changes in that policy. Consequently the United States had been supplying certain kinds of
armaments directly to Israel.

President John F. Kennedy had begun by authorizing the
sale of Hawk missiles. Johnson had agreed to sell Patton tanks.
A contract had been signed providing for the sale of Skyhawk
light bombers. In 1964, when Eshkol had visited the White
House, Johnson had entered into firm agreements regarding
the security and integrity of Israel.

It would be difficult to pretend that this pro-Israel attitude
had aroused much enthusiasm among the officials of the State
Department. Now that there was again an actual crisis, the
White House and the State Department could not completely
agree on what policy to take toward the Middle East. The
State Department made many neutralist statements, and the
White House expressed disturbance at Nasser's action. The
State Department instructed its ambassadors in the Arab capi-
tals not to damage any existing good relations and to pacify the
Arabs by dealing obliquely with them, whereas the White
House issued more forcible directives. Ambassadors had to
rack their brains and decide for themselves what tack to take.

So it was that on May 23, Nolte, the new Ambassador to
Cairo, received instructions signed by Rusk for the text of a
verbal communication to Nasser and also an urgent cable from
President Johnson that he was to transmit to Nasser. Nolte
hurried to deliver the message to Foreign Minister Riad. Johnson reminded the Egyptians that the United States was firmly
opposed to any act of terrorism on the territory of neighboring

states. He demanded unconditional observation of the agreements of the armistice, advised a gradual reduction of the
troop concentrations, and expressed support of U Thant's
efforts. The cable emphasized the following points:

> The emergency force of the United Nations was to re-
> main in Gaza and in Sharm el Sheikh until the General
> Assembly could reach a decision on the subject.
> Egypt was not to allow its armed forces to enter the
> Gaza Strip.
> The concentration of troops in the Sinai peninsula was
> endangering the peace, and both the Egyptian and the
> Israeli forces should return to their bases.
> The Egyptian government should send no trooops to
> Sharm el Sheikh until it had promised to respect free
> navigation through the strait of Tiran.
> The United States wanted freedom of navigation in the
> strait, and would regard the closing of it as an act of aggres-
> sion.
> The United States requested the Egyptian government
> to show restraint in an actual crisis. In order to tighten
> the bonds between the two nations, the White House pro-
> posed sending a distinguished American to Cairo or receiv-
> ing an Egyptian emissary in Washington. President John-
> son was ready to send Vice President Hubert Humphrey
> to talk with the Egyptian leaders about all the problems
> that had not been settled between the two countries.

Riad reacted violently, attacking the pro-Israel attitude of
the United States and asserting that the closing of the strait
was perfectly legal and would not be reversed. He even con-
tested the legality of the existence of the State of Israel.

"Israel seized Elat in 1949," he said, "after the armistice had
been signed. We therefore have a right to forbid Israeli navigation in the strait of Tiran and also shipments of strategic
materials to Elat."

Nolte politely recited the statements that Rusk had instructed him to make: The United States was opposed to

aggression and would support the integrity and independence of all the nations in the area.

Actually the United States was in a very embarrassing position. Some Israeli politicians had interpreted the American request to wait forty-eight hours as meaning, "Wait forty-eight hours, and then do whatever you consider best." The truth was simple. The decision to close the strait had dealt the Americans a blow to which they could not respond because of their struggle in Vietnam. They feared a new involvement. That fear virtually paralyzed American diplomacy. On May 23 the huge State Department building was striving feverishly to do all it could to avoid war. Some witnesses have reported that Eugene Rostow kept repeating, "We must come to some agreement with the Russians, at any cost." Others thought any concession justified as long as it did not call for an abandonment of basic policies.

But, as in France, the American executive had taken the power of decision away from the State Department as soon as the crisis increased—it was lodged only in the White House.

May 23 was also the day for the "Tuesday breakfast," an extremely important institution in American political life during the Johnson administration. The President's chief advisers attended it: Rusk, Robert S. McNamara, Walt W. Rostow, George Christian. The talk always dealt with immediate problems. When the guests took their seats around the table, President Johnson had already yielded to strong pressures from corporations, industrialists, and politicians who were demanding an immediate statement about the Middle Eastern crisis. On the previous day the State Department had expressed opposition to such a statement, but in the meantime Johnson himself had decided to issue one.

Several departments had prepared their versions, all of which had been submitted to the President. Johnson had adopted the one that Eugene Rostow had prepared on Sunday. It would have been delivered if just then a call had not come in from a telephone booth on Connecticut Avenue.

Mr. A., one of Israel's most influential partisans, had been on his way to a meeting with Hubert Humphrey, whom the President had designated as his representative to Cairo, when he had been informed that the White House was searching for him in order to acquaint him with the statement. Walt Rostow, Eugene's brother and Johnson's closest adviser, had read it to him over the telephone. In astonishment Mr. A. found that it contained nothing about the closing of the strait or about the United States' position on freedom of navigation. The statement contained another startling sentence: "No act of aggression has yet been committed."

"But what about the closing of the strait?" Mr. A. exclaimed. "Isn't that an act of aggression? A statement like this is not only useless but dangerous. The United States is refusing to take a position on the essential point. Better no statement at all than one like this."

A few minutes later Johnson was told of the conversation. He was furious. "If A. thinks that it would be better not to make any statement at all, then tell him that there will be no statement!"

But shortly he changed his mind. The pressure on the White House had reached incredible proportions. Twenty-four members of the House of Representatives issued a statement containing the following passage:

> We pledge the fullest support to measures which must be taken by the Administration to make our position unmistakably clear to those who are now bent on the destruction of Israel, that we are now prepared to take whatever action may be necessary to resist aggression against Israel and to preserve the peace.

George Meany, a labor leader of great influence, let the White House know that he was preparing to make a public statement of a similar character. The White House advised him not to do so. "There will soon be a satisfactory statement from the White House. Instead of making one of your own, you would do better to support the President's."

A feverish argument ensued over which of the alternate texts the President should use. The overcautious version prepared by the State Department was discarded in favor of one that Walt Rostow and his assistants had prepared. At 6:30 P.M. President Johnson appeared on American television screens and delivered the following message:

> The United States considers the Gulf to be an international waterway and feels that a blockade of Israeli shipping is illegal and potentially disastrous to the cause of peace. The right of free, innocent passage of the international waterway is a vital interest of the entire international community.

When Nasser announced that he would close the strait, the Israeli tanker *Samson* was moored in Elat harbor after unloading oil. That night it received orders to leave the port before the strait was actually blockaded. The tanker headed south under full steam and passed through the strait at daybreak. No one stopped it.

On May 23 many foreigners left the country with all possible speed. Among them was Erich Leinsdorf, conductor of the Boston Symphony Orchestra, who said that the American government was advising its citizens to leave the Middle East. But Richard Tucker and Roberta Peters decided to stay, and that evening in Tel Aviv's Palace of Culture an enthusiastic audience applauded them.

The governments of eastern Europe did not order their nationals to leave the country. But the same day a Hungarian circus that had been performing in Tel Aviv packed up its tents and loaded its animals and clowns on the first boat leaving Haifa.

On the other hand, another visitor was politely requested to cut short his stay in Israel: he was Raphael Passio of Finland, who had arrived two days previously on an official visit. As a result of the increased tension both the Finnish and the Israeli Foreign Ministers suggested that Passio curtail his visit to the Holy Land. At Lydda airport Eshkol gave his guest a silver chessboard—a symbolic present at that moment—and left for Jerusalem where he was to address Parliament.

The key phrase in his speech was: "I demand that the great powers respect without delay the right of free passage to our southern port, a legal right for all states without exception."

That phrase expressed the position of the Israeli government. It also characterized the essential differences between the generation of leaders who had come to Israel from foreign lands—those of the Diaspora—and the generation that had been born and raised in the land. During the Diaspora it had been customary for Jews to seek aid and protection from persons in high office. To the young Israelis, however, it had been clear from the beginning that neither Great Britain, the United States, nor France would reopen the strait. In the Middle East, Arabs and Israelis would confront each other alone. No one was going to pull Israel's chestnuts out of the fire. Only Israel, relying on its own strength, could do that.

That afternoon a cable from Eban reached Washington, informing the Israeli embassy that he was coming to the United States to talk with American leaders.

It was Eban's own decision, one not entirely supported by Israeli leaders. The government and the Maarakh Alignment were in disagreement. Eshkol's personal opinion was that this step would provoke American pressure on Israel to follow the American line. He would have preferred to send Golda Meir. She was equally familiar with problems of defense and was less easily swayed than was Eban.

At 7:00 P.M. Eshkol saw Eban in his office and slipped him a note: "Perhaps Golda ought to go instead of you." Eban flew into a rage. According to high Cabinet officials, he forcibly insisted on going and even threatened to resign. For the time being nothing was decided. Later a cable was received from Israeli Ambassador Eytan in Paris: "I have a chance to see

De Gaulle tomorrow, but if Eban could come, the chance would be better." Ady Yoffe dashed into Eshkol's office with the cable in his hand. The head of government sighed. "All right. If we can't do anything else, let him go."

At 3:00 A.M. a special El Al plane took off for Paris with Eban and Raviv aboard.

Yitzhak Rabin fell sick in his house in Zahala. The physical and nervous exhaustion of the last several days had taken their toll, and chain-smoking had weakened his general condition. His doctors ordered complete rest. He transferred his functions to General Ezer Weizmann, Chief of Operations.

Late that night Bittan telephoned the American Ambassador in Tel Aviv to say that the Israeli government, much against its will, would postpone any response to Nasser's provocation. "We are ready," he said, "to wait forty-eight hours."

PART TWO

·

Decision

•

DE GAULLE: "DON'T MAKE WAR!"

HUGE PLANES LOADED to capacity were landing one after the other on the runways of Lydda airport—El Al's blue-tailed Boeings, air force double-decker Stratocruisers, and jets belonging to travel and transportation companies, including a few from Air France—a breathlessly improvised airlift that was fighting the clock. Representatives of the Israeli Defense Ministry in the western European capitals had been besieging factories and military bases day and night, fighting with local diplomats every step of the way for authorization to use the airports. In the Middle East war could break out at any moment.

The wave of sympathy for Israel that had swept over all the capitals also invaded the war industries and the military bases abroad.

In France the manufacturers of war matériel welcomed Israeli emissaries. Even orders from other countries were canceled to facilitate prompt shipments to Israel. Every request for essential matériel was cleared in a few hours by telephone, without the red tape of paperwork and conferences. Authorization to use the airports was granted at once, and soldiers loaded the armaments onto planes. At every field the Israelis found an officer in charge willing to help them.

At 7:00 A.M. May 24 the El Al Boeing carrying Eban and Raviv landed at Orly airport. Ambassador Eytan greeted them as they alighted and informed Eban that the interview with

President de Gaulle would take place soon after the weekly meeting of the Council of Ministers, about noon. Eban shut himself up in the Hilton Hotel at Orly to prepare to plead his cause before the President. (About 10:00 A.M. he received a telephone call from London informing him that Prime Minister Wilson would receive him at 5:00 P.M.)

Eban consulted his files. He spent two hours planning what he would say to President de Gaulle. "I wanted," he said later, "to talk like a Gaullist in order to bring to mind the obligations France had undertaken and indicate that the moment for decision had come. I worked on two phrases in particular. 'We have a choice between submission and resistance. We are determined to resist. We have made our decision.' And 'We are going to spend a few days finding out whether we stand alone or whether those who have pledged themselves in this affair will honor their word.' "

Meanwhile the French government was studying the situation in the Middle East. Couve de Murville had produced such specific details on navigation through the strait as the exact number of Israeli ships that used the Gulf of 'Aqaba, which he considered insignificant. De Gaulle accepted his Minister's opinion that the closing of the strait was not a serious blow to Israel and therefore did not justify going to war. The Israelis' right to send their ships through the strait was a complex legal problem, one of many bones of contention between the Israelis and the Arabs.

De Gaulle was afraid that a military conflict in the Middle East would require the intervention of the great powers and might turn into a world war. He proposed as a means of resolving the crisis a conference among the four powers who alone could impose their solution on the litigants.

When Eban reached the waiting room of the Élysée Palace with Eytan by his side, M. Tricot, one of the Presidential associates told him: "The President is going to end the Council of Ministers soon. I have told him that you are here. When he wants to," Tricot added with a smile, "he can end a meeting very quickly."

And indeed just a few moments later the French ministers passed through the waiting room in single file. Before entering their cars they shook Eban's hand. Eban was amused by those eighteen men, each with an identical black portfolio and each going off in an identical black Citroen.

At 12:30 P.M. Eban was ushered into the Presidential office, where he found Couve de Murville and a tense, almost anxious De Gaulle. Eban remembered what Eytan had told him: "As you sit down, he will say, 'Sir, you have my attention.' Then you can say whatever you want."

But this time the President acted differently. He stretched his arm toward Eban and said loudly: "Do not make war! Do not make war! In any event, do not be the first to fire!"

Eban's response was rapid and firm. "In no way would we be the first. A hostile act has already been committed by the Egyptians."

It was clear that President de Gaulle did not like that answer. "So far as I am concerned," he said, "whoever fires the first shot is the one who begins the hostilities."

"This is the most critical moment for our survival that has arisen in the past ten years," Eban said. "That is the reason why my colleagues and I have come to you for advice at this moment of decision, for you have been a great friend. There are three reasons for the present crisis: the guerrilla attacks from Syria, the concentration of Egyptian troops in the Sinai desert, and, most of all, the closing of the strait of Tiran. These three causes will evolve into one inevitable disaster: The Egyptians will grab us by the throat, the Syrians will knife us in the back, and then the Egyptians will find a way to stab us to the heart. I have come here to say that we have decided not to live in such danger any longer. To us, the closing of the strait means that he who decided to do it has chosen to make war, for we have given notice of our attitude toward that act. In the several years that we have maintained diplomatic relations with Asia and Africa, we have added a new dimension to international diplomacy. We have ceased to be a completely Western-oriented nation. We have developed a sphere of aid in the Third World. We cannot accept the present situation."

De Gaulle interrupted Eban impatiently. "Please, be precise. Just what are you going to do?"

Eban then presented the basic formula he had devised: "Having no choice between submission and resistance, we have decided to resist. There will be no departure from that decision." Then he added: "But we have also decided to wait a few days,* in order to ask the advice of those who are, by their pledges, involved in the situation. Meanwhile, we shall do nothing. We do not foresee any definite counteraction for today or tomorrow or the day after."

Eban noticed that Couve de Murville gave a sigh of relief at that. He seemed to have been afraid that war would break out at any moment. But Eban did not grasp that, like De Gaulle himself, Couve de Murville had misinterpreted his words and had understood by them that Israel was promising to undertake no military action whatever. The two Frenchmen did not comprehend that by the term "resistance" as Eban had used it Israel meant that it intended to fight.

Still tense, De Gaulle said: "The situation is a difficult one. It must not go on. Don't rush into things. The four great powers must consult one another. Don't look to the West for a solution to the problem." De Gaulle spoke of the West as of something foreign. He repeated: "The four powers must act together. I will take charge of that. Together we will find a way to get the ships through the strait."

"I am inclined to be pessimistic about the Soviet attitude," Eban said. "If Russia had acted differently, we would not be in this crisis. Russia has never been of the same mind with us in respect to freedom of navigation in the strait."

"True," De Gaulle replied, "but neither has Russia taken a contrary attitude. We have got to have time. Be patient. Meanwhile you should not do just what the Egyptians want you to do—namely, be the one to open hostilities."

De Gaulle then returned to the problem of "the West":

---

* In reporting this talk to a friend, Eban himself used the expression "a few days."

"There is no such thing today as purely Western solutions. By looking too much to the West for attaining its objectives and finding solutions for its problems, Israel misses the point. The Soviet Union must participate in finding a solution." Then he added, "You are not yet secure enough to solve all your problems alone."

Eban later said: "I found the French Chief of State worried, nervous, and tense. He gave me the impression that he was terror-stricken. I was astonished to find that what he so feared was not a localized conflict but a confrontation between the East and the West that might involve the whole world."

Eban told De Gaulle: "Years ago many countries pledged to support us and stand by us if the strait is closed again. The strongest and clearest expression of that promise was made by the French representative in the United Nations in 1957."

"True, but that was in 1957, and this is 1967. Georges-Picot's statement," De Gaulle continued, astonishing Eban by his keen memory, "on the freedom of the seas was made rather emotionally. Now the strait of Tiran must be considered in the same light as the Dardanelles. It is up to the four great powers."

Feeling that there was nothing left for him to say, Eban decided to end the talk on a polite note. "Now that we are faced with a test, we wish to thank you for all France has done and for what France is still doing in the way of giving us courage and boosting our morale and our military strength."

Without knowing it, Eban had made a serious blunder in calling the President's attention to the increasing military assistance from France to Israel.

De Gaulle replied, "All that we have done in that connection was an act of friendship, but now that same friendship compels me to speak as I have just done."

Eban interpreted the remark as a veiled threat. "Of all the many ways of showing friendship, you cannot choose only those which will be of advantage to you."

Eban rose. While Couve de Murville was talking to Eytan on

the threshold, Eban went up to De Gaulle and asked him, "Do you recall what you said to Eshkol in 1964?"

"Yes, I remember," said the President. "He was sitting in the same chair as you were. I expressed the wish that Israel might survive and prosper. That is the essential thing, the essential thing." Eban and Eytan left the Élysée Palace, the former less depressed than the latter.

In De Gaulle's eyes the talk had produced only one important point. He had said to Eban, "Don't make war!" and Eban had assured him that Israel had decided to wait. Eban had said not "We will fight" but "We will resist."

As a result of that talk, De Gaulle sent two cables, one to Kosygin and the other to Nasser: "Israel will not make war." Minister of Information Gorse read an official statement to the press: France had decided to propose a conference of the four great powers.

Couve de Murville telephoned Secretary of the Army Pierre Messmer to demand that no more military matériel be sent to Israel without the consent of the Foreign Ministry within the framework of the interministerial committee for the exportation of arms. Simultaneously high officials of the Foreign Ministry were phoning several military bases to stop at once all shipments to Israel that had not been approved by the committee.*

France's position was clear.

It was raining torrents in London when Ambassador Remez's car deposited Eban at 10 Downing Street. The street was jammed with people. Eban remarked to his escorts: "These Britishers fascinate me. In a crisis they throng around the Prime Minister's house, but what for? Especially in all this rain."

Wilson took his visitors into his own office, where he settled himself behind a large table and placed Eban on his right. The strong tobacco Wilson used offended Eban, and the tea that was served was too strong for him also, but the conversation was friendly and pleasant. Wilson proudly showed his guest a

---

* Interviews with high French officials in Paris, November 9–30, 1967.

copy of the speech he had made a few hours earlier to the unions in Margate: "Her Majesty's government shall promote and support international action to uphold the right of free passage in the gulf of 'Aqaba. Britain is prepared to join with others to secure a general recognition of that right."

Then Wilson turned to Eban: "I see that De Gaulle has proposed a conference of the four powers. I doubt that anything will come of it, but we shall see. I think the Soviets will eventually refuse to participate. But why should we say no? As for the matter of navigation in the strait, the British government believes, as I have told it, that Nasser cannot pull it off. I have sent Thomson to Washington to coordinate our action with the Americans'. If you should run into him there, keep in touch with him. We are discussing nuts and bolts with the Americans."

Of all the heads of government with whom Eban conferred during his trip, Wilson was the only one who did not urge Israel to appease Egypt. Eban was much encouraged by the interview. He went to the Hotel Savoy and that evening paid a visit to his mother, who was living in London.

In Moscow the Soviet leaders gave Foreign Minister Brown to understand that they did not approve of Nasser's closing the strait, but at the same time they declared that they did not want war and expressed the hope that the crisis could be resolved peacefully.

That afternoon the Israeli General Staff met in Tel Aviv with Eshkol. Rabin was absent, and General Ezer Weizmann, as chief of operations, outlined for Eshkol a campaign predicated on penetration of the northern part of the Sinai peninsula by Israeli troops, first toward El 'Arîsh, then toward the Suez canal.

In Washington an executive of the German intelligence service met with a friend from the C.I.A. "According to our information," said the German, "Israel is going to attack Syria."

"You don't know your Bible," said the American. "Israel is getting ready to attack in the south. It's Egypt!"

That same evening President Johnson received a report from

the C.I.A.: "According to our forecasts, Israel will attack Egypt on May 26."*

Late that night Dayan received authorization to join S Brigade.

British Minister Thomson and Admiral Henderson were meeting with Rusk, Eugene Rostow, and their assistants in the State Department. The Britishers explained their strategy for opening the strait, one that involved three steps: an attempt to persuade the Security Council to adopt a resolution demanding that Egypt open the strait to free navigation; in case that effort failed, a coalition of several maritime powers to issue a warning that the strait of Tiran was an international waterway that they intended to use; third, if Egypt remained immovable, assembly of a fleet of ships from various nations to break the blockade under the protection of naval units.

Both the State Department and the White House agreed to this plan. As the United States did not want to take unilateral action, the British proposal, which ensured that the United States would not have to act alone, was certain to meet with approval from Congress and to be endorsed by public opinion.

The general outlines of the project were submitted to the Pentagon for the opinions of McNamara and the naval chiefs. The Army was requested to prepare adequate operational measures.

On May 24 the Israelis in Washington were very nervous. Eugene Rostow had promised Evron only that the United States would call an informal meeting of the Security Council, saying, "We hope that there will be no shooting if anybody can avoid it." When Evron had asked about the American pledges, Rostow had replied, "There is no intention to abandon any of the commitments to you that either Eisenhower or J. F. Kennedy undertook."

"We do not see the use of a meeting of the Security Council,"

---

* Interview with a high American official in Washington, November 1, 1967.

Evron said. "What will you do if it does not guarantee freedom of navigation?"

"We will act in the framework of the United Nations or independently. Events are taking a serious turn. You should refrain from any provocation. I hope that for the time being you will send no ship through the strait to raise the issue."

Evron gathered from this conversation that the Americans did not know what to do. He had no illusion about the forty-eight-hour delay. The United States simply wanted more time.

Ambassador Harman flew on that morning of May 24 to former President Dwight D. Eisenhower's farm in Gettysburg, Pennsylvania. No one else knew about the trip. Eisenhower cordially greeted his guest and confirmed the interpretation Israel had given to the pledges of the United States in 1957. "Nasser," Eisenhower said, "has created an illegal situation and illegality cannot be admitted. The Russians will take heed of a strong attitude on the part of the United States. I don't think that Israel will be deserted."

Johnson's statement condemning the closing of the strait had aroused various reactions in Congress. The House of Representatives had endorsed it enthusiastically. White House advisers therefore concluded that, if the question of American participation in an international undertaking to open the strait or even an operation by the United States alone arose, Johnson could be assured of a majority in the House.

In the Senate, however, the reaction was different. The Foreign Relations Committee had met in closed session that morning, and the majority of senators present had definitely pronounced against any unilateral action on the part of the United States. Haunted by the specter of the Vietnam war like all other responsible Americans, the senators were strongly opposed to any action likely to draw the United States into war abroad. Senator Mike Mansfield attacked Nasser vigorously, but he also recommended action only within the framework of the Security Council. Senator John Stennis, a "hawk," insisted that the United States should not act alone. Many other senators supported his opinion. From then on it was clear that the United States would not take any action to open the strait until it had succeeded in organizing active assistance from several other nations.

The White House let some indications of this attitude seep out to the press and the television newscasters. CBS's well-informed Eric Sevareid said:

> President Johnson has probably not made any decision yet as to whether the United States would take military action on its own, if fighting does begin. If fighting begins and Israel is endangered, the pressure for action from pro-Israeli groups in this country would be very heavy; but American action without benefit of major allies, on top of the same situation in the Far East, would probably blow the lid off the American Congress.

At the same time a bizarre little drama was being acted out in the Security Council. Canada and Great Britain had demanded an immediate meeting of the Council to discuss the strait. But the debate never came up. Three nonaligned nations refused to have the question put on the agenda. The French wanted to postpone debate for twenty-four or forty-eight hours. Nikolai Fedorenko, the delegate from the Soviet Union, preferred to deliver a harangue against the "Chiang Kai-shek gang" because the presiding officer that day was the delegate from Taiwan. Finally, as might have been expected, there was a heated discussion between Fedorenko and Goldberg that became quite funny. Goldberg quoted from *Alice in Wonderland* and Fedorenko replied with Oriental proverbs about monkeys falling out of trees. When the laughter subsided, the Council meeting ended.

In Cairo Nasser assembled his political and military advisers. Almost all his people were optimistic, saying, "For the first time since the Suez war, Egypt has taken the initiative." The closing of the strait was going to be a heavy blow to Israel, for the concentration of troops it had made on the frontiers was immobilizing its reserves and creating economic problems which might become unbearable.

For the first time also Israel believed that its survival was at the mercy of a truly dangerous opponent. It could not go to war with Egypt by itself. It needed the support of foreign powers, and it had little chance of obtaining it. France, which only a little while earlier had been a loyal ally, was pursuing a policy of conciliation with the Arab states and would take no action on Israel's behalf. For proof who needed more than the statements, the cables, and the frequent talks between the French Ambassador in Cairo and the President of Egypt? Great Britain was opposed to the closing of the strait but would not help Israel to assert itself by force. Like France, Britain had avoided invoking the tripartite agreement. Perhaps the United States envisaged helping Israel, but it would back down if confronted by Soviet opposition.

Israel's lack of determination and its powerlessness paved the way for further Egyptian action. Neighboring countries, more favorable toward Nasser's policies than not, were taking note of that fact. One example was Hussein's announcement in a radio broadcast that he was authorizing Saudi and Iraqi troops to enter his territory. Previously he would not have dared, for Israel had let him know that it would regard the presence of foreign troops in Jordan as a *casus belli*. But Israel's threats no longer put off the Arabs as they had two or three weeks earlier. Saudi Arabia had declared its approval of Nasser's policy and had also decided to revive the question of a united Arab command. Algeria, Iraq, and Kuwait had put troops at Egypt's disposal, and in the Gaza Strip Shukairy's army had received heavy armaments.

Nasser was taking emergency measures to increase his military strength. He recalled several battalions from Yemen and mobilized fresh units in Egypt itself. He sent War Minister Badran to Moscow to buy tanks and planes.

That evening Nasser dined with U Thant, who was glum and depressed. Nasser had made him wait twenty-four hours before receiving him, and a "spontaneous" demonstration had taken place opposite his hotel. In addition U Thant had a painful toothache, which had begun as soon as he had landed in Cairo.

When the two men finally met in Nasser's dining room, U Thant saw quickly that the Egyptian President was not going to back down one inch. "The closing of the strait," Nasser said, "wipes out the last smears of the triple aggression in 1956."

Once relieved of that opinion, Nasser turned on all his charm and considerably impressed his guest with his gracious yet forcible personality. He solemnly swore that he did not intend to attack Israel and indicated his readiness to make a gesture that might decrease tensions. He would, for example, willingly receive an envoy from the United Nations to negotiate an agreement between the two nations. He was also ready, he said, to revive the armistice commission of Israelis and Egyptians that had languished since the Suez war. He even proposed an agreement on the matter of the strait—he would permit the passage of ships to Israel, providing they were not Israeli vessels and were not carrying strategic materials.

Candidly Nasser also proposed a solution for the problem of the U.N. troops—why not station them in Israeli territory?

U Thant fell into the trap. Deeply impressed by Nasser's restraint and sincerity, he failed to recognize that all the Egyptian President's "concessions" merely restated in different terms the official policy of Egypt. The U.N. force was not to return to Egyptian soil, and essential materials like oil, the principal product that Israel imported through the strait, would never reach Elat. On the Israeli sire of the frontier, the U.N. force would be proof of Nasser's total triumph.

Thant decided to cut his stay in Cairo short by twenty-four hours and began to draft his proposals for a solution of the conflict. The first was for a two-week truce over the strait, during which Israel would not send any ships to Elat and the U.A.R. would not prevent the passage of non-Israeli vessels. That was just what Nasser wanted. Two weeks would give him the time he needed to consolidate.

In the corridors of the U.N. building, the Israeli delegates noticed the pitying smiles they received from their fellow delegates. Lloyds of London raised the insurance rates on freight bound for Elat. The governments of Liberia, Panama, and Greece ordered ships flying their flags not to enter the strait. The Israeli press printed the legal opinions of authorities on international law in London, New York, and Paris. All that seemed to prove was that Israel had lost confidence in its own strength and was seeking comfort in the views of learned academicians.

Lieutenant Guy Jacobson was happy in the army. His company was well organized, its morale was good, and its equipment was all in order. On the afternoon of May 24 he even got a message from his wife. The only matter of concern was one of his soldiers, Yossi. A tall, red-haired, apple-cheeked member of a kibbutz and a tank sergeant, Yossi had distinguished himself in an incident with Syria a few months back. Since then he had changed. "I'm a pacifist," he kept saying. "I have reached the conclusion that it is wicked to shoot people. If there should be a war, I wouldn't fight."

In a steady, friendly, soothing voice, Jacobson had undertaken to explain to Yossi that it was necessary for the people of Israel to fight bravely for their survival. "You are young, and you are single, but some day you will have a wife, a home, and children. To them you must stand for certain things. They will not be proud of saying that their father spent the time of the war for survival in prison."

Although he had had no success, Guy was not angry with the young sergeant, nor was he deceived into thinking that he had managed to convince him somehow. He just felt sorry for the taciturn red-head who would be sent to prison, ostracized by many of his friends, and would have his life ruined. "Tonight," he said, "I will make my report to the company commander."

But Yossi had promised not to make any pacifist campaign among the soldiers of the company until he was sent back to his base.

•

INTELLIGENCE NIGHT

THE ISRAELI PRESS was swamped with unusual statements and advertisements under blazing headlines. On May 25 *Ha'aretz* published several petitions for the immediate formation of a coalition government; they had been signed by intellectuals, professors, students, and ordinary citizens. Their numbers doubled and redoubled in the coming days.

An enormous advertisement directed to Israeli women read: "Our duty in this time of crisis is to keep calm, to attend to our daily tasks, and to make ourselves beautiful, without getting worried or panicky. Take care of your appearance, and be charming and cheerful, even if it seems hard!" That advertisement was inserted not by the Union of Working Mothers but by the Helena Rubinstein laboratories.

Advertising slogans acquired double meanings: For example, there was the slogan of the Epirotiki Lines: "Sacrifice a week of your time, and add a year to your life." The titles of the motion pictures being shown in Israeli theaters seemed to have been inspired by current events: *Let's Live, The Suez Affair, The Night of the Generals, The End of the Game, The Eve of Surrender, For Whom the Bell Tolls,* and, most disturbing of all, *The Russians Are Coming, The Russians Are Coming.*

The Russians had not yet arrived, however. They had satisfied themselves with a brief statement rejecting President de Gaulle's proposal for a four-power conference on the Middle

East. The British and the Americans, therefore, had been safe in accepting the proposal, certain as they were that Moscow would refuse.

That morning President Johnson flew to Canada for a quick visit with Prime Minister Lester Pearson, who entertained him at lunch in his handsome summer residence on the shore of Lake Harrington. For the first time Johnson introduced the plan for an international force to open the strait of Tiran. Pearson liked the idea, and promised to send a Canadian ship, even a warship, to help break the blockade.

Pentagon experts were less enthusiastic, as their report on the project, which was delivered that same day, revealed. Navy officials gave an unequivocal "no."* Sending warships just to open the strait, the admirals insisted, would do no good. In any event, it would take a good deal of time to install an intervention force in the area, and even if it could be assembled restricted naval action alone would not break the blockade. Key positions would have to be occupied on land, and many soldiers would thus have to be landed in the Sinai peninsula to handle such land engagements as might arise—engagements that could assume large proportions.

The American General Staff was categorically opposed to any action of that kind. Nevertheless, it was ordered to prepare a military operation for the Sinai peninsula. On the morning of May 25 officials of the operations division began to sketch a plan for a second front—air transport of paratroops, naval bombing, and large-scale open fighting in the peninsula.

A second action was also plotted: quick intervention on the Israeli coast in the event of a successful Arab attack and invasion.† Flying mobile forces into Israeli territory, in order to provide a buffer between invading Arab troops and the Israelis, who would retreat toward the center of the country, was also considered. For this operation the 6th Fleet was to furnish some of the units, for it was already enroute to the eastern

* Information procured at the Pentagon, October–November 1967.
† Information gathered in the Pentagon and confirmed by White House officials.

Mediterranean. A supplementary division was to embark that day. But the principal force would come from American bases in Germany and North Carolina. A huge airlift was to transport 30,000–100,000 men if need be.

The American army in Germany was alerted. The Pentagon's final estimate, dating from January 1967, was that Israel was strong enough to defeat its enemies. All the experts agreed on that point. They could even foresee how the campaign would shape up: Israel would attack first, launching a smashing armor attack under cover of air power.

About noon on May 25 these estimates were taken to the White House.

In the afternoon Israel received official word of the naval plan. Harman was summoned to the State Department, where Eugene Rostow and Battle were waiting for him. They told him the details of the project, which Walt Rostow labeled with his sharp wit "the Red Sea Regatta."

"If the Security Council or the United Nations does not confirm the principle of free navigation in the strait," Eugene Rostow said, "several maritime powers will be organizing 're-gattas.' Egypt cannot withstand such a force, whose very presence will prevent an actual blockade of the strait. But we must wait until the Security Council has finished debating the matter, and that will be another ten days to two weeks."

Harman was outraged. "The time is past for talking about guarantees and promises! You told us forty-eight hours. Now you are asking for two weeks. It shocks us. We cannot agree to that!"

The Americans explained that every decision of their government in respect to participating in an international conflict required the consent of Congress. They had to exhaust all possibilities to avert war. "Our military experts," they said, "are of the opinion that a naval operation alone will not be enough to open the strait. Much more extensive operations must be prepared for. We must be extremely prudent."*

When Harman rose, Eugene Rostow asked him: "Couldn't

* This version of the conversation comes from American sources.

the U.N. forces be stationed on your side of the frontier? What
do you think of that?"

In Paris an actual, if not a legal, embargo had been placed
on shipments of arms to Israel. Finally, after emergency negotiations, a compromise was arrived at: As in the past France
would supply Israel with everything that had been promised
its representatives. The first attempt at stopping arms shipments to Israel from France had failed.

In Tel Aviv, Rabin and Eshkol left at 10:00 A.M. to inspect
the units that had been stationed in the south. They took along
Kashti, Zvi Dienstein, Allon, and General Haim Barlev, who
had been recalled two days previously from France. The military attaché in Paris had located him on May 23 while he was
touring the Midi, and as soon as he had reached Orly he had
been shoved onto a plane leaving for Israel without even time
to see his family.

In the command car of Shaike Gavish, commander on the
southern front, Eshkol and his retinue talked with the three
division leaders: Tal, Sharon, and Abraham Yoffe. Tal explained the plan of operations to Eshkol, who made no comment on the plan itself but was very interested in its technical
and tactical details. Nevertheless, some of the officials of the
Defense Ministry dared to ask him for the first time: "When
are we going to begin? We've had enough of these endless
hesitations."

The head of government replied, "We must be absolutely
sure that any action by the Israeli army will not be impeded by
pressure from foreign powers."

Early in the afternoon, Eshkol admitted a visitor to his room,
then locked the door. Allon sat down by a table. He had had
time to do a great deal since he had been recalled from the
Soviet Union by a cable from his party; he had arrived the
previous evening at Lydda airport. In Moscow he had met with
the Labor Minister, but he had waited in vain for an interview
with Kosygin that an influential British socialist had promised
him. Since his return Allon had spoken on the telephone with
Rabin and had been closeted in a long interview with Barlev,

who had given him a complete rundown on the situation. Newspapers had carried pictures of him swaggering in his light-colored shirt and khaki pants as he left with Eshkol for a tour of inspection in the south. In the afternoon he had talked with several generals and had checked plans for the campaign. "War is inevitable," he had said at the end of that meeting.

Now Eshkol was questioning him.

"Yigal, what do you think?"

"We should go to war."

"When?"

"Yesterday."

Eshkol studied a map of the Middle East and for a moment said nothing. Then: "Good. I am going to call a cabinet meeting and propose the beginning of hostilities."

"Put my name on your speakers' list," Allon said.

At the close of the talk Allon showed deep satisfaction. He told Galili, who shared his apartment in Ramat Aviv, "Israel, at the next cabinet meeting, Eshkol will propose war."

The fourth Egyptian tank division, Nasser's mailed fist, took up its position in the Sinai peninsula that morning.

Yariv went to Eshkol's house with a mass of disturbing bulletins on the increasing military preparations of all the Arab countries.

"Wait a moment," Eshkol told his colleagues after Yariv had left. "We sent Eban to lay the question of the strait before the heads of foreign states. Now it appears that the very survival of Israel is at stake. We must enable him to lay heavy emphasis in his talks upon the concentration of Egyptian troops."

A little later an urgent cable was sent to Eban, informing him of the sudden escalation and endeavoring to impress him with the current military situation: the trip of the Egyptian War Minister to Moscow; the movement of Iraqi, Syrian, and Jordanian troops toward the Israeli frontier; the entry of important Egyptian military units into the Sinai peninsula.

"You should explain to President Johnson that the danger no longer lies simply in the closing of the strait but also in the concentration of troops and in the prospect of an Arab attack on Israel. Can President Johnson advise us what to do in this situation?" That was the first cable. A few minutes later it was followed by a second, even more disturbing.

At 3:40 P.M., Jacob Herzog, Director General of the Prime Minister's office, arrived in Tel Aviv. An hour earlier, in his Jerusalem office, he had finished drafting a cable to Eban with final instructions on the line to take with Johnson. But before sending the cable he had telephoned the Defense Ministry in Tel Aviv. He had been told: "The situation has completely changed. Come at once."

Herzog hustled Levavi into his car and headed for Tel Aviv. In Eshkol's office he found Rabin and other officials. There was a militant atmosphere in the room. Some thought that the Egyptians might attack Israel the next day, Friday. The anxiety approached panic. The troop movements and reports of artillery fire from the Gaza Strip made a dark picture.

A new move was suggested: make a dramatic appeal to the United States and thus ensure that it would come to Israel's aid in the event of an attack. Herzog settled down to draft another cable. Unlike the first one, which had been merely informative, the second was the cry of a drowning nation. Its substance: "As a result of events during the last twenty-four hours, be advised that we expect a surprise attack from the Egyptians and the Syrians at any moment. The United States government should declare at once that any attack on Israel would be regarded as an attack on the United States. It should also issue instructions in that spirit to its forces in the area. It is recommended that you show this cable to the highest officials, the President himself or the Secretary of State."

The text of the cable was read and approved by the highest officials of the Foreign Ministry and the Prime Minister's Office. At that moment no one suspected that the cable would be one of the Israeli government's worst blunders. It was transmitted to Washington.

Early in the afternoon a BOAC plane from London landed at New York's Kennedy airport, where Evron was waiting for Eban, who followed him to the plane for Washington. On the way they reviewed the latest proposals for an international force. "If not enough countries agree to join with the United States," Evron said, "perhaps the U.S. will act alone, though they don't like that idea."

Evron also outlined the program that had been arranged for Eban: that evening talks with Rusk and other top State Department people, the following morning McNamara, and later Johnson. "This evening, we will arrange an appointment with the President, who is expected back from Canada," Evron said. "You will probably see him around noon tomorrow."

Meanwhile, the Israeli embassy had received one of the ill-advised cables from Israel. Somehow the second one—that from Herzog—had arrived first, but both were signed "Eshkol." Harman took the messages with him to the Washington airport, where hundreds of reporters and television newscasters were waiting.

Eban held a press conference there.

"Has France offered a solution?" they asked him.

"Yes," he said. "France proposes to settle the problem of the strait of Tiran along the same lines as those agreed to at the Montreux Convention in respect to the Dardanelles."

If Eban had taken the trouble to review that agreement, he might have seen that he had fallen into the trap the French had set for him. According to the convention the nation that held the Dardanelles had the power to close them in the event of war. Now, a state of war did exist between Israel and Egypt.

Harman took Eban to an embassy official's apartment and informed him that, according to the cables, a surprise attack by the Egyptians was expected at any moment. Eban turned pale. Then Evron telephoned Rusk to ask for an earlier appointment. Rusk agreed to see them at once.

At 4:30 P.M. Rusk, Battle, and Eugene Rostow received Eban, Harman, and Evron. Evron informed the Americans of the cables and requested that the United States issue a statement at once to the effect that any attack on Israel would be regarded as an attack on the United States.

Rusk's face betrayed his anxiety. "Have you informed the

British and the French about this?" he asked. Then he hurried
to the White House to report to the returning President as soon
as he returned.

Once he had the information, Johnson immediately had the
report checked against the data collected by the American
secret services, cabled Kosygin in an attempt to persuade him
to restrain Nasser from committing any act of war, and dispatched a cable to the Egyptians asking them to promise not to
engage in any military action and warning them of serious
consequences if they did.*

That evening Egyptian Ambassador Mustapha Kemal was
called to the State Department offices. The Israeli diplomats
were already there for a working dinner on the ninth floor. The
Israeli participants were Eban, Harman, Rafael, Evron, T.
Meron, and Military Attaché General Joseph Geva; the Americans were Eugene Rostow, Joe Sisko, Foy Kohler, Battle, and
their assistants.

While they were having cocktails on the terrace, Kemal, a
moderate, sociable man deeply disturbed by the events of the
moment, was waiting alone in Eugene Rostow's huge office.
The day before Johnson had summoned him and issued severe
warnings about the closing of the strait, but Kemal knew that
no one in Washington thought him powerful enough to influence Nasser.

Excusing himself from his guests, Eugene Rostow returned
to his office. "President Johnson," he told Kemal, "has requested me by telephone to transmit through you a warning to
your government. We have heard rumors that Egypt may soon
attack Israel. If such should occur, we wish to inform you that
the United States will act in accordance with the Charter of
the United Nations and also in accordance with its guarantee
of the independence and integrity of Israel. The President's
words to me were 'We will be against whoever fires the first
shot. We will honor our pledges. The status quo must be re-
established in the area.' An attack on Israel would be suicide
on your part," Rostow added.

* According to American sources of information.

Kemal took the memorandum that Rostow had hastily drafted, and Rostow showed him out. That same night the two messages reached Moscow and Cairo. A little before the Americans and the Israelis sat down to dinner, Rostow was called away again. When he returned he told Eban that Rusk wanted to see him at once.

Eban hurried to Rusk. "Our service has checked on your reports," the Secretary of State said. "We have no reason to believe that the Egyptians are getting ready to launch a surprise attack. The Egyptian troops in the Sinai peninsula have not been put into offensive formation. Our experts do not think that Nasser will order an attack until U Thant has returned from Cairo and reported to the Security Council."

"My government," Eban said, "would not have sent such urgent cables if they were not sure of their information. May I ask you to have the matter checked again?"

Rusk agreed.

The working dinner proceeded in a strained atmosphere. Eban was frequently called down to Rusk's office. Eugene Rostow had to go to the telephone several times to report to the White House or to receive instructions. Nevertheless, the guests tried to concentrate on the purpose of the meeting: to review the American guarantees of free navigation in the strait of Tiran.

"Those American guarantees," Eban said, "were given to me by John Foster Dulles himself in 1957."

The Americans frowned in disbelief. Eban calmly took out of his briefcase the official memorandum of his talks with Dulles. There could be no doubt that the documents were authentic; they had been emended in Dulles' easily recognizable handwriting. With some embarrassment the American diplomats had to admit that they had no copy of the memorandum. Rostow had to ask Eban to lend him his copy so that he might show it to President Johnson on the following day before the conference between the President and Eban.

The talk then turned to a different topic: the plan to use an international force to open the strait. The Americans gave a detailed explanation of the British proposal. One of the Israeli diplomats, believing that this discussion was a waste of time in "diplomatic onanism," said, "Such a conference might have been of advantage a few days ago, but now events have caught up with us."

Rafael, the Israeli delegate to the United Nations, spoke at length. Eban looked gloomy and ate scarcely anything. Toward the end of the meal, while Eban was absent on another trip to Rusk's office, Sisko read a note that one of his friends had slipped him: "If you manage to get Eban to accept the project, it will probably be the last time we'll see him acting as Foreign Minister."

At exactly midnight on the night of May 24–25 Yeshayahu Newton, a tall, thin man of thirty-five who had been a second-class officer in the Israeli merchant marine was mobilized. He had with him a small bag containing his work clothes, his gloves, a seaman's knife, and his toilet articles. He had spent the night at the base and in the morning was one of 150 seamen, most of them officers, being questioned one by one in a small office by Colonel Menachem Cohen, formerly a captain in the Israeli navy, and by Captain Yoram Friedman and other officers.

"Have you put your affairs in order?" Newton was asked.

"What affairs? My three brothers were mobilized the first day, and no one bothered about their affairs. Why is anyone bothering about mine?"

He was asked to sign the following affidavit: "I submit to state discipline, and I will follow my captain wherever he leads me."

In a nearby room a photographer from Haifa was snapping the smiling sailors. Sixty were chosen from the group and divided into two squads. "Go home at once," they were told, "and report back at 6:00 with a suitcase—not heavier than forty pounds."

At 6:00 a big Egged tour bus was waiting at the gate of the

camp. As soon as it was loaded, it sped off south, bypassing Tel Aviv, and pulled up before Sarafend Hospital. A squad of doctors and nurses was waiting to vaccinate the sailors against smallpox and yellow fever. Newton gathered that they were going somewhere in the south.

From Sarafend the bus drove to Lydda airport, where the sailors were herded into the waiting room. When they received their El Al tickets, they learned that they were going overseas. Company directors from Zim Lines and Cargo Ships El-Yam shook their hands, gave them refreshments, and handed them each a present—a medal commemorating the "Tenth Anniversary of the Opening of the Strait of Tiran."

An El Al Boeing had been kept waiting on the runway for an hour until official orders arrived. Stewards climbed aboard and asked about sixty passengers to disembark: "A party of foreign students must leave the country at once by government order." The travelers left the plane without comment, only to see their places taken by brawny, well-tattooed "students" using profane language.

The plane took off at midnight. Newton looked at his ticket. "Destination: Nairobi," it read, but he was sure that they would be going farther. "How much will you bet," said one of the sailors, "that we're going to man a test ship?"

In Washington three sets of experts spent the night checking reports on military preparations in the Middle East.* One was from the C.I.A.; another from the National Security Agency, a less well known but equally efficient department; and the third composed of State Department officials. All had been organized in response to Eban's emergency appeal to the American government. They worked until daylight, inspecting hundreds of documents, information bulletins, aerial photographs taken by reconnaissance planes and satellites, and dispatches from correspondents and various other sources. In the morning a weighty memorandum on the possibility of a surprise attack in the Middle East was sent to the White House.

* Interviews with several top officials in Washington.

•

JOHNSON: "DON'T PUT A PISTOL TO MY HEAD!"

AFTER STUDYING THE memorandum compiled by the three groups of experts, President Johnson found that each reported no indication that Egypt would attack Israel in the next few hours or even the next few days. "If war does break out," said one Pentagon expert, "Israel will win a decisive victory within a few days." The generals predicted that there would be heavy Israeli tank penetration toward the Suez canal, accompanied by an air attack. They based their opinion on the offensive strategy that the Israeli army had been using for some years.*

Johnson did not want to see Eban, at least, not for a while, for he did not know what to say to him. The projected maritime force was still in limbo, and without the consent of Congress Johnson could not involve his country in a new conflict. He asked his aides to postpone the meeting with Eban as long as they could.

At 9:30 A.M. Rusk telephoned Harman to ask whether or not Eban would be in Washington on Saturday, when the results of U Thant's trip to Cairo would be known. Harman gathered that this question was a polite way of postponing the interview with Johnson at least twenty-four hours.

At 9:45 A.M. Eban telephoned Rusk: "No, I will not be in Washington after tomorrow. In fact, I ought to leave tonight, because on Sunday morning there is to be a decisive cabinet

---

* The substance of this memorandum was given to me by top officials in Washington.

meeting in Israel, which may be the most important in our
whole history. Anything decided in it will depend to a great
degree on what the President has to say to me. Israel would
like to hear an absolute and unreserved pledge of American
assistance. U Thant's report will change nothing, one way or
another. I am afraid that war will break out in the Middle East
next week. The Egyptian closing of the strait is an act of war,
against which we must defend ourselves. The only way to
avoid war will be a firm statement from the President that the
United States will open the strait either alone or with its allies.
Such a statement, supported by a letter from Johnson to Eshkol
which contains details of the strategy to be employed in the
operations the Americans are contemplating, will be, I think,
the one means of resolving the crisis. . . . Everything we hear
about the matter being put before the United Nations only
depresses us, because such procrastinations only make our
chances less."

"I understand," Rusk said and hung up. Then he hurried to
see the President.

When Rusk reported that conversation, Johnson was furious.
"If the gentleman from Tel Aviv is in such a hurry," he said,
"he can go home right away." Then he remarked irritably to
one of his aides: "I don't like anyone to put a pistol to my head.
This Sunday cabinet meeting of his to decide on peace or
war—it's an ultimatum, and I don't like it."

Still he let it be understood that he might see Eban after all.
"But not right away," he said. "Later. Maybe this evening."

Meanwhile, Eban and the Israeli military attaché, General
Geva, were meeting with McNamara in the Pentagon. Eban
had expected a rather private interview with a small committee. He was therefore astonished to find the Secretary of
Defense with his assistants, Cyrus Vance and Hoop, the army
chiefs, and the Chairman of the Joint Chiefs of Staff, General
Earl C. Wheeler.

In his briefcase Eban had a cable from Eshkol expressing
disappointment at Rusk's proposals of the previous evening and
again requesting Eban to emphasize the danger represented by
the concentration of Egyptian troops. When Eban did so, he

met with general skepticism. Wheeler went to the wall and dramatically pulled aside a heavy curtain, revealing a large map of the Middle East. He explained briefly why he thought Egypt could not win and Israel would emerge triumphantly from any military engagement. "We have had the matter checked by our experts," he said, "and we are all in agreement that you will win."

"But what if they attack our airfields?" Eban persisted.

"No matter which of you strikes the first blow," Wheeler said, "you are the stronger, to our minds. You will win in either case."

The conversation turned to the international force for opening the strait. McNamara definitely stated that he was strongly opposed to it and that he had no faith in the "regatta." "Suppose," he said, "that we did assemble an international fleet. It might pass through the strait two or three times and stay in the area for one or two months, at a cost of billions—and then what? It couldn't stay there forever. What would happen if, after the fleet withdrew, a single Israeli ship showed up without convoy in the strait? That would be the real test."

At 11:00 A.M. Presidential adviser Walt Rostow telephoned Evron (who had known Johnson before he became President and whom Johnson respected). When the crisis had first developed Johnson had asked Walt Rostow to keep in close touch with Evron.

"We are aware that we are confronted by a very serious situation," Rostow said. "After what Eban told us last night, the President would like their talk to be constructive, and he wants to study the matter at some leisure. That's why it would be desirable to delay the meeting until this evening or perhaps until tomorrow morning. The President would also like to hear a report of U Thant's trip to Cairo before he makes up his mind on what should be done."

"If the talk between Eban and Johnson seems that important to you," Evron said, "it's only natural that the President will want some time to think about it. But the meeting shouldn't be delayed too long."

At that very moment a special military plane was landing in

Washington; the State Department had sent it to Eisenhower's farm in Gettysburg, and American officials had finally located in the former President's files a copy of the memorandum of the Eban-Dulles talk; they were bringing it to the President with all speed so that he might study it before he met with Eban.

At noon Rusk and McNamara submitted a joint report to Johnson in preparation for that meeting. In that top-secret document they enumerated the various courses that might be undertaken and came to this conclusion: "In sum, it seems that there are only two solutions for the United States: first, organize a multi-national naval force; second, leave Israel to act alone."

Rusk recommended the former.

That morning in Cairo *al-Ahram* ran the weekly editorial by Hassanein Heikal, Nasser's confidant:

> An armed engagement with Israel is inevitable. The psychological factor involved compels Israel to take up the challenge of war, for there is a question of Israel's security and even its survival. It is not only a matter of the Gulf of 'Aqaba but also of a more important question, namely, Israel's conception of its security, which is the entire basis for its defense.

Heikal was right. That was exactly the foundation of all Israeli political and military thinking. For years the country had based its strategy on the strength of its army as a deterrent. This policy had kept the Arabs from attacking. It was the strength of the Israeli army that had stopped the diversion of the Jordan waters and had kept Egyptian saboteurs out of the country. The strait of Tiran had remained open; the Jordanians had forbidden any Arab troops in their territory; and innumerable hostile acts had been avoided because the Arabs had lived in terror of Israeli military power.

But the myth of the "forbidding force" had been exploded. Egypt had concentrated 100,000 men and 800 tanks in the

Sinai peninsula, had chased out the U.N. troops, and had closed the strait. Jordan had permitted Iraqi and Saudi Arabian forces to enter its territory. Egyptian leaders had announced that the Gaza Strip would once again be a launching pad for saboteurs against Israel. The question of the strait had already become a side issue. It made little difference how many Israeli ships used that passage to the sea. The important thing was that Egypt was no longer afraid of Israel and could take bolder and bolder steps.

Even if an international force had been organized and put into action in order to reopen the strait to Israeli shipping, the situation would not have changed in Israel's favor, for it had lost prestige. Israel appeared a weak country, whose defense and survival depended upon the great powers. This evolution of circumstances could provide Nasser with new triumphs. Without attacking Israel directly, he could activate sabotage, demand Israel's retreat to the boundaries of the 1947 plan, provoke local incidents, and wield a greater influence on international attitudes. Israel's power would gradually diminish, and the country's existence would become precarious. If Israel were to survive, it would have apparently only one alternative: to make war, at the cost of heavy losses, to recover its power.

Heikal understood this situation. But the Israeli government, which was desperately clinging to the idea of an international fleet seemed not to understand this simple truth.

That morning Nasser addressed the central committee of the Arab Trade Unions:

> In ten years, the Arab people have changed. The Arab people now want to fight and recover the rights of the people of Palestine. . . . If Israel attacks Syria or Egypt, we will all declare war against her, and our ultimate objective will be the destruction of Israel. Four or five years ago, I could not have said this. But I do not promise what I cannot deliver. Now I am convinced that we will win. Egypt is waiting the attack of the Israelis at any minute, and then we will destroy Israel.

Intoxicated with his success in the previous few days, Nasser was sure of victory. Just a few weeks earlier he had spoken in more reserved tones, saying that it might be years before Egypt would be a match for Israel. But the sight of his huge forces concentrated in the Sinai peninsula distorted his vision. Hundreds of tanks and planes, tens of thousands of soldiers, Arab mobs so dizzy with excitement that they were dancing in the streets, promises of support from the Arab capitals, irresolution among the great powers, Soviet support, France's pro-Arab policy—all these elements had clouded his judgment.

The previous evening there had been a four-hour conference in the headquarters of the Egyptian General Staff. Some officers had recommended that Egypt begin hostilities against Israel. Nasser, however, had been of a different turn of mind, preferring a plan that Amer had outlined to him: to wait for the Israelis to attack and then to react with a well-planned counteroffensive. Three lines of defense had been established in the Sinai peninsula, the first for the purpose of halting Israeli tanks. Failing that, the Egyptian troops could fall back to the second line and even to the third. The Sinai desert would be a deadly trap for the Jews. Then would come an offensive on Israeli territory.

A few officers observed that those three lines did not exist in fact, for most of the units were massed on the Israeli frontier, and only the fourth division was backing them up. Amer, however, could not be bothered with such details. Instead he favored a limited campaign against Elat and strategic points in its vicinity. It should be mentioned that this attack, as well as an airborne offensive against the Israeli airfields, was to take place only in the event of an outbreak of hostilities in the area.

Sometime that morning, Colonel Talibeh, commander of the 2nd Air Brigade, signed order no. 67/6 for the bombing of Elat. The alert for the execution of that order went into effect at dawn on May 26.

That same morning a long cabinet meeting was in progress in Tel Aviv. Some of those present—Galili, Minister of Transport Moshe Carmel, Allon, and Minister of Commerce Sharef insisted on immediate action, but the religious ministers and Moshe Kol, Minister of Development and Tourism, opposed it, fearing that the Israeli army was not strong enough to defeat Egypt. In the end the government decided not to decide anything until Eban came home.

At 2:00 P.M. David Ben-Gurion arrived in Beersheba and shut himself up in the Desert Inn Hotel for a long conference with Dayan. The former leader analyzed the situation. He was convinced that, for the time being, Nasser did not intend to attack Israel; he had won quite a few victories already without having to fight. On the other hand, if Israel attacked on the Sinai front, it would appear to the world as the aggressor.

"Nasser will not force either the time or the place of an offensive on us," Ben-Gurion said. "We shall have to choose that for ourselves. It will be a long war and a hard one, and it will last a month or more. Losses will mount. We should be certain of the sympathy and the aid of the great powers and ask them, not for soldiers or for airplane coverage, but for arms, planes, and tanks to replace those we shall lose. We must mount a diplomatic campaign to persuade the United States, Great Britain, and France to supply us with armaments. The offensive should not be in the Sinai peninsula but rather an air attack on Sharm el Sheikh. International opinion will favor us, for the closing of the strait is an act of aggression. To counter our attack on the strait, Nasser will attack Israel. We can stop him and then launch our counteroffensive. That way we shall not seem to be aggressors in the eyes of the world."

Ben-Gurion spoke convincingly, but there were errors in his reasoning. Lacking precise information on the strength of the Israeli army, he did not count on its being able to win in a short time, without the need for supplementary equipment. The old lion seemed obsessed with his recollections of 1956, when Israel had been judged an aggressor as a result of the Sinai campaign and both the Soviet Union and the United States had adopted a common policy against the Jewish state. To avoid a similar hostile attitude on their part, Ben-Gurion was inclined to forgo whatever advantage a surprise attack might give Israel. A limited operation in the area of the strait would, however, give Nasser the advantage of attacking first and would cost Israel heavy losses in men and matériel.

Dayan did not wholly agree with Ben-Gurion. He did not believe that Nasser was preparing to attack Israel, and he sided with Ben-Gurion in thinking that it would be disastrous to let Nasser force Israel into war at a time and in a place of his own choosing. Nevertheless, he insisted, Israel could not afford to wait. "Nasser," he said, "will drag out the crisis and in the end will attack us when and where he wants to. We must declare war at once."

The Jordanian sector of Jerusalem was deathly still. The shops were closed, and the streets were empty. In Israel, in Lydda, there was a short ceremony to welcome President Shazar home from Canada.

In Moscow the Egyptian War Minister Badran signed an agreement with the U.S.S.R. for future supplies of basic armaments. Soviet Defense Minister General Gretchko said, "Our army, our people, and our government are on the side of the Arabs."

In London, *The Observer* printed an article by its correspondent in Israel, which touched the hearts of many, with its statement "I am almost ashamed that I am not a Jew."

In Cairo Nasser expressed his thanks to the French Ambassador for De Gaulle's friendly attitude toward the Arabs.

In Paris a correspondent from an Israeli daily newspaper stopped Foreign Minister Couve de Murville on the street near the Foreign Office and asked him whether or not France had really abandoned Israel. "Never fear," Couve de Murville replied. "You will eventually see that France is acting in Israel's best interests." The reporter excitedly cabled that good news to Tel Aviv.

The El Al plane landed in Nairobi after a stopover in Tehran. The steward said over the loudspeaker, "We wish our students a profitable stay." The sixty sailors who had been mobilized the previous night disembarked on African soil. At the same time a light Auster plane took off for Cyprus from Biggin Hill airport near London. On board was "peace pilot" Abie Nathan, who had told reporters that he was going to Damascus or Cairo to persuade Arab leaders to make peace with Israel.

At 6:00 P.M. Evron entered Walt Rostow's White House office. Rostow told him that the President would receive Eban that evening: "He has been studying your case all afternoon with State Department and Pentagon specialists."

Evron telephoned the Hotel Mayflower to ask Eban to wait for him there. "I'll pick you up a little before 7:00," he said, "and Abe too, and take you to the meeting with the President."

He had just hung up when the telephone rang. "Yes," Rostow said, "I have told Epi Evron. . . . Yes, he is here. . . . Right away? . . . Yes, sir."

"Come along," he said to Evron. "The President wants to see you."

In astonishment Evron followed Rostow to the President's office.

Johnson was sitting on a sofa and invited Epi and Walt Rostow to sit at his sides. The Filipino photographer who recorded every moment of Johnson's life for the President's personal album was also there, silent like a shadow. In one corner, two teletype machines were humming. Johnson was complaining to his companions about Lester Pearson's denunciation of the Vietnam war, which had been published in Canada that morning a few hours after the President had visited him at Lake Harrington. On the other hand, Pearson had agreed to take part in the "international force" to open the strait of Tiran.

Johnson did not conceal his reservations for the coming interview with Eban, which would be influenced by the forthcoming "decisive" cabinet meeting in Tel Aviv. "I have spent the entire afternoon discussing your affairs," Johnson said. "I will not be able to tell Eban anything more than what McNamara and Rusk have already told him."

The President expressed the hope that he would not have to

take military action. "I do not believe," he said, "that Egypt will attack you. Frankly, this six-foot-three Texan* would love to see that blue-and-white flag passing through the straits, but I have to get Congress' approval. I'm not going to repeat the mistake that Truman made in Korea. Italy will go along with us, and so will Canada and Great Britain and other friends likewise." Johnson explained again why he could not undertake any action without the consent of Congress.

Meanwhile, Eban and Harman, who were waiting for Evron at the Mayflower, were growing nervous. When he had not arrived by 7:00, they decided to go to the White House without him. But Harman took a wrong turn, and they arrived at the service entrance. A little later a guard telephoned the chief security officer of the White House: "There's a guy here says his name's Eban and has an appointment with the President of the United States."

Eban and Harman were escorted to the President's office. The American specialists who were to take part in the talk were already there. Some were to be present during the entire conference; others had been summoned to give their opinions on points within their special fields. The Israelis went down the line, greeting Rusk, McNamara, Pentagon experts, the Rostow brothers, Sisko, and a few others. The two groups sat facing each other over nonalcoholic drinks. (The Johnson White House never offered hard liquor during diplomatic conferences.)

Eban took the floor to remark on the concentration of Egyptian troops in the Sinai peninsula, which was putting the very existence of Israel in danger. "Nasser is going to war with us," he said. "He is ready. This is concrete information."

Johnson turned to McNamara, who said, "All our information services agree that Nasser has neither the intention nor the strength to attack Israel."

The talk bypassed the question of the strait and of the international force. "If anyone did go through the strait," Johnson said, "it would be a severe blow to Nasser's prestige."

* Johnson liked to speak of himself in the third person.

Walt Rostow added: "That's the point where you roll over the carpet. If an international fleet went through the strait, there would be belly laughs all over the world."

The basic problem, the Americans said, was the strait—first, because of the clear and firm commitments of the United States in regard to it, and, second, because Nasser had closed it with such a grand gesture. If Nasser could be made to back down on the strait, the blockade would be raised, the whole maneuver would founder, and Nasser would find himself in a dubious position as overlord of Egypt.

"I think we can do it," said Johnson, "but it isn't what Lyndon Baines Johnson thinks that matters, it is what the President of the United States says. That I cannot say without the approval of Congress." Then he added with caustic irony: "The fellows who ask me not to send one more soldier to Vietnam, now keep pressing me to send all our aircraft carriers to the Gulf of 'Aqaba."

Johnson picked up a sheet of paper, and read a carefully worded statement of his official position:

> The United States of America has its own constitutional processes which are basic to its action on matters involving war and peace. The Secretary General has not yet reported to the United Nations Security Council, and the Security Council has not yet demonstrated what it may or may not be able or willing to do, although the United States will press for prompt action in the United Nations.
>
> I have already publicly stated this week our views on the safety of Israel and on the strait of Tiran. Regarding the strait, we mean to pursue vigorously the measures which may be taken by maritime nations to assure that the strait and gulf remain open to free and innocent passage of the vessels of all nations.
>
> I must emphasize the necessity for Israel not to make itself responsible for the initiation of hostilities. Israel will not be alone unless it decides to go alone. We cannot imagine that it will make this decision.

Johnson laid down the paper and said: "You can act within the framework of an international organization. What do you lose by trying?"

"We have reached the conclusion that we cannot live that way," Eban said. "There has never been a moment for my country such as this. We are on the pathway of a grave decision. We are faced with a clear cut choice: surrender or fight. We are unanimous not to surrender. It might be a bloody business—but we are sure we can win the war. We want to know who will stand by us, and whether the United States will reaffirm the pledges it made in 1957. In Paris I have talked with De Gaulle, who has proposed a conference among the four great powers. I think, however, that he may now have changed his mind, since the Russians have not agreed to such a conference. At least the arms factories of France are open to us. In London, I was agreeably surprised to find a willingness to act, provided that you also take action. Consequently everything depends upon you. I have two questions to ask: Do we fight alone or are you with us? And what is the practical extension of your commitment?"

"We must consider a legal action against the blockade," Johnson said. "We have a vital interest to see that this blockade is not carried through. The basic question is whether you want to involve us or not. You keep telling us there is a cabinet session on Sunday. I can't do much about that. If you want to involve us, we must act in the framework of the United Nations. It must be a multilateral action. We might get the support of Canada, Italy, and Norway. We are not retreating, we are not backtracking. I know that your blood and lives are at stake. My blood and life are at stake at many places. My purpose is to see that Israeli ships go through. This will have consequences far beyond the immediate blockade.

"If you want to get some proximity with us in your future deeds," Johnson continued, "then you have got to invest some time. I am no mouse. I am neither weak nor scared. I've got to face out this thing." He rose and escorted Eban to the elevator.

As they parted, Eban said: "I go with a heavy heart. What will happen is obscure."

After Eban had left, Johnson said to one of his advisers: "I was ready for heavy bargaining, but I found myself up against a lightweight, and I could get away with the niceties." Johnson admired Eban's ability as a speaker and his fine mind, but he was disappointed in his lack of firmness.

In Israel, everyone in the government, the General Staff, and all other leaders were anxiously awaiting news of the outcome of Eban's talk with Johnson. But Eban would not permit Johnson's statement to be cabled to Israel. He took the stenographic transcript, which Abe Harman edited, and returned via New York and Paris.

That night it was Moscow's turn to send emergency cables. After receiving President Johnson's apprehensive cable of the previous night, Kosygin had dispatched three urgent cables to Tel Aviv, Cairo, and Washington. The U.S.S.R. was also trying to calm all parties concerned and to avoid the outbreak of war in the Middle East.

At 2:15 A.M. the telephone rang in Ady Yoffe's room at the Dan Hotel. Secretary Bikov of the Soviet embassy was on the other end of the line. "Ambassador Chuvakin wishes to talk at once with the head of the government," he said.

"At this hour?" said Yoffe, looking at his watch. "Couldn't it wait till morning? The Prime Minister is asleep."

He could hear Bikov talking to someone beside him, whose voice came through clearly: "Nyet!"

"The Ambassador," Yoffe suggested, "might be willing to meet with Arie Levavi, Director General of our Foreign Ministry"

"Please," Bikov persisted, "do not take the responsibility for postponing this meeting."

Yoffe sighed, but he woke up Eshkol and Levavi. As befitted a professional diplomat, Levavi jumped into his formal clothes with the speed of lightning. Eshkol and Yoffe settled for pull-

ing their trousers on over their pajamas. That was how Chuvakin and Bikov found them at about 3:00 in the morning. The
hotel staff was asleep, and there was no room service, but Yoffe
managed to rustle up some orange juice and some toothbrush
glasses, which he offered to his guests.

Chuvakin brought Kosygin's cable:

> Acting in the interests of peace and wishing to avoid any
> spilling of blood, the government of the Soviet Union has
> decided to make this appeal to you. We request you to do
> everything in your power to avoid a clash of arms that will
> have serious consequences for the cause of peace and inter-
> national security. We appeal to you not to create a new
> area of war that could bring indescribable suffering to all
> nations. . . . It is absolutely essential that a means be
> found to settle this dispute in peaceful ways, for it is easy
> to light a fire, but to put one out is not so easy as may be
> imagined by those who are pushing Israel toward the abyss
> of war. We hope that, after serious reflection on the situa-
> tion and on the responsibility of the party that opens hos-
> tilities, the Israeli government will do everything to see
> that an armed conflict does not break out in the Middle
> East.
>
> Respectfully,
> A. Kosygin

Eshkol was impressed by the restrained tone of the message,
which contained no threats or accusations toward Israel. He
was also touched by the "respectfully." Eshkol remembered the
harsh and violent cable that Nikolai Bulganin had sent to Ben-
Gurion after the Sinai campaign and in which he had threatened Israel with extinction and had not taken the trouble to
address his correspondent "respectfully."

"You know that there is no concentration of Israeli troops on
the Syrian frontier," Eshkol said to Chuvakin in fluent Russian.
"May I suggest that you have someone sent from Moscow to
verify that with his own eyes?"

Yoffe remembered the conversation between Chuvakin and

Eshkol in October 1966, when the Ambassador had charged that Israel was concentrating troops in the north and Eshkol had replied: "Mister Ambassador, my car is at the door. Come along; let's drive up to the Syrian frontier, and then you can see with your own eyes that you have been misinformed." Chuvakin had responded with a typically Soviet diplomatic silence.

"You can easily send someone to Israel for a while," Eshkol said. "Although our country is not as important or as advanced as Syria, a minor official of the U.S.S.R. would probably consent to pay us a visit. On the other hand, I would gladly go to Moscow at once to explain our position to your government."

"Are you going to fire the first shot?" Chuvakin asked.

Eshkol did not answer, as Chuvakin had taught him not to.

"Are you going to fire the first shot?" Chuvakin asked again.

Bikov spoke to the Ambassador. "You have asked that question three times now without receiving a reply."

Eshkol broke his silence. "When an Ambassador presents his credentials to a chief of state, he states that his mission is one of peace. I regret to say that your efforts in that direction have not met with much success. Mines have been planted on our soil. Is not that the first shot? Wasn't the bombing of Nahal 'Oz the first shot? If not, then just what constitutes the first shot?"

Chuvakin did not reply.

A few hours earlier Nasser had received Johnson's cable asking him not to engage in combat. At 3:30 A.M. the Soviet Ambassador arrived at his house with a frantic message that had been cabled after Kosygin had received a cable from Johnson the previous night: "We request you not to undertake any military action." Nasser assured his visitor that he had no intention of doing so. Why should he? He had won his points without shedding a drop of blood.

At about the same time a cable for President Johnson arrived from Moscow:

Information that Egypt is getting ready to attack Israel is utterly false. On the other hand, according to our sources,

Israel is planning an armed action against its Arab neighbors. We know that the Arabs do not want war. The Soviet
Union requests the United States to take all measures possible to avoid a military conflict, for the Soviet, the Arab,
and the Israeli people do not want war.

The cable also contained the following sentence: "If Israel
begins hostilities, the Soviet Union will come to the aid of the
attacked countries."

•

D-DAY?

ON THAT MORNING of May 27 the sun rose on one of the biggest picnics in the history of the Jewish people. For several days the desert had been the most heavily populated region of the whole State of Israel. On every hill and under every clump of dried bushes, units of the regular army or the reserves were stationed. Stones by the roadside had become dressing tables or desks. Twisted and pierced pipes served as showers in the camps. The roads and crossroads were choked with Israelis in khaki and wide-brimmed Australian hats.

On May 27 the throng was even greater than usual and of a different sort. From Tel Aviv, Haifa, and Jerusalem, from villages and kibbutzim, long caravans of cars were arriving, most of them driven by women with just one end in view: to find a fiancé, a son, a brother, or a husband who had been mobilized. All anyone knew was that the units were somewhere in the Negev. The desert was vast. The cars went from camp to camp, stopping at every squad of reservists to ask for Shmulik or Yoske or Gingi. Miraculously most of the women succeeded in finding the men they were looking for—and in loading them down with cakes, drinks, sandwiches, shoes, and sweaters.

Ben-Gurion's dream of populating the Negev seemed to be coming true.

The same morning the sixty airborne sailors landed at Massawa airport in Ethiopia. The previous afternoon they had

131

toured Nairobi, visited the safari region, and seen an elephant dance. They had taken off by plane at night. In Massawa they were lodged at the luxurious Red Sea Hotel.

Feverish negotiations were being conducted simultaneously in Piraeus and Massawa between the Zim Lines of Israel and Greek ship owners. An old Greek ship of 3,500 tons that had reached Massawa with a cargo from Kuwait had become the property of Zim; its name had been changed from *Arion* to *Dolphin*.

The sixty sailors at last learned the purpose of their trip—to force the passage of the strait of Tiran in the *Dolphin* and one other vessel. As soon as they received the order the boats would sail north and enter the gulf of 'Aqaba through the strait. They were to carry no arms except for the captain's traditional revolver. Their final destination was Elat, but the sailors doubted that they would go much farther than Sharm el Sheikh, where the Egyptians had set up a battery of cannon and would certainly use it to stop the Jewish ship. Then what?

All the sailors were willing and eager to go on that perilous mission. As soon as they arrived, the officers went to the harbor to ready the *Dolphin* for what might well be the last voyage of its long career.

The odor of gunpowder was in the air at the Defense Ministry and at General Staff headquarters. According to the foreign press, Israeli units in the desert were ready to move at dawn the following day. That morning Rabin was talking with Eshkol, who gave him to understand that war was imminent. The government was becoming increasingly impatient to hear from Eban about his talk with President Johnson, but the hours ticked by, and no cable came. Eshkol ordered the Director of the Prime Minister's office, Jacob Herzog and Joseph Tekoa to telephone Washington at once. Herzog asked Harman where the report of the interview with Johnson was.

"The Minister gave me explicit instructions not to cable anything about it," said Harman. "When he gets home, Eban will report directly to the government."

Eshkol was furious. Ady Yoffe then telephoned Washington and ordered Harman, on Eshkol's authority, to send a cable at once with the substance of the conference. Harman did so. A few hours later the cable arrived. A high official of the Defense Ministry who was in Eshkol's office that morning remarked, "If war comes, victory will cost us 15,000 casualties, but defeat will cost us hundreds of thousands."

Another official, one connected with the Prime Minister's office, went into panic. "I know we'll win," he told a friend, "but we will lose tens of thousands of soldiers. Nasser knows that we are stronger, so why does he push us into war? He's acting like an idiot, a madman. There's only one possible con- clusion—he's got secret arms!"

U Thant delivered his report to the Security Council and asked the two parties for a two-week delay to reassess the situation and to try to resolve the crisis. Egypt, eager to exploit her success, demanded an emergency debate on Israel's aggres- sive policies over the previous eighteen years.

At 7:30 P.M. Paula Ben-Gurion admitted an unexpected visitor to her Tel Aviv house. He was Menachem Begin, a leader of the Gahal, an opposition bloc. For fifteen years Begin and Ben-Gurion had been fierce political adversaries, but the two had become closer after Ben-Gurion left power. Neverthe- less, a meeting between them could have been brought about only by a crisis.

For a week Begin had been struggling to bring Ben-Gurion back to power, for he wanted war, and he believed that Ben- Gurion was the best person to direct it. Begin had met several times with the ministers of the Religious National Party to obtain their support for replacing Eshkol with Ben-Gurion. But the leaders of the Religious National Party did not agree with Begin. They were afraid of war and wanted to avoid it. They also knew that Ben-Gurion had taken a conservative position and was not in favor of immediate declaration of war. They therefore concluded that if they brought him to power again the worst would not happen. Consequently, for diametrically opposite reasons, the two leaders, H. M. Shapiro and Begin, were working toward the same end. Each went to see Eshkol. Begin suggested that Ben-Gurion become Prime Minister again, with Eshkol as his assistant, but Eshkol categorically refused. "We're two horses," Eshkol said, "who can't pull together."

Meanwhile public opinion was increasingly in favor of a government of national union. For the people in general, that phrase took on a magical significance. It meant that the actual direction of the country, as far as its defense was concerned, would be in the hands of the strongest, most experienced, and most capable men during time of war.

Eshkol was aware of that significance. It hurt him deeply that his partners in the coalition, the members of the Gahal and Rafi parties, and even some influential members of his own party had asked him to surrender his Defense portfolio to someone else. He correctly interpreted this request as lack of confidence in his abilities as Defense Minister. He could have avoided this attitude by appointing Allon as his special adviser for defense problems without relinquishing his own position, which would have encouraged people to think he was putting experienced men in charge of things.

But his stubbornness had only increased the momentum of the political movement that was sprouting in Israel. The influential circles in the Mapai were urging Eshkol to invite Rafi and Gahal to share in the government. Carmel of the Achdut Ha'avoda was in favor of a national union. The newspapers were swollen with articles, letters from readers, and petitions from various groups of citizens, students, parties, associations, and intellectuals—all demanding a national union government. On the other hand, the old guard of the Mapai led by Golda Meir and the leaders of the Mapam were opposed to the change. One Mapam leader said, "The day the Rafi gets into power will be a black one for the working class."

The efforts by the "religious" members of Gahal and by the Rafi and many members of the Alignment for the Unity of Israel's Workers (comprising the Mapai and the Achdut

Ha'avoda) were supported by most of the people, but in the eyes of the old guard these calls for unification were only intrigues to push the old guard out of office. Everyone in the country except the government leaders seemed to have grasped how late the hour was.

When Begin came to Ben-Gurion's house on the evening of May 27, he was wearing a jacket and tie despite the unbearable heat in Tel Aviv. Some Gahal friends were with him. Peres and Joseph Almogi were already with Ben-Gurion.

The meeting was friendly, but Begin and Ben-Gurion did not see eye to eye on the policy to be adopted toward Egyptian aggression. Like Dayan, Begin thought that time was of the essence and that war should be launched at once with a large-scale attack on the Egyptians. He did not endorse Ben-Gurion's proposal for action restricted to the area of the strait of Tiran. In the course of the conversation, Ben-Gurion declared that he would not be a candidate for the post of Defense Minister.

After their meeting with the old lion, the delegates of the Gahal and Rafi went to the Hotel Yarden restaurant to settle on another candidate for the post: Dayan.

Meanwhile, in the plane that was carrying him back to Israel, Eban was carefully preparing the report he would make to his colleagues. He was more than ever determined to prevent war and to cut short any project for an offensive against Egypt. His opposition to any military action by Israel was based on his confidence in the United States, for he was convinced that the Americans would take action to open the strait. He also feared that if Israel undertook a military operation without the approval of the United States, it would be in the same position it had been in after the Sinai campaign, when the United States had joined the Soviet Union in imposing a cease-fire and demanding the withdrawal of Israeli forces.

His plane landed at Lydda at 8:30 P.M. Bodyguards and policemen restrained the reporters who tried to push through to it. Eban and his secretary entered a car, which headed for Tel Aviv's Red House, where all the national leaders were gathered. The meeting of the Cabinet began at once, although the Israeli radio had announced that it would not take place until the next day.

Several generals and Foreign Ministry specialists were present. Eban reported in detail about his trip to Europe and the United States. From his briefcase he took the documents of his talks with Wilson, De Gaulle, and Johnson. The transcript of the conference with Johnson filled nine pages.

Eban reported word for word what Johnson had proposed: his request that Israel wait two or three weeks while the United States tried to find a solution, either within the framework of the United Nations or independently of that international organization.

Eban read almost entirely from his papers, but, according to some evidence, his report of his talks in the United States and France was inaccurate at several points. Eban said many times that Johnson had pledged him that the United States would open the strait at any cost, in concert with other nations or, if need be, alone. But Johnson had promised nothing of the kind in the name of the American government; even when he had mentioned a "multinational project," he had emphasized that his country could not participate in it without the consent of Congress.

Nor was Eban's report on his conference with De Gaulle accurate. He stated that the French President was opposed to war, but he did not refer to the General's clearly antagonistic attitude toward Israel or his repeated warning, "Don't make war!" which had had the tone of an ultimatum. The gist of Eban's story of his meeting at the Élysée Palace seemed less pessimistic than would have been expected from the disappointment he had expressed in his first cables after that meeting.

During a brief recess an important Israeli leader met with some officials of the Foreign Ministry who were openly critical of Eban. They maintained that he was deceiving the government with his inaccurate report of his talks in France. "The cables he sent," they kept saying, "were quite different." The man went up to Eshkol. "I have something serious to say to you," he said. "Some officials of the Foreign Ministry do not agree with their minister's report. Here are their names. I advise you to listen to them." Eshkol took the names, but he did not question the officials.

At that moment the Foreign Minister was talking with some of his colleagues in a corridor. "I would not stay in the government," he was saying, "if it decided to make war at once. First, every avenue of diplomacy must be explored." Furthermore, he strongly opposed the formation of any coalition government.

The meeting lasted late into the night. Eban went into a nearby room, where the Committee on Foreign Affairs and Defense was meeting, in order to report on his trip to its members. In picturesque language he described what had happened in Washington during the previous twenty-four hours and the "astonishing force of Israeli diplomacy." But the members of the committee did not seem convinced that the United States would open the strait just to please Israel.

At the same time there was great activity in the Negev, as columns of tanks and half-tracks left their bases and divisions prepared to move forward.

After midnight, Eshkol put the vital question to the government: "Should we go to war at once?" The ministers were divided. One member of the Mapai said, "I want it, yet I am afraid of it." Another said, "Why make war when Ben-Gurion himself does not approve?" Ben-Gurion's opinion seemed to have influenced several ministers, including Eshkol, who continued to look to him for final authority in matters of defense.

Finally, the matter came to a vote. The voting was conducted in simple fashion; each minister gave his opinion. The eighteen Israeli ministers were split equally. Nine favored immediate war: Eshkol, Minister of Justice Yaakov Shimshon Shapiro, Galili, Allon, Carmel, Minister of Posts Israel Yeshayahu, Minister of Police Eliahu Sasson, Minister of Agriculture Haim Gvati, and Sharef. Nine others were opposed:

Aranne, Eban, Minister of Finance Pinhas Sapir, H. M. Shapiro, Minister of Health Israel Barzilai, Minister of Housing Mordecai Bentor, Burg, Minister of Religious Affairs Zerah Warhaftig, and Kol. It was a tie.

This vote reflected the personal tragedy of Prime Minister Eshkol. He was an experienced man who understood the entire situation perfectly and knew that war was inevitable and that he should declare it without delay. Nevertheless he did delay, for he was incapable of forcing a decision by pounding the table and threatening to resign unless his opinion was adopted. It was a crucial moment for Israel. Eshkol was convinced that Israel's survival depended upon opening hostilities. The government would not have risked provoking the retirement of its Prime Minister at such a critical juncture. But he did not fight. (Two days later, Eshkol told a friend that in fact he had intended to resign from office at that very moment.) The personal tragedy of Eshkol was that, despite his correct analysis of the situation, he was completely paralyzed by lack of authority and indecision.

Eshkol put an end to the debate in his customary way: "It's late. Let's get some rest. We'll meet tomorrow to make up our minds."

General Weizmann pulled off his general's stars in a gesture of despair and flung them on the table in Eshkol's office.*

In the Sinai peninsula and at the strait of Tiran, the Egyptian army was put on the alert. In Cairo a general remarked to an American diplomat, "The Egyptian General Staff thinks that, if an Israeli attack comes, it will be on the last Sunday in May—that is, tomorrow—at daybreak."

In the Negev the units returned to their bases. Israel was not going to make war in the morning.

While the meeting of the Israeli Cabinet was in progress, Washington was becoming more and more nervous. It was still

---

* So a major French newspaper reported.

early evening there. President Johnson had left the capital for his Texas ranch. The official explanation was that he wanted to rest over the weekend, but some said that he was trying to escape the increasing pressure from Jewish and other pro-Israel organizations. From his ranch Johnson telephoned every hour to Rusk and Walt Rostow, in order to keep abreast of the situation. Rostow bombarded the Israeli embassy with calls.

As night fell, Johnson was handed Kosygin's reply to his cable of May 26. He decided to send a fresh cable to Eshkol asking him again to refrain from any act of war. It was sent to Ambassador Barbour in Tel Aviv, with a message from Rusk asking him to assure Eshkol that the United States was earnestly pursuing its study of the "international force" project. Rusk even telephoned Barbour to reinforce the message personally. He asked the Ambassador to transmit the cable to Eshkol as soon as the complete text had been received in Tel Aviv.

In Washington Eugene Rostow called Harman to tell him that the British were already organizing a fleet. Other contributors would include Canada and the Netherlands. The United States was also applying to France and other nations. Israel would doubtless also be invited to participate in the "multilateral action." The United States asked that Israel wait two or three weeks until after debate in the Security Council and until Congress might have given its approval to the President's action.

•

THE GENERALS VERSUS ESHKOL

PRESIDENT JOHNSON'S CABLE to Eshkol reached Tel Aviv at 5:00 A.M. on May 28. Barbour immediately called the Hotel Dan to transmit the message. Ady Yoffe was by then accustomed to the nocturnal visits of the great powers' ambassadors to his boss, but he asked Barbour not to come until morning. Eshkol had just retired, for after the government meeting he had talked for a long time with Herzog and Kashti about purchasing planes and munitions abroad.

At 10:00 A.M. Barbour handed Johnson's cable to Yoffe. It was brief, merely reporting the substance of Kosygin's cable to the White House and emphasizing in particular the sentence in which the Soviets said they would help the Arabs if they were attacked: "As I am your friend, I repeat with more emphasis what I said to your Foreign Minister, that Israel should not commence the hostilities."

Yoffe considered it the most important cable that had yet been received from the United States. For the first time it specifically referred to possible Soviet intervention against Israel.

It rained diplomatic notes in Tel Aviv that morning. The British Ambassador, for example, received the following message for delivery to Eshkol: "We understand that you have reached the moment of decision. We urgently request you to maintain your attitude of restraint as long as efforts are being made to solve the problem through diplomatic channels."

140

A third cable came from De Gaulle, who had finally deigned to reply to Eshkol's letter of May 19. De Gaulle stated that he was in favor of keeping the *status quo* in the Middle East. He acknowledged that free navigation through the strait of Tiran was important for Israel, and he expressed the opinion that neither the Israelis nor the Egyptians wanted war. His conclusion that only a conference among the four great powers could solve the issue was a disappointment, however.

In the Sinai peninsula the long columns that had been rolling all night toward El 'Arîsh continued their advance. According to observers in Cairo, an Israeli attack could have taken place at any moment, probably in the region of El 'Arîsh. Consequently the Egyptian high command decided to bring up fresh troops—veterans from Yemen who had been hastily recalled and reservists or recruits from training camps in Egypt. There was also a third category of combatants, whose beardless faces indicated the alarm that started to spread in the Egyptian General Staff. They were boys of seventeen and eighteen who had been recruited in the streets of Cairo by hastily improvised mobilization centers, given weapons, and sent immediately into the Sinai peninsula. Soon the Egyptian forces there would reach a total of 100,000 soldiers, 1,000 tanks, 1,000 pieces of artillery, and 215 airplanes.

None of the General Staff's anxiety was visible on the confidently smiling face of President Nasser as he opened an important press conference in the Koubba Palace, the first he had given for years. Three hundred Egyptian and foreign reporters attended. Nasser's remarks about Israel could be boiled down to a few key phrases:

> If Israel wants war, then we say again, "Make war!" I will close the Suez Canal to any nation who intervenes on Israel's behalf. Elat was built on Arab territory, which the Israeli army occupied after the armistice with Egypt had been signed. Egypt will support the war of liberation of the people of Palestine, and in the event that that provokes

retaliation from Israel, Egypt is prepared for a general conflict with Israel.

In Tel Aviv experts on Arab affairs analyzed Nasser's statements. It was already known that he was preparing for war and that his threats to close the Suez canal were designed to prevent the Western powers from aiding Israel. But his two last remarks were the most disturbing. According to the analysts, his allusions to the "illegality" of Israel's presence in Elat suggested that his next action, military or diplomatic, would be aimed at driving the Israelis out of Elat. His mention of the "war of liberation of the people of Palestine" was the first outspoken allusion of readiness to support the campaign of al-Fatah and other saboteurs against Israeli territory. The Egyptian President was clearly not going to be satisfied with merely closing the strait. The more he ate, the hungrier he became.

This attack by the regime on all its enemies, real or imaginary, made a great day for Egypt. As Nasser was telling his news conference how he would destroy Israel, his deputy, Mohieddin, was appointed "organizer of the nation" and entrusted with preparing propaganda against "foreign invaders." Tharwat Okasha, the Egyptian Minister of Culture, forbade the showing of spy films (especially those dealing with James Bond, 007) that made heroes of "spies and imperialist warmongers."

At 4:00 p.m. the Israeli government met again to consider the decision that had been put off the previous evening: war or delay? But during the intervening hours the situation had changed radically. Eshkol had received cables from various heads of state and particularly the one from Johnson urging him not to declare war. In addition, Eshkol was deeply impressed by the threat of Soviet intervention on behalf of the Arabs.

Eban took the floor to repeat some of his arguments of the previous night and to analyze the cables that had been received since then. He still strongly opposed the opening of hostilities. "Johnson has stated," he said, "that he has decided

to force the opening of the strait, either with allies or without.
He has promised us international action designed to open the
gulf of 'Aqaba to the ships of all countries. The Egyptians will
not put up a fight against such a powerful international fleet
when it appears at the entrance to the strait. The naval powers
have likewise promised to allow us to participate in that international fleet. That is very important, for we will not be
fighting alone for the strait, but in the framework of a collec-
tive enterprise. A unilateral act on the part of Israel, in the
present circumstances, would be ill advised and would result in
serious consequences."

Eshkol said: "President Johnson has cabled me in a very
friendly tone, asking me to wait two or three weeks. We should
agree to do so."

Allon was of the same opinion, and, one after another, many
ministers agreed to "give Johnson a chance" to do what he had
promised and to avoid isolating Israel diplomatically. The
truth was that many of them were afraid to go to war, doubting
the strength of the Israeli army. One minister confided to a
friend, "If I had ever thought that this government would have
to deal with such serious problems of defense, I would never
have accepted a place in it."

Only one member of the government was still in favor of
war—Carmel, a taciturn, heavy-set man, who kept stubbornly
repeating, "Now is the time." In a show of hands, seventeen
ministers voted for delay. Carmel alone voted for war at once.

All plans for an attack were put back into cold storage. A
long and tedious waiting period began for the several thousand soldiers already sitting in their tanks and half-tracks awaiting final orders.

Rabin advised Eshkol to inform the General Staff of the government's decision in person. *Dolphin* remained at anchor in
Massawa. No test boat would sail for the strait. The sailors
stayed at the Red Sea Hotel, awaiting orders.

The meeting broke up at 8:00 P.M. Eshkol felt obliged to
speak to the people and to explain why Israel had decided to
wait. Two technicians were rushed from the nearby Kol-Israel

broadcasting station to record the Prime Minister's statement.

Galili and Herzog drafted a text, which they submitted to Eshkol, who did not like it and changed a number of passages. Yoffe sat down at a typewriter and with one finger typed the edited version. Eshkol had no time to read it over, for the technicians had already arrived. "We haven't time to record it," they said. "Come to the studio and speak it live during the 8:30 newscast."

"Let's go!" said Eshkol, dashing out with them. He and his aides piled into a car, which whisked them to Kol-Israel. Eshkol went straight to the broadcasting studio and began to read. He described the anxiety that the concentration of Egyptian troops had caused the government. The closing of the strait of Tiran, he said, constituted "an act of aggression against Israel." Then he announced that the government had decided to wait: "The government has defined the line to follow in its diplomatic activity abroad, which is to insist that the international institutions take measures to secure free passage for ships of all nations through the strait of Tiran."

When he came to the last paragraph, beginning "We have also decided on the action we will take for . . . ," the statesman stopped abruptly. On the paper before him "troop movements" had been replaced by "withdrawal of troops." He did not like that substitution, which he did not think listeners would understand. He began to stammer into the microphone as he kept turning the sheet of paper in his hands, not knowing what to say next. Eshkol's colleagues outside the glass broadcasting booth panicked as they heard him mumbling. Yoffe signaled by pointing to the microphone that he was on the air and must finish somehow. Eshkol signaled back to cut the broadcast short. At last, after much stammering and many signals, Eshkol finished reading.

Throughout the country hundreds of thousands of civilians and soldiers were glued to their sets. The Prime Minister's stammering threw them into despair. It seemed to mean that Eshkol was in a quandary and the government powerless. The publisher of an important evening newspaper, who had been listening to a transistor radio as he climbed the stairs to his office, said to a reporter who was with him, "That's the end of Eshkol!"

In army camps, at tank bases, in trenches, inside field tents, tens of thousands of soldiers had listened to the head of government as he stammered. Many soldiers, and officers too, broke down and sobbed pathetically. A dedicated nation ready to make any sacrifice whatever and a fearless army felt they had no leader.

Eshkol was perhaps the only one who was unaware of the seriousness of his blunder, which after all was not such a serious one. As soon as the broadcast was over, he left for General Staff headquarters in order to explain to the generals what the government had decided. Satisfied with having achieved almost complete unanimity in the Cabinet, he strode briskly into the conference room, expecting to have an easy time explaining the government's decision to wait. With Allon beside him, he opened the meeting with some funny Yiddish stories that he told well. He even told the generals how he had received the Soviet Ambassador the night before while still in his pajamas. Then he informed the generals of the government's decision. They reacted violently.

"You can and you should say anything you like to me," Eshkol said. "Talk as if you were out of uniform."

And so they did. "If we go on begging protection from Paris and Washington," shouted General Abraham Yoffe, "we shall be lost."

Weizmann said, "Our leaders cannot get together to confront the Arab menace."

"Your shilly-shallying," Sharon said directly to Eshkol, "will cost us thousands of deaths." Some generals even thought of resigning.

As Eshkol rose to leave, Rabin said to his colleagues, "It looks as if the only strength the country can rely on is the army."*

* These exchanges were published as authentic in *France-Soir* in July 1967 and also in Zeev Schiff and Eliahu Ben Elissar, *La guerre israélo-arabe* (Paris: Julliard, 1967).

Eshkol left the meeting depressed and astonished. He was especially haunted by the charge of diffidence that had been hurled at him: "Why are we always begging protection from others?"

On one hand it was a sad evening for the people of Israel, but on the other it was a gay one, for May 28 is the festival of Lag Baomer.* Throughout the country hundreds of marriages were being joyfully celebrated, for life had to go on. Even though they felt the presence of death people were able to summon the hope and joy necessary for dancing. Many bridegrooms had twenty-four-hour leave from the trenches of the Negev or from Galilee. Many were married in uniform with their eyes on their watches. Once the ceremonies were over, they jumped into military jeeps, which would take them back to their posts. Some never showed up at all, as their duties had kept them in camp. In Naharia, Esther Rosenthal's wedding guests drank, ate, and danced while her parents and the rabbi spent the evening on the telephone. But her fiancé, Yitzhak En Gal, never came. His unit was on the alert.

At a lavish wedding party in Tel Aviv one half-drunk reporter joked cynically, "Eat, drink, and be merry, for tomorrow we die."

* The traditional day for celebrating marriages.

•

FEAR

THAT MORNING MEIR Park in the center of Tel Aviv was almost deserted. One old man was sunning his back as he read his newspaper, and on a nearby bench a tiny child munched a banana beside his mother. Two taxis drew up at the park entrance, and about ten bearded, black-clad men with their heads covered climbed out and formed a knot in the south corner of the garden. Then they marched seven times around it, chanting, "The spirit of the Almighty is in the secret places of the heavens."

The old man was curious; he asked one of the rabbis anxiously, "What are you doing?"

"Consecrating the park for an emergency cemetery."

Wide-eyed with terror, the woman grabbed her child and ran. She would have been even more terrified had she known that the rabbis were going to consecrate other gardens and empty plots in Tel Aviv and Jaffa for the same purpose.

Tel Aviv was preparing for war. A few days earlier the Committee for Evacuation and First Aid had met to discuss its morbid duties toward bombing victims. Some members thought the casualties might reach 40,000, for the Egyptians had bombers, bombs, and poison gas.

Undertakers claimed there was not enough room in existing cemeteries and were therefore readying emergency burial grounds and morgues in the Levinski Normal School, in the auditorium of the Nahmani Theater, and the Noga and Zlil

147

motion-picture theaters. Centers for the wounded were prepared in the lobbies of big hotels.

Instructions for identification and burial of victims were
mimeographed. Miles of nylon sheeting for wrapping bodies
were stockpiled—two yards for each. Fifteen thousand Israeli
pounds were spent for the purchase of coffin boards, shovels,
concrete gravestones, and plaques for the names of the de-
ceased. Death certificates were prepared for completion, and
shrouds, candles, and matches were collected. Squads of rabbis
and theology students, gravediggers, doctors, and police photographers were organized to identify corpses. Documentary
films on the rescue of bombing victims were shown in a little
theater in the Allenby Road.

Everyone knew that the war, when it came, would be total—
life or death. The dead would be so many that no one knew
where they might be buried.

The frantic citizens of Tel Aviv wrote to newspapers to find
out where they could find bomb shelters. Students began
digging trenches in earth that the May sun had dried, in alleys,
courtyards, and empty lots. In newspapers and on billboards
there were notices about discipline in bomb shelters, first aid to
the wounded, and other civilian-defense measures.

Nasser had gas—mustard gas and plenty of other kinds—
manufactured near Cairo. For several years he had been wip-
ing out whole villages in Yemen with these gases. There was no
reason to assume that he would not use them on Tel Aviv.
Israel had no protection against them.

Kashti sent cables all over the world asking for gas masks.
The English ones were no good, nor were the French, but the
United States sent 190,000 masks to Israel in special transport
planes. The German government agreed to supply 20,000, but
Defense Minister Schroeder forbade their shipment, thus trig-
gering a crisis in the German government.

The gas masks that did arrive were given not to the civilians
but to the army. But the army had no fear of gas or of bombing
attacks. It was sure of victory.

The fear took hold away from the front. In country towns and among women and the old men. In Israel there was no desire for war. Instead there were terror of blood flowing in rivers and doubt that Israel could stand up to the attack.

At the same time, however, the people knew there was no other way.

"Mr. Eshkol was not cut out to be Prime Minister and Defense Minister in a crisis," stated *Ha'aretz's* lead editorial that day. "The way it is constituted now, the government cannot successfully direct the nation, threatened as it is. It must yield to a new team."

Ben-Gurion told the press, "Our behavior and our leadership, in the days to come, will decide our fate." H. M. Shapiro of the Religious National Party told Eshkol, "My party will leave the coalition if Dayan is not made Defense Minister."

In Washington Harman was summoned once more to the State Department. "The President," its officials told him, "is studying the possibility of increasing economic aid to Israel during the period of mobilization and emergency. Can you give us details on the effect of mobilization upon Israel's economy, upon its loss of tourist revenues, and upon the financial damage that the blockade of the gulf of 'Aqaba will cause?" They also let it be understood that until the crisis was resolved, the United States might furnish Israel with oil from Texas or Venezuela. "As for the naval project," they said optimistically, "everything is proceeding according to plan."

The plan was a very curious one, for at that very moment other steps were being taken. Two special American envoys were on their way to Cairo with instructions to arrange a compromise with Egyptian authorities. At the same time officials of the State Department had given *The New York Times* to understand that they had a temporary solution in mind: to send non-Israeli ships into the strait of Tiran. Also under consideration was a treaty similar to that of the Montreux Convention (by which the Dardanelles could be closed in the event of war by the government controlling the straits). Those two pieces of information could be interpreted only as a trial balloon, but they seemed to disclose a secret plan of the State Department for the solution of the crisis—a project different from the "Armada" plan that had been promised to the Israeli leaders.

Eshkol declared in Parliament, "I believe that I can hope that the nations who favor maintaining freedom of navigation will act together to guarantee that the strait and the gulf be kept open to vessels of all countries, without distinction, in the near future." When State Department officials in Washington heard about the speech, they congratulated the Israeli Ambassador on Eshkol's restraint.

Nasser took the floor in the Egyptian parliament: "The problem presently before the Arab countries is not whether the port of Elat should be blockaded or how to blockade it—but how to totally exterminate the State of Israel for all time. Just as Egypt has succeeded in abolishing the results of aggression of 1956, so, with the help of Allah, it will succeed in eliminating the consequences of the war of 1948."

That afternoon the Egyptian National Assembly granted him unlimited powers, permitting him to govern by decree. He exercised these powers at once. New units were transferred from Yemen to the Sinai peninsula, and mobilization continued. Cairo seemed electrified. Giant posters called the Arabs to a holy war. In countless meetings huge purple banners were unfurled; they bore the skull and crossbones, the traditional pirate emblem, which the Palestine Liberation Organization* had adopted as its own. Inflammatory speeches roused the people of Cairo, and everyone was shouting, "On to Tel Aviv!"

Nevertheless, the world at large felt great sympathy for Israel. Tens of thousands paraded in New York, Rome, Zurich, Paris, and London. Millions of dollars were contributed to an emergency fund. Long lines of volunteers formed outside the Israeli embassies. A flood of gifts and encouraging letters

* Organization of the Palestinian refugees, aiming at the destruction of Israel and recovery of Palestine to the Arab nation.

descended on the desks of diplomats. Thinkers, intellectuals, artists, from Jean-Paul Sartre to Sean Connery, signed petitions proclaiming the justice of the Israeli cause and Israel's right to survive.

Yet Israel had never stood so alone.

•

WHERE IS *DOLPHIN?*

MAGNIFICENTLY ATTIRED IN a suit of gunmetal gray, President Nasser stood waiting on the ground at Cairo airport for the landing of the royal Caravelle bearing the emblem of the Arab Legion. A few moments later little King Hussein of Jordan, in a marshal's uniform and a black forage cap and with aviator's wings on his green tunic, stepped from the plane.

"Nasser, my brother!" he exclaimed as he embraced Nasser.

"Welcome, Hussein, my brother!" replied Nasser as he embraced Hussein.

Nasser's black Cadillac moved majestically through the streets of Cairo, which were jammed with happy, singing, dancing crowds. The Egyptian President and his guest alighted at the Koubba Palace. All during the trip from the airport the two leaders had been exchanging smiles, claps on the shoulder, and handshakes. Cairo had not seen such a love affair for a long time.

Only two days earlier, on May 28, Radio Cairo had been describing Hussein as a "Hashemite whore," a "British agent," a "chameleon," an "imperialist slave," an "Anglo-American spy," and similar admirable characters and urging the people of Jordan to rid themselves of him. Then on May 29 the situation had changed for the better after Jordanian Chief of Staff Hamash, who had been unceremoniously chased out of Cairo only a week earlier, had returned on a secret mission to propose a reconciliation between Jordan and Egypt and an alliance against their Zionist enemy. After a few hours of talk it had been decided that Hussein should come the next day—May 30—to sign a mutual-defense pact in Cairo.

Everything went as expected. After a brief talk among Nasser, Amer, and Hussein at the Koubba Palace all three reached an agreement. They telephoned Baghdad to obtain President Abdul Rahman Muhammad Aref's assurance that Iraqi troops would start for Jordan in order to reinforce the frontier against the enemy. Then the three went into the sumptuous conference room to sign the treaty on a long table covered with green cloth. There a fourth man joined them—Ahmed Shukairy, head of the Palestine Liberation Organization. Once expelled from Jordan, he had been rousing the Jordanian people to depose their traitor king until the day before, but he was all smiles as he embraced Hussein.

The treaty was signed with great ceremony. It provided, in particular, that "in the event of hostilies, the Commander in Chief of the Egyptian armed forces will assume command of operations in both countries." Practically speaking, Jordan had put its army and its territory at the disposal of the Egyptian high command.

The Egyptians took their guest to inspect the units in the Sinai peninsula. Apparently joyful, the little king returned to Amman that evening in the company of the friend with whom he had been reunited, Shukairy. A delirious mob welcomed them at the airport and cheered them all along the road to the city. Excitement reached a peak in the Old City of Jerusalem, and shouts of joy rang out until dawn. All over Jordan the offices of the Palestine Liberation Organization were reopened. For the first time portraits of Nasser appeared on houses, in shops, and in the constricted *suks*. Jordan had joined the battle.

Hussein had been worried about keeping his throne and had feared a revolution. He knew that the Syrians, Shukairy, and the Egyptians were conspiring to oust him. He had to jump on the Egyptian bandwagon.

But why had Nasser changed toward Hussein? Only recently he had contemptuously rejected the King's overtures. Why had he now thrown himself into the arms of the "Hashemite whore" and flown in the face of Syria, which had broken with Jordan in the meantime? Israeli analysts, in explaining Nasser's *volte-face,* recalled his intention to destroy Israel by attacking it from all sides. But the true explanation was that Nasser was afraid.

Nasser had been carried away by his initial success, and every day was bringing him one step closer to armed conflict with Israel. The concentration of Israeli troops on the frontier opposite his own disturbed him. Despite everything that had happened, he hoped Israel would not attack. But what if it did? If the Zionist tanks invaded the Sinai peninsula and struck at the Egyptian army before it could mount a counteroffensive, what then?

Such apprehensions had forced Nasser to mobilize all his available troops, to recall more troops from Yemen, to order arms from Russia, to dig new trenches and to build new fortifications. He also needed Hussein on his side. Jordan's appearance on the military scene would weaken the concentration of Israeli troops on the Egyptian frontier, for the Jews would have to withdraw many of their soldiers in order to protect their long frontier with Jordan, which had become a declared enemy. One army stretched out on two long frontiers in rough terrain—not to mention the Syrian border—and fearing attack from either side would not dare to take the offensive.

Rabin learned of the Egyptian-Jordanian pact while he was in a helicopter inspecting the troops in the south. He continued his tour of inspection before returning that evening to Tel Aviv, where he was to meet with Eshkol. At General Staff headquarters, officers took out of locked files the action plans that had been prepared for a possible attack from Jordan. Instructions were sent at once to unit commanders stationed in the center of the country, so that they could take their positions on the frontier.

The army knew that if war broke out it would be total—a war against all the Arab countries. The General Staff had studied that eventuality more than once and had given it the code name "All of Them."

The ceremonious reception of Hussein in Cairo and the signing of the treaty alarmed the Israeli government. What next? The enemy was no longer only the triumvirate of Nasser (Egypt), Noureddine El Atassi (Syria), and Shukairy (P.L.O.); for some days it had been increased by Emir Sabah as-Salim as-Sabab of Kuwait, President Henri Boumédienne of Algeria, Hussein with his Arab Legion, and Aref and his troops. The new danger that threatened Israel's survival had made the issue of the strait of Tiran almost a minor one.

What could Israel do against the vast support that Nasser had just acquired? The last reservists had been called up on May 27. On May 30 Eshkol was receiving a delegation of Druzes who wanted to enlist in the Israeli army after having staged a demonstration for several days before the Defense Ministry. Inmates of the Tel Mond prison also wanted to enlist for the duration of the war. That morning an astonishing demonstration had taken place in Tel Aviv—a parade of criminals. Prisoners who had stolen, killed, and looted, each of whom had spent some years in an Israeli jail at the expense of the taxpayers, were demanding to be allowed to fight for their country. "We want to enlist," they shouted. Their records included desertion from the army and the reserves. "We are Israelis too," they shouted. "We, too, have a right to fight for our country!"

The Israeli newspapers shrank from twenty pages to eight, for their reporters had also been mobilized. The inner pages were devoted to long lists of soldiers scattered over the country who wanted to send greetings to their families. The radio broadcasted messages for soldiers, occasionally informing a reservist in the Negev sands that his wife had given birth to a son or a daughter. One reserve lieutenant from Tel Aviv had a son on the morning of May 30; he named him Tiran.

Colonel Cohen's crew, twenty-five of the sixty sailors who had been taking it easy at the Red Sea Hotel in Massawa, received orders to board *Arion*. Felix, an amateur painter, took a pail of yellow paint and a big brush and on the sides of the vessel lettered its new name: *Dolphin*—Haifa. The Israeli flag was run up the mast. The boat was dirty, had no air-conditioning, and was rusty and ready to fall to pieces, but none of that mattered. The old tub was good enough to force a passage through the strait. From another Zim boat, *Fenice*, 1,000 tons of cotton, iron, rubber, and dried meat were transferred to *Dolphin*. The sailors themselves repaired its boilers, its safety equipment, and its sick bay. The Greek crew went ashore.

Dolphin weighed anchor and put out to sea, where it awaited orders to proceed to the strait. The remainder of the sixty sailors went "sailing" in the swimming pool at the Red Sea Hotel.

Washington received a cable from the intelligence officer of an American warship anchored off Massawa that *Arion* had changed its name and its flag.* Eugene Rostow telephoned the Israeli embassy and casually asked, "Do you know whether *Dolphin* is still in Massawa?"

Following a well-established procedure, the Rostow brothers called the officers of the Israeli embassy in Washington to assure them (as usual) that the prospects for the "international fleet" were improving, that the statement by the powers had already been almost fully drafted, that official application had been made to many countries, and that the chances were good that certain nations would join.

In the White House, Johnson was taking every important visitor into a corner and asking him for a few boats for the international force. Generally speaking, he met with little suc-

* Interview with an American official in Washington.

cess. The President had been hoping to persuade an Italian delegation that was in Washington, but after a few hours with Eugene Rostow the Italians said no. The Americans, however, did not tell the Israeli diplomats. They continued to insist that the fleet was being organized and was already gathering near the strait. They also revealed in the greatest of confidence that a resolution on multilateral or unilateral action to open the strait was being drafted for submission to Congress.

Up to that time, however, no one had seen the draft. The State Department officials responsible for contacts with Congress had never even heard of it. Nor had they been asked to sound out any senators on the subject. On the contrary, they had been expressly told to calm the senators and to allay any apprehension that the United States would go to war over the strait.

Doubtless the White House was sincere in its lavish assurances to Israel, but the State Department was playing a double game. On one hand, it was restraining the Israelis by extending the diplomatic talks for days on end, and at the same time promising congressional support for definite action. On the other, it was cooling any enthusiasm Congress might have had for any military undertaking whatever. The truth was that the United States was trying to gain time, to obtain the support of many nations for the "regatta" project, and simultaneously to come to some agreement with Nasser through the two envoys who had been sent to Cairo.

On May 30 the United States began to wake up. As soon as the agreement between Nasser and Hussein had been signed, the Americans realized that they had been on the wrong track. Late that night Walt Rostow called Evron and confessed for the first time that he could see no solution.

•

JOHNSON'S WRATH

AT NIGHT ISRAEL's cities were ghost towns, and the hot summer winds swept through dark, empty streets. Few people were outdoors and even fewer in public places. The motion-picture theaters in Jerusalem held only one showing each evening. The major theaters in Tel Aviv were closed, for the actors were performing in camps, with brushwood fires for footlights. Discotheques, night clubs, and meeting halls were deserted.

One evening, however, the Mandy discotheque filled up to persuade rich playboys to donate blood to military hospitals. The few cars on the streets drove with their headlights painted blue, except for slits through which tiny beams of light could shine. The great agricultural exposition Agr-Expo, which had cost so much time and effort, closed. The Soldiers' Committee lottery, the election of beauty queens, parties, and anniversary celebrations were canceled. Foreign correspondents lounged in the bars of the big hotels, bored to tears. Hundreds of thousands of Israelis had been mobilized, and those who had not been called up because of age, health, or administrative mistakes were embarrassed to go out for fear of being taken for deserters.

It was the season when Israelis were ordinarily reviving after the winter rains and planning vacation trips to other parts of the world, when café tables were set out on sidewalks, when bodies lolled beside swimming pools and on beaches. That year, however, the Israelis had only grim smiles for the adver-

158

tisements that kept appearing in newspapers for "summer va-
cations in Greece, Switzerland, Czechoslovakia's watering
places, Nahariya, and Elat." Amos Kenan, the famous writer
on food, described a meal of combat rations as Nasser's worst
punishment for the Chosen People.

Rumors flew: The Arabs in Israel were preparing a rising.
Caches of arms had been found. Spies had been arrested. Russian submarines were off the coast. War would begin at midnight.

But not that midnight or the next one.

Military pressure for immediate action was increasing on the
morning of May 31. The Egyptian-Jordanian pact, which Iraq
had endorsed, was a bad omen. Israeli generals and many national leaders among whom were those who had previously had
confidence in Eshkol, were demanding an end to delays. Let
the fighting start before it was too late!

"Johnson has promised an interventionary force," Eshkol
kept saying. "Johnson does not lie."

But he was persuaded to send an important political figure
to Washington on a top-secret mission which was to have two
purposes. American confidence in the Israelis had been shaken
by the false alarm of May 25, when panic-stricken Israel had
screamed that Egypt would attack at any moment.* It was
therefore necessary to repair the damage and to recapture the
confidence of the Americans. The second purpose was to make
sure that Eban had actually been promised American action to
open the strait. Early that morning the secret emissary flew to
the United States.

But on May 30 Eshkol had sent Lyndon Johnson a cable in
which he had cited the question of the strait and the danger
presented by the concentration of Egyptian troops and had
called to the President's attention that time was working
against Israel. The key phrase of the message had been based
upon Eban's report to the government: "I welcome the assur-

---

* Information from American sources.

ance that the United States will take any and all measures to open the strait of Tiran to international shipping."

Johnson reacted violently to the cable when it reached Washington on the morning of May 31. In a rage he summoned Walt Rostow. "I have no right to make such promises without the consent of Congress," the President roared. "This is not what I told Eban. Tell the Israelis so."

Rostow called Evron to come to his office on the double and demanded that he transmit Johnson's answer at once to his government emphasizing that the President had made Eban no such promise.

It was the first indication that the Americans and Eban had interpreted the White House meeting differently.

Eugene Rostow called Harman to his office and handed him a draft of the statement of the maritime powers:

> Our governments reaffirm the view that the gulf is an international waterway into and through which the vessels of all nations have a right of passage. Our governments will assert this right on behalf of all ships sailing under their flags, and our governments are prepared to cooperate among themselves and to join with others in seeking general recognition of this right.

Rostow called Harman's attention to the fact that the text had already been submitted to twenty-eight governments for their signature. It was also being sent to Israel. The signatures of the United States, Great Britain, the Netherlands, and Canada were already certain. A congressional resolution was also being drafted.

Harman was delighted to see that the future apparently looked bright, for he believed, even more than the Americans did, in the value of the international fleet. But the true story was quite different. Most countries had already indicated, even before reading the draft, that they would not sign it. France had given a very firm no. The Rostow brothers then asked Harman some disquieting questions: "What would you say to a

compromise? Do you think it would be possible to offer Nasser
a way out that would not hurt his prestige? Do you believe
that he really wants war?"

At the same time Vice President Humphrey and Rusk were
explaining the international situation to various Senate committees. In reply to one question Rusk answered unequivo-
cally: "You should not draw any conclusions from what the
press says about military intervention. Those reports are only
guesses. The United States is not contemplating any unilateral
move in the Middle East, but only within the framework of the
United Nations and with other countries."

"Rusk's attitude toward even 'the prospect of a multilateral
force' is very lukewarm," an American told an Israeli diplomat
friend. Other State Department officials were already talking
about an "objective attitude toward the conflict," which would
take into account the "oil interests of the United States." It
would be necessary, they said, "to leave a door open for
Nasser." "Very few Israeli ships use the strait of Tiran," State
Department experts told receptive reporters. "Israeli complaints about the damage the closing of the strait is causing
its economy are greatly exaggerated. It certainly is not worth
going to war about." Except for some Israeli diplomats, no
one in Washington thought the "regatta" would ever come
off. "It's strange," commented Joseph Alsop, "how much more
optimistic the Israeli embassy seems than the Americans. War
will surely break out within a week."

"A war? There will be no war!" declared Ambassador Chuvakin to some Israeli friends in Tel Aviv. "The situation is
calming down. There will soon be a diplomatic solution."

"Why are you so worried?" Fedorenko asked Arthur Goldberg during a pause in the wearisome debate in the Security
Council. "There's no need to get excited. There's no fire. The
Middle Eastern crisis will doubtless calm down in the days to
come."

"We are opposed to any war in the Middle East," Kosygin
told the British Foreign Minister, who was ending his visit to
Moscow. During a sparkling reception in Rome, two Soviet

diplomats extended their best wishes for Israel to their Israeli colleagues. "The Soviet Union," they said, "helped create the State of Israel and so will never be a party to its extinction. Israel is only a pawn on the chessboard of the great powers. All you have to do is to wait patiently and keep the peace, and everything will turn out all right."

The promises and the good wishes expressed that day by Soviet diplomats in every capital were part of an effort to lessen tensions. The Kremlin thought the Arabs were going too far. It seemed advisable to keep what had been won, and the best way to do so was to lower the temperature, appease the West, direct the crisis into diplomatic channels, and let it stay there until it was forgotten.

The Soviet campaign for appeasement all along the diplomatic front, did not, however, prevent the Kremlin from stating officially on May 31 that it was refusing De Gaulle's invitation to a conference of the four great powers. Nor did it prevent a new Soviet fleet from passing through the Dardanelles headed for the eastern Mediterranean, where it was to join an already impressive fleet cruising off Egypt.

Chuvakin cabled from Tel Aviv that Israel could not attack Egypt for the moment. From Cairo Podyedyeev confirmed that Egypt did not need protection. Nevertheless, as units of the 6th Fleet and British ships were rushing into the area, the Soviets thought it advisable to reinforce their naval detachment in the Middle East.

They also decided to increase their diplomatic efforts. For a week Ambassador Podyedyeev had been blamed for the failure of his mission in Cairo. The Kremlin finally announced that he would soon be replaced by an experienced diplomat of the highest rank—Sergei Vinogradov, who had been Ambassador to Paris for many years and had become a personal friend of De Gaulle. If he could gain De Gaulle's confidence, it appeared to the Soviets, he might also succeed with Nasser. But such comparisons are always dangerous in the game of politics.

In Paris 30,000 people were blocking traffic on the Avenue Wagram as they milled around the unpretentious house that contained the Israeli embassy. Most of them were Jews demonstrating their support for Israel; they carried signs reading: "Israel is our friend and our ally." "Nasser is a murdererer." "Let Israel live." Angry young people were shouting slogans and singing Israeli songs and the *Marseillaise*. Old people were weeping. A flock of distinguished guests pushed through the crowd to join the Israeli Ambassador on the balcony of the embassy. Among them were politicians like Sanguinetti and Bourgès-Maunoury; prominent Jews like High Rabbi Kaplan and some of the Rothschilds; and many artists, including Artur Rubinstein, Michel Simon, Guy Béart, Adamo, Johnny Halliday, Sacha Distel, and Claude Lelouch. French Jews who had been saying for years that they were French first and Jews second were proclaiming at mass meetings: "We are Jews first. The Israeli war is our war!"

Echoes of the demonstration reached the Élysée Palace. The French authorities reacted with a curt order to the security service to check on the Israeli embassy's part in organizing it. The various services handling the shipments of arms to Israel were instructed to examine every order in great detail. Unexpected difficulties arose every time Israelis asked to use an airport, and French customs officers scrutinized every document and every piece of luggage with greater care than usual. A special interdepartmental committee was appointed to make an emergency survey of the possibility of placing an embargo on arms shipments to the Middle East—in other words, to Israel.

Late in the morning of May 31, the political committee of the Alignment met in Tel Aviv with several ministers and political leaders, among whom were Golda Meir and Shaul Avigur. Eshkol was melancholy at the thought that he might not be Defense Minister much longer, for the number of those who wanted the post separated from that of Prime Minister was increasing by the minute. The previous evening Eshkol had been literally forced to attend an excited meeting of the Alignment. He would have liked to avoid it, but he had to consent after Moshe Baram, the coalition leader, told him:

"The bloc wants to revolt. You ought to be there." After that session a clear majority did declare itself in favor of appointing Dayan Defense Minister. Eshkol left the meeting bitterly angry.

Now, on May 31, with the help of old friends, he was trying in vain to find a magic formula by which he could retain his portfolio as Defense Minister or at least keep it from falling into Dayan's hands. Y. S. Shapiro proposed a revolutionary plan by which Eban would resign to become Deputy Prime Minister responsible for international matters and information abroad. The vacated office of Foreign Minister could then be given to Dayan and the Ministry of Defense to Allon. Eban merely slipped a note to Shapiro, "I am prepared to resign from the government but not to change my job."

Finally, the political committee decided to nominate Allon as Defense Minister. Eban volunteered to bring the religious parties, which were much in favor of Dayan, around to Allon and put an end to their insurrection.

But M. H. Shapiro, leader of the Religious National Party, clung stubbornly to his opinion that only Dayan could manage Defense at that critical time. Paradoxically he hoped that if Dayan became Defense Minister, Ben-Gurion would be able to convince him not to declare war. Shapiro knew that Dayan's nomination as Defense Minister was absolutely essential to bring the Rafi and the Gahal into the government. As a devout Jew, he was motivated by a mystical sense of the importance of a unified government at such a perilous time.

At 4:30 P.M., Eshkol called Dayan to the Dan Hotel. He seemed to be resisting every effort to make Dayan Defense Minister. With Avigur beside him, he offered Dayan the Deputy Prime Minister spot, with Allon as Defense Minister. Dayan refused, however, saying: "I have no talent for giving advice, and I cannot accept a position as consultant. I want actual powers." When Dayan learned that Eshkol was contemplating making Allon Defense Minister, he asked to be made commander of the troops on the Egyptian frontier. Eshkol leaped at the unexpected chance. If Dayan were given other military responsibilities, he would no longer be available for the Defense post.

That evening Eshkol called the government into special session, in order to discuss broad changes in the Cabinet. He told the ministers that he had offered Dayan a place in the government but that Dayan had preferred to command the troops on the Egyptian front under orders from the Chief of Staff. Characteristically, Eshkol failed to mention that he had offered Dayan not the post of Defense Minister but only that of Deputy Prime Minister.

The secretariat of the Mapai was meeting at the same time, and a storm was brewing. A large majority demanded the appointment of Dayan as Defense Minister. Despite the strong opposition of Golda Meir, the secretariat decided to demand that any attempt of Eshkol's to change the composition of the government be first submitted to the secretariat for approval.

The special session of the government ended late that night. The religious ministers would not give in to the appointment of Allon as Defense Minister, but his nomination nevertheless seemed probable, for Eshkol had finally agreed to resign one of his posts. A committee of five ministers, including Eshkol, was appointed to propose a redistribution of Cabinet positions to the government on June 1.

The daily newspaper *Davar* was asked to announce in its early edition the next day that Dayan would be given a high military command. This announcement was Eshkol's way of trying to pacify Dayan's partisans.

Allon was almost Defense Minister.

•

NASSER RECEIVES A SECRET ENVOY

IN WASHINGTON ON the morning of June 1, there were more and
more demands for compromise with Nasser. A television com-
mentator accredited to the White House declared:

> President Johnson is convinced that Egypt is not for com-
> bat at this time; that President Nasser, having reestablished
> himself as the tough leader of the Arab world, can perhaps
> be induced to accept some compromise that preserves his
> new prestige without war.
> Allowing all ships except those flying the Israeli flag
> through the strait of Tiran is one such compromise. The
> Israeli government has said it cannot accept this, even if
> the Arabs are willing. But the White House remains hope-
> ful.
> Mr. Johnson is also hopeful that if the Egyptians force a
> running of their blockade, it will be done with a combined
> big-power naval force, . . . not just United States ships.

Success in achieving a compromise with Egypt depended on
two men: Charles Yost and Robert Anderson. On May 27
Charles Yost, then of the Council on International Relations in
New York, had received an urgent telephone call from the
State Department in Washington, asking him to leave for Cairo
in the very near future, in order to jolt the United States
embassy there out of its rut. Four days had been enough to
make Washington lose faith in Ambassador Nolte, whose lack

166

of diplomatic experience had already involved him in an argument with Egyptian Foreign Minister Riad, to whom he had transmitted Johnson's cable. The day after that fiasco he had been savagely attacked in the headlines of all the Egyptian newspapers. Yost, on the other hand, was very familiar with Middle Eastern problems and had been one of the eighteen civilian advisers to the Middle Eastern division of the State Department. A lean, polite, and learned man of sixty years, he had also served as Ambassador to Damascus and later as head of the American delegation to the United Nations. He was on friendly terms with many Arab leaders and especially with Riad.

On May 29 Yost reached Cairo, where he stayed in Nolte's apartment. On the morning of June 1 he finally met Riad, who was full of smiles, apologies, and compliments. The Egyptian Foreign Minister repeated that Israel was preparing to attack Syria. "The Soviets," he said, "warned us in time, and we have taken the necessary precautions. Then events caught up with us. We were compelled to demand that the U.N. force, which we had asked merely to return to its encampments, be completely withdrawn. We had no alternative. We did not want to occupy Sharm el Sheikh or to close the strait, but the army had gone too far, much farther than the government wished, and had seized Sharm el Sheikh. As it was therefore in our hands, we were obliged to close the strait."

"Is there any possibility of a compromise?" Yost asked.

Riad gave him to understand that indeed there was. The Egyptians were not considering war with the Israelis. The matter of the strait might well be settled, though Riad did not say how.

Unconvinced, Yost believed that his mission had failed. He nevertheless cabled the United States that it would be advisable to give Nasser a way out.

Meanwhile the Egyptians undertook a broad and astutely managed campaign to sweeten their reputation abroad. They told the French that a solution could be found. At a press conference in Washington, the press attaché of the Egyptian embassy declared that the strait had been closed only to shipments of strategic materials, but when he was asked to define that term he had nothing to say. The experts in the Egyptian Foreign Ministry were preparing a new plan: an appeal to the International Court of Justice at The Hague. If the United States agreed to it, then Israel could say goodby to the strait, for the wheels of justice turn slowly. Before The Hague would render a decision, months would pass.

In addition to Yost, who was officially accredited, a confidential emissary arrived in Egypt in the greatest secrecy, with precise instructions from the White House to meet with Nasser. This envoy, who knew Nasser well, was Robert Anderson, former Secretary of the Treasury under Eisenhower.

An economist connected with oil companies, Anderson had frequently visited the Arab capitals. In 1955 he had been Eisenhower's secret envoy to Jerusalem and Cairo, with his mission then to make peace between Egypt and Israel. At that time he had met Nasser and Ben-Gurion several times, but he had been stymied by Nasser's remark, "I am ready to meet Ben-Gurion to talk peace, but three hours later, I would be assassinated by the Arabs."

Anderson landed at the Cairo airport on May 31 and was met by a group of Egyptian generals, who escorted him to the Nile Hilton in the greatest secrecy. Nolte saw him for only a few moments there, for Anderson was not to use the embassy to transmit his reports to Washington. On June 1 he was taken secretly to Nasser's office.

The conference lasted a long time but proved disappointing. Nasser refused to back down on the question of the strait. "My decision is final," he said. After much discussion, he agreed to only one of Anderson's suggestions—that he send a prominent Egyptian to Washington to talk with American leaders. Johnson had suggested sending Humphrey to Cairo or receiving an Egyptian envoy at the White House. Nasser was opposed to Humphrey's coming: "It will be interpreted as pressure on Egypt, and I do not want that." He proposed sending Mohieddin, who was known for his pro-Western sympathies, and the date was set for Wednesday, June 7.

When this decision became known at the U.S. embassy in Cairo, everyone was optimistic. It seemed that everything could be settled if Mohieddin went to the United States to arrange a compromise and calm things down. Anderson, however, was not so elated. That evening he left for Lisbon to file his report from there.

Under Egypt's leadership the Arab countries continued to prepare for war with Israel. On the morning of June 1 all airports were put on a state of alert. Civilian flights to the Sinai peninsula and Gaza were canceled. Student pilots who had not yet finished their training were transferred to operational squadrons in Egypt and the peninsula. Orders for an alert reached to the highest levels. Pilots spent the day in their airplanes, equipped with ammunition and full tanks of gasoline, waiting on the runways to take off at any moment. In Baghdad President Aref told his aviators, "With the help of Allah, we will meet next in Tel Aviv or Haifa." Two battalions of Egyptian commandos were transported to Jordan, and, from his office in Amman, General Riadh, Chief of the United Arab Command, began to coordinate Jordan's and Egypt's military operations pending hostilities.

In Paris De Gaulle was very busy with the Arabs. That same morning of June 1 he saw Syrian Foreign Minister Makhous. The next day he was to lunch with King Faisal of Saudi Arabia. De Gaulle was the only political figure in the West who could influence Nasser, the only one with enough leverage to ask him to raise the blockade of the strait of Tiran and expect an answer. He was also the only one to do nothing.

During those feverish days, France was the only nation that could have prevented war.

Broadcasts on Arab stations kept picturing the disasters that would be visited upon Israel when the powerful fleet of Egyptian bombers turned Tel Aviv into a heap of ruins. "Death will come upon you!" pronounced the speaker against a background of military marches. "The night will come when death will

enfold you in his black cloak. . . . Death will surround you on
all sides. . . . Inhabitants of Tel Aviv, pack your bags and flee
from Palestine, for the Arabs are coming, and you know the
Arabs."

A calm, strong voice with a distinct Anglo-Saxon accent
replied to these hysterical predictions; it belonged to General
Haim (Vivian) Herzog, who had served as military commen-
tator on Kol-Israel since the crisis had first worsened. Every
day he made a complete survey of the situation, reassuring
hundreds of thousands of Israelis in the interior of the country.
When the Arabs threatened to destroy Tel Aviv by bombing,
Herzog said, "I must say in all sincerity that if I had to choose
today between flying in an Egyptian bomber bound for Tel
Aviv or being in Tel Aviv, I would out of a purely selfish desire
for self-preservation, opt to be in Tel Aviv."

The last episode of the long struggle for power began in Tel
Aviv that day; it was an absurd struggle in which the stakes
were the formation of a coalition government and the post of
Defense Minister. The previous evening the appointment of
Allon as Defense Minister had seemed certain.

At 7:00 A.M. the telephone rang in the house of Mayor Abba
Houshi of Haifa, one of the Mapai leaders. The caller was an
executive of the Mapai central committee in Tel Aviv. He had
learned the true story of Eshkol's conference with Dayan the
day before, and he knew that Dayan had asked for a command
only after he had been given to understand that he could not
be Defense Minister.

Mrs. Houshi answered the phone. "Where is Abba?" she was
asked.

"I don't know. He's making an inspection of the city."

"If you don't find him right away, he'll regret it the rest of
his life."

Mrs. Houshi telephoned the city hall, and two motorcycle
policemen were dispatched to scour the city. When they finally
found the Mayor in a park, he dashed to a telephone. The
conversation convinced him that he should redouble his efforts

to have Dayan appointed Defense Minister. He summoned a dozen friends to the Mapai secretariat and put them to work.

The party secretariat met at 10:00 A.M. Eshkol took the floor to try once more to convince the members that Dayan had wanted a military command. "We asked him," Eshkol said, "and Dayan answered that he preferred the Negev. That is, therefore, better for us than making him Defense Minister."

This time the members were cautious. While the debate was in progress, Asher Yadlin went to the restaurant next door and telephoned Rafi leaders, asking them to tell him exactly what Dayan had said to Eshkol. "Would his being given a command in the south," he also asked, "solve the problem of a national union government?"

The Rafi answer was emphatic. Dayan wanted to be Defense Minister. He had said to Eshkol the previous day: "I am ready to be Prime Minister or Defense Minister or both. But if I am not to be put in charge of Defense, then I prefer to be mobilized as commander of the southern front. I know the Sinai peninsula and the Egyptian positions in it well. To serve in the army, I would even drive a half-track."

Yadlin reported these words to his friends, and the debate continued. The meeting ended at 3:00 P.M. The great majority of members was opposed to Dayan's being given a command in the south and insisted that he be made Defense Minister.

General Weizmann came to Eshkol's office. He was a tall man, spick-and-span in appearance. The public regarded him as a sort of flying cowboy, but under his facade the aviation general was a serious man, capable of leadership and organization; he had made Israel's air force one of the best in the world. His one fault was perhaps to be too forthright about what was on his mind, whether he was talking to military men or to civilians. Weizmann found Y. S. Shapiro in Eshkol's office, where the two were having a quick lunch, and proceeded to tell Eshkol what was on his mind.

"The strongest army since King David's is at your command," he said. "Order that army to march, and you will become known as the conqueror in the war for the survival of

Israel. If you do not, you will be responsible for the destruction of our country. Your policy will bring the total annihilation of the Third Jewish State." Shapiro broke down and sobbed.*

At 3:05 P.M. Igal Yadin came to the Defense Minister's office. As Eshkol's special adviser on defense problems, he had made a special trip from Jerusalem. He paced the waiting room nervously, puffing on his pipe, until Eshkol admitted him. Then he went straight to the point. "I had to see you," he said. "The situation is now such that you have no choice. You must appoint Dayan Defense Minister."

The Alignment ministers also met that afternoon. For half a day Allon had believed himself about to be Defense Minister, and he is said to have already rounded up old friends from the Palmach for his staff. He had also met with the high-ranking officers and had paid a visit to the Defense Ministry.

About noon, however, his hopes began to wane as he observed the pressure being put on Eshkol. When the Alignment ministers met, he knew that his appointment was beyond recall. He issued a statement: "I am withdrawing my candidacy for the post of Defense Minister. I am ready to accept any post in which I may be of help to the war effort, either in the government or outside it."

Eshkol thanked Allon for his chivalrous attitude, but Allon was very bitter. He thought he might have been able to prolong the debate a day or two more, and, had he been forcible enough, perhaps have become Defense Minister. But he also thought that the maneuver would ruin the coalition and delay the attack that had to be made on Egypt at once.

Disappointed and discouraged, Allon and his wife went to the Negev, where their son Iftakh was a noncommissioned paratroop officer. The unit commander offered him coffee. Allon became emotional. "Don't forget two things," he said to his son before leaving. "This will be a hard war, with shells, shrapnel, and bombs. Wherever you land, if the advance is

---

* See a series of anonymous articles published in *France-Soir* in July 1967; also see Schiff and Ben Elissar, *op. cit.*

halted, hit the ground right away. Then, when you go into battle, wear your helmet. Don't try to be smart!"

In Tel Aviv Eshkol summoned Dayan.

At 4:15 P.M., when Dayan arrived at Eshkol's office, the Prime Minister offered to appoint him Defense Minister. Dayan accepted. That same evening Rafi approved the appointment. Ben-Gurion had opposed it, hoping that Eshkol would resign all his portfolios, but he finally agreed.

At the same time Eshkol called in General Haim Bar Lev and appointed him Deputy Chief of Staff.

At 10:00 P.M., the government met at the Red House in Tel Aviv. Dayan arrived in khaki clothes in his Saab. Begin, who had been appointed a minister without portfolio, arrived at the same moment. On the following day Yoseph Saphir became the second representative of the Gahal in the government.

The last news broadcast from Kol-Israel on June 1 was an announcement of the formation of a national union government. All over the country—in cafés, in homes, in camps, in ships at sea, under camouflage nets, in tanks and tractors—spontaneous cheers burst forth. Bottles of cognac were opened. Said one sergeant major, "I would never have thought there was so much cognac in the Israeli army!"

The appointment of Dayan was a decision in itself—to take up Nasser's challenge.

•

THE END OF THE ARMADA

THAT FRIDAY, JUNE 2, plans for the "international force" collapsed. Anderson had flown from Cairo to Lisbon, where he had communicated to Washington a very pessimistic report on his mission. The cable had depressed Rusk. On the previous day he had talked with Iraqi Foreign Minister Pachachi, whom he had taken to meet Johnson secretly.

The President and the Secretary of State had finally concluded that Nasser would not back down. On June 2 Nasser's answer to Johnson's May 23 cable was received. "A typical Egyptian answer," Eugene Rostow remarked ironically. It was a long letter, which reviewed the whole matter from the beginning, in order to justify the position of the U.A.R. in respect to the U.N. force and the strait of Tiran. "We have erased the consequences of the aggression of 1956," Nasser had written, adding many compliments to the United States and thanking it for its brave attitude during that crisis. These thanks represented the only glimmer of hope left—a very feeble glimmer indeed.

British Prime Minister Wilson, who arrived in the United States that Friday, brought a no more optimistic point of view. Before he had left London the British government had come to no decision on the eventual use of arms to force the blockade. Canada's Pearson had emphasized to the American Ambassador that he was opposed to military action, no matter what happened. Wilson had met with Pearson before coming to

Washington, and then he too had backed down. "The British don't trust their own courage," cabled an Israeli reporter, "and still less the Americans'."

After having met with Johnson in the White House, Wilson held a press conference in which he cautiously backed down from his previous statements about Great Britain's possible use of force. Negative replies from the various governments to which the United States had appealed piled up on Rusk's desk. The only leader who seemed truly ready to go to war over the strait was—strangely enough—the Australian Harold Holt, who was also to meet with Johnson that day. But his willingness changed nothing.

Lyndon Johnson was also sending Eshkol a long letter in response to the latter's cable of May 30. Its tone was friendly, but the substance contradicted what Eban had told the Israeli government about an American promise to act alone if other powers refused. Johnson stated that all he had promised to do at the time of his conference with Eban was his written statement: "We mean to pursue vigorously the measures which may be taken by maritime nations to assure that the strait and gulf remain open to free and innocent passage of the vessels of all nations."

In his letter Johnson repeated everything he had said to Eban, once again emphasizing that it would be unwise as well as most unproductive for him to act without the full consultation and backing of Congress. The United States was continuing its efforts in the United Nations and among the principal maritime powers to obtain from them an international declaration. As long as all the possibilities in the United Nations had not been exhausted, he did not know whether or not other nations would subscribe to the British plan for an "international naval presence in the area of the strait of Tiran."

At the end of the letter the following sentence appeared: "Our leadership is unanimous that the United States should not act alone." That letter was sufficient to dash all hopes for unilateral American action to open the strait.

Eshkol's secret envoy returned from the United States that

day, bringing with him the disappointing news that the United States did not contemplate any direct action to open the strait of Tiran.

The plan for an international force gave up the ghost at the end of the week preceding the war. Nevertheless, efforts continued to be made in that direction for another few days. They were pathetic and absurd, for the plan had already failed and it would have had no chance of success even if it had gone through. In fact, on the day after the closing of the strait, Egypt had secretly informed representatives of the great powers that the troops stationed in Sharm el Sheikh would not fire on any ship that was trying to force the blockade under the protection of foreign warships. The American government knew of this promise.* But why had it then fooled around for two weeks with such a concoction as the "Red Sea Regatta," or, as Ambassador Harman called it, "the Armada"? It was clear that nothing would be resolved by the passage through the strait of a fleet the Egyptians had been ordered by their own government not to fire on. Why did they try so hard? The simple answer is that they did not know what else to do.

In Cairo the high command met for a long time with Nasser. There were several indications that international tensions were subsiding. Soviet appeasement was bearing fruit. Dayan's appointment created no undue excitement. The intelligence experts figured that by appointing Dayan, Eshkol was trying to defuse criticism from his political opponents and to restore faith in his government. Mohieddin's imminent trip to Washington was another positive factor. For exactly these reasons it seemed advisable to avoid military action at any price. "Don't give the Israelis an excuse to attack. Gain time! That's an order. This very morning cables have been sent to various friendly countries to ask the same of them: 'Don't provoke us to action! Don't enter the strait of Tiran!'"

At the same time Nasser decided to make the blockade of the

* Information from the State Department.

strait appear to be a concerted action by all the Arab countries. He advised his Syrian friends to be cautious, but Syria did not intend to heed instructions from Egypt. The morning of June 2 Colonel Mustafa Talas, commander of the Syrian central sector, stated: "We shall use a strategy of slow death on Israel, which will bring Israel to bay. Then we will destroy Israel."

In any event Egypt continued to send reinforcements into the Sinai peninsula. Amer issued a new battle order: "Israel may attack the U.A.R. soon. Our plans have provided for that eventuality. Keep your eyes open."

Egypt was not preparing to make war.

Israel was.

Dayan began his career as Defense Minister with breakfast in his house in Zahala, to which he invited his friend Zvi ("Chera") Zur, formerly the sixth Chief of Staff of the Israeli army. The Minister asked Zur to become his assistant, to take charge of civilian affairs in the Defense Ministry. Zur agreed and went to work at once.

Dayan arrived at the ministry in uniform. One of his first orders disturbed his subordinates greatly. He asked them to ready a half-track for him, so that he could go to the front at any moment if hostilities broke out. The chiefs of Ministry remembered the Sinai campaign, when Dayan had been Chief of Staff and, instead of staying at headquarters, had dashed off to the south with the fighting units. They were afraid that once again the Minister would close his office in order to watch the Egyptian army from the front row.

At 9:15 A.M. Dayan, Eshkol, and the ministers of the war cabinet met at General Staff headquarters. Eshkol opened the meeting. He was upset because he was no longer Defense Minister, and because he had not forgotten the generals' harsh remarks about him. And above all, he had not forgotten that some army leaders had blamed his government for looking to foreign powers for protection.

Several ministers asked questions. Some, still hesitant about a decision, wondered whether it would not be better to wait still a little longer. It was apparent that many were clinging to the magic formula of "waiting" and that they would use it as an excuse to delay a final decision once more.

After the ministers had left, Dayan asked the generals to bring him the operational plans of the General Staff. About noon a limited ministerial meeting was convened by Herzog in Eshkol's office. Present were Dayan, Eban, Allon, and Rabin. Dayan outlined his plans for war, the object of which was to destroy the Egyptian army in the Sinai peninsula and to occupy the shores of the strait.

Other ministers also took the floor. To the astonishment of some, Eban declared himself in favor of military action. He had changed his mind overnight, independently of the appointment of Dayan. He had lunched with Rabin, Yariv, and other generals, who had explained to him in detail their military and political estimates. Eban had said nothing then, but after spending two hours alone in his room at the Hotel Dan, he confided to a friend, "Time has come to disconnect the military timetable from the diplomatic one."

An urgent cable recalled Harman from the United States.

In Paris that morning a cable from Eshkol was brought to De Gaulle in the Élysée Palace. It was a last attempt to change the French President's attitude. Israel wanted peace, Eshkol said, but the Arabs wanted to destroy the nation. The closing of the strait was in itself an act of aggression against Israel. "We might have retaliated sooner," Eshkol continued, "but we followed the advice of our friends, including you, and we decided to wait. Unfortunately, the results of that decision have been disappointing. The Soviet Union has rejected your proposal for a conference of the four powers, and the Security Council is again paralyzed by futile debate. Destruction threatens Israel. One-third of the Jewish people were exterminated by the Nazis, and now the question of our survival has come up again." The cable ended with a pathetic appeal: "It grieves us to see that until now, France, the land of liberty and of the highest ideals of humanity, did not let its voice be heard. Mr.

President, I beg you to act so that France may be heard, and show her loyalty to us as a friend and ally so that our friends as well as our enemies may see that your country is the friend and ally of Israel."

When the French cabinet meeting ended, a statement was issued to the public, emphasizing four points:

1. France is pledged in no way to any of the nations involved.
2. In the words of its President, France believes in every nation's right to exist.
3. France will give neither approval nor aid to whatever nation takes up arms for any reason, and fires the first shot.
4. Problems of navigation in the gulf of 'Aqaba, as well as those of Arab refugees and relations between nations in the area, must be resolved by consultations among the four great powers.

France was no longer Israel's ally. The aggressor was no longer the one who had closed the strait of Tiran, but the one "who would fire the first shot." It was easy to see to whom that warning was directed. France considered the closing of the strait a *fait accompli,* one of many points of dispute in the Middle East and one that would be better to settle diplomatically, along with the many others that had accumulated over the previous nineteen years.

The Arab world was gratified by France's statement.

De Gaulle did not answer Eshkol's cable. But that afternoon the French government put an official end to arms shipments to Israel.

France imposed that embargo even before "the first shot" had been fired.

Israel found some small consolation in the decision of the West German government, over Schroeder's opposition, to furnish the requested gas masks. "If Schroeder had continued to block us," Chancellor Kurt Georg Kiesinger said to a friend that morning, "I would have demanded his resignation."

But was there anyone who still believed there would be war? "The war is over," said the editor in chief of a Malmö newspaper and cabled his correspondent in Israel to come back to Sweden.

In London, at a news conference for journalists accredited to the Foreign Office, the official spokesman announced: "The crisis is over. The time bomb has been disarmed."

In Tel Aviv the General Staff met at 9:30 P.M. to submit its operational plans to the Defense Minister.

"If you don't have any plans," said Dayan, "I have."

Everyone knew what Dayan's strategy was, for he had described it to the generals more than once and had also discussed it with Rabin during the waiting period. Just before this meeting the commander of the southern front, General Gavish, had presented his own bold project, which was almost the same as that of Dayan, as both of them knew—a strike into the Sinai peninsula along several different axes, the destruction of the Egyptian army there, and the occupation of the strait area. When he met with Dayan, Rabin came up with this very bold plan for moving into the peninsula on four axes: two in the north around Rafah and two more in the south, in the El Quseima sector, toward the fortified position of Abu 'Aweigîla.

Dayan accepted this plan as a whole; he insisted only that the objectives of the war be clearly understood: destruction of the Egyptian army and occupation of Sharm el Sheikh.

That evening there was a big party at the Hotel Neot Midbar near Beersheba. The pilots of Arie Ben Or's squadron had their wives along, and the fun lasted until morning. The pilots all had new berets, which they had contrived to resemble the tank soldiers' helmets with the squadron's insignia. It was a picturesque reminder of the fact that the enemy tanks were their main objective.

Arie came to the dance straight from some exercises that had occupied him all afternoon, for he was experimenting with a new attack method.

There was also a party for the men of Amos Katz's unit,

which was encamped in the sands of the Negev. At 1:00 A.M., when it broke up, Katz jumped into his jeep and headed north for a short home leave in Rehovot, which he reached at 3:00 A.M. Not wanting to awaken his family, he parked outside the house, crawled into the back seat, and went to sleep.

At the Soviet embassy in Washington, there was also a lively party. "The crisis is over," the Russians told the foreign diplomats among their guests. "Nasser has won a total victory."

The Soviet military attaché went up to a group of attachés from other embassies. "Israel has been liquidated," he said loudly, pressing his palms to each other and turning his hands slowly to indicate the total crushing of the Zionist state.

•

A CONFIDENTIAL CHAT WITH DE GAULLE

AT 11:00 A.M. on June 3 M. Lebel, director of the Africa-Levant division of the French Foreign Office, telephoned the Israeli embassy in Paris and asked to speak to Minister Jochanaan Meroz. "Could you come here right away?" he asked. "I have something to tell you."

Meroz went at once to the Foreign Office, where Lebel told him: "France, I must inform you, has decided to put a temporary halt to its shipments of arms to the Middle East." (Of course, no Arab country was buying arms from France, with the exception of Lebanon, which had acquired some French planes for an air show on its Independence Day.)

Lebel explained to Meroz the reasons for the embargo. The unofficial reason was that the press had made too much fuss over the shipment of arms from France to Israel and particularly over the Bordeaux incident. (Two days previously four El Al Boeings had landed at Bordeaux, where they had been loaded with arms and spare parts. As the airport at Bordeaux accommodated both military and civilian flights, it had not been difficult to obtain pictures of those four planes for newspapers issued on June 2.)

But the official reason had already been determined, and Lebel repeated it to Meroz: "France is not bound to any of the parties presently in opposition. That is why we are not sending any more arms to the Middle East."

"Is this the thanks we get for being patient and restrained as

182

we were asked to be?" asked the astonished Meroz. "I wonder,"
he added with a touch of irony, "whether or not the Soviet
Union has promised you that it would place an embargo on its
shipments of arms to Egypt?"

At the same time Armed Forces Minister Messmer was ap-
pealing to Premier Georges Pompidou to lift the embargo.
Pompidou made a quick check and answered that shipments
already on their way would not be recalled. A little later Israeli
Admiral Limon arrived at the Defense Ministry, where a reception was held for the guests of the Bourget air show, and Messmer welcomed him there. Limon took Messmer aside. "I know
why you are here," Messmer said. "You will continue to get arms
and equipment as in the past." Several French generals and
officials of the Ministry of the Army also promised Limon that
shipments would continue. "The embargo," said one of them,
"is simply the result of a little overdoing on the part of the
Foreign Ministry, but the Premier has set everything straight."

Nothing, however, had been set straight. Pompidou had
merely permitted the cases of arms that had already been
packed to be loaded; after that the loading of planes already in
Paris would end. The embargo had been delayed only twenty-
four hours.

At 7:00 P.M. Israeli Ambassador Eytan arrived incognito at
the Élysée Palace. Burin des Rosiers talked with him briefly,
and after ten minutes he was taken to De Gaulle in complete
secrecy. The two men spoke alone.

De Gaulle seemed calmer than he had been ten days earlier
when he had talked to Eban, but his opinion on the crisis had
not changed. On the morning of June 3 he had analyzed the
situation for one of his confidants: "The Russians intended to
aggravate the difficult situation in the Middle East. That is
why they encouraged the Egyptians to march into the Sinai
peninsula. They thought that if incidents on the frontier, the
infiltration of saboteurs, and the concentration of Egyptian
troops went on for several weeks or even several months, the
situation would come to a boiling point. The United States

would then be obliged to send troops to the Middle East to defend Israel against an Arab attack. That would have produced another Vietnam. But Nasser got out of Russia's control. He sent a much larger force than had been planned to the frontier, and he also closed the strait without consulting Moscow. Consequently the danger of escalation increased again, and the situation can deteriorate until it produces a military conflict between the two great powers. That must be prevented at any cost."

In the secret interview with Eytan, De Gaulle repeated his warning: "Don't be the first to fire!"

The main subject of the conversation was obvious—the embargo that France had just imposed on the delivery of arms to Israel. De Gaulle did not even try to hide behind official pretenses but stated directly that he had decided to stop the arms shipments in order to prevent the outbreak of war. He believed that when France's customers—in other words, Israel —saw their sources of supply drying up, they would refrain from rushing into war.

Eytan explained at length that the embargo affected Israel alone, for Israel had been buying almost all its arms from France, whereas the Arab countries had been receiving considerable amounts of military equipment from the U.S.S.R., and no one had thought for a moment of stopping the shipments of cannon and tanks to Egypt and Syria.

De Gaulle was firm as a rock in his refusal to lift what he called a "preventive embargo" on arms shipments to Israel. "Don't make war!" he repeated. "I know that the other party does not want war. I have done everything in my power to avoid war. There is only one solution—and that is in the hands of the four great powers."

"Egypt committed an act of aggression in closing the strait," Eytan said, "and thus has produced threats from the Arab countries that they will destroy Israel."

"If you are attacked," De Gaulle said, "you will not be abandoned to destruction.* I am convinced that a war will cost

* During a press conference on November 27, 1967, De Gaulle insisted that he had told Abba Eban, "We will not let you be destroyed." His

you many losses and much blood and that it will settle nothing. In ten years you will have to fight again."

"I do not know whether or not there will be war," continued the General, as if thinking aloud, "and neither do you, Mr. Ambassador. But don't pin your hopes on the United States. It will not rescue you."

Deeply depressed, Eytan left the Élysée Palace. France had unilaterally stopped arms shipments to Israel at the most critical moment of Israel's existence as a state and before Israel had fired a shot. Eytan hurried to cable his government the substance of his conversation with De Gaulle. The attitude of the President, Eytan reported, had not changed at all for the better. On the contrary, he had personally ordered arms shipments to Israel stopped, in order to keep the Israelis from taking any military action.

That day Israeli representatives in Paris faced the total wreck of their diplomacy. For years they had been sending optimistic reports stressing the French President's friendly attitude toward their nation and ignoring all the signs—which had been clear—that France was cooling toward Israel and warming toward the Arab countries.

And they still did not know everything. They did not know, for example, that De Gaulle had severely lectured Pompidou about the support that the Premier's patrons of long standing, the Rothschilds, were openly giving Israel. The awakening of Jewish national sentiment in some Frenchmen angered De Gaulle, who saw it as a kind of betrayal. "Tell your friends to stop criticizing the government's policies," Pompidou said with some embarrassment to one of the Rothschilds, "for they do not know what is best for them."

"We are disappointed in France's attitude," said Rusk during a conference with Evron, at which Battle was also present. "We are used to France's failure to honor her obligations in the framework of the United Nations, but we are really disap-

---

exact statement was "You will not be abandoned to destruction," which he said to Eytan, rather than to Eban. The difference in meaning is obvious.

pointed in this matter of yours. Couldn't you try to exert some influence in Paris to get France to sign the international declaration?"

Rusk was not aware that at that moment Israeli influence in Paris was close to zero. "We should know," Rusk continued, "what France's attitude will be if Egypt uses force to prevent the passage of your ships through the strait of Tiran. If the Egyptians fire on one of your vessels, would France consider it 'the first shot'?" Then he added, "We don't understand the Soviet attitude either."

He had reason to be baffled. On June 3 in the Security Council Fedorenko had made a vehement attack on the United States and its policies toward Vietnam and Cuba. He had also mentioned several other crimes the United States had committed, in Russian eyes, but he had not touched on the question of the strait of Tiran, which was what the debate was about in the first place. U.S. Ambassador to Moscow Llewellyn Thompson had been recalled to Washington to explain the Soviet Union's attitude toward the blockade of the strait and the crisis in general.

At the end of the conference with Evron, Rusk repeated that Congress was unhappy about Vietnam and therefore did not want the United States to act alone in the Middle East. Shortly after Evron had returned to his own office, Eugene Rostow called him. "Is *Dolphin* still at Massawa?" Rostow inquired nervously.

Dolphin was still at Massawa, moored by a rusty anchor near the entrance to the harbor, its crew suffocating in the Red Sea heat. The sailors spent their days and nights in the swimming pool they had rigged on the deck. Naked and motionless as hippopotamuses, they lazily fished over the side, only to drop what fish they caught into barrels on the deck to try to hook them again. From time to time someone called attention to suspicious activity on board a Saudi ship moored nearby. Jonathan Kramer, who owned a printing press in civilian life and was cook on *Dolphin,* surpassed himself, but his dishes were concocted of fish and only fish. The sailors were convinced that half the fish in the Red Sea had passed through their digestive systems.

The sailors in the other Israeli group were still waiting in the Red Sea Hotel. One more day crept by. Nothing happened.

The same question— "What's *Dolphin* doing?"—was being asked in Sharm el Sheikh and Cairo. A few days earlier Egyptian agents in Massawa had reported that the little ship was preparing to sail, and the garrison at Sharm el Sheikh was expecting the test boat on June 3.

The Egyptians had taken one further step to postpone their enemies' plan to force the strait. After the conference with Anderson it had been thought advisable to keep Mohieddin's visit to Washington secret, but now the government did release details of the trip in hopes of discouraging promoters of the "international force." On the eve of a summit conference between Egypt and the United States, who would send a ship through the strait? In order to prove that relations with the Americans were improving, one of Nasser's associates telephoned the American embassy to invite Ambassador Nolte to present his credentials on Monday, June 5.

The positioning of the Arab troops in the Sinai peninsula was finished. A force of 200 tanks, under the command of General Shazli, the hero of the Yemen war, was concentrated opposite the southern boundary of Israel. According to Israeli information, its objective was to cut off Elat and thus to establish land connections between the peninsula and Jordan.

Seven Egyptian divisions were positioned in the Sinai peninsula. Across the frontier three Israeli divisions faced them— those of Tal, Abraham Yoffe, and Sharon.

"My grandfather needed Hitler so that he could get into power," said young Winston Churchill, the journalist, at a luncheon at Dayan's house in Zahala.

"It took 80,000 Egyptian soldiers in the Sinai peninsula for me to get to be Defense Minister," replied Dayan.

He gave the youthful journalist to understand that war

would not break out for a while. Churchill hurried to reserve a seat on the first plane for London the following day.

At 3:00 P.M. Dayan went to the Ministry and at 4:00 to the press club, where he held his first press conference with hundreds of foreign correspondents in attendance. Two of his answers to the many questions put to him particularly attracted their attention. When asked about the diplomatic mess Israel had become mired in since the closing of the strait, he replied: "At present, it is either much too soon or much too late. Too late to take military action against the closing of the strait of Tiran and too soon to draw conclusions as to what diplomatic action should be taken in respect to that matter."

From those remarks the reporters inferred that Dayan did not expect war for some days to come. His second answer caused a sensation in Great Britain and the United States: "I expect nothing from anyone, and I do not want anyone fighting for us. . . . If war should come, I do not want American or English boys getting themselves killed here. I don't think we need them."

The new Defense Minister left the press conference to talk with Eshkol in Jerusalem. The inner Cabinet met again that evening: Dayan, Eban, Allon, Yadin, Herzog, and Rabin. Soon Harman would arrive from the United States.

A decision would be made that night.

Many soldiers had brief leaves that day of June 3. Several thousand reservists were demobilized and told the password, which would be broadcast over the radio if the situation took a turn for the worse.

At Sede Boqer, not far from Ben-Gurion's prefabricated house, Guy Jacobson parted that evening from his wife Ruth and his father. He had spent several days with his family, which had been allowed to visit him. Other soldiers' families had come to the barren desert where Guy's company was encamped. At daybreak they would return to Tel Aviv.

Arie Ben Or took Yonina home after a fine weekend with her at Neot Hamidbar. Arie's mother was waiting for them outside the house. "Is there going to be a war, son?" she asked, trying to hide her feelings, for Arie was her only son. "Mother," he said, "be brave. Whatever happens, be brave."

Amos Katz had spent the whole day at home. When his father had come out on the doorstep that morning, he had found Amos asleep in his jeep. His father and mother had awakened him in order to stuff him with good food before letting him sleep again in his own bed. They even sent for Jenny to come from Hedera. She gave him all kinds of advice: "Don't try to be a hero. Don't pretend you're some kind of a superman. Don't do anything you don't have to." Katz was not worried. He did not imagine for a moment that he might be killed.

That night he returned to his unit. He had hardly arrived before he sensed that something was going to happen. Men were running back and forth. Orders were being given. Couriers were hurrying from one unit to another. Presently Katz was ordered to move his company to another sector. The well-trained soldiers did not waste a moment. Tanks rolled away into the darkness at top speed.

That evening the Soviet Ambassador in Cairo paid a visit to Nasser to tell him that the Soviet government believed the crisis to be over and that Israel would not attack.

In Tel Aviv Chuvakin cabled Moscow his opinion that Israel would not start anything for two weeks.

Ambassador Anatoly Dobrynin cabled the Kremlin from Washington that efforts to solve the situation through diplomacy would last another week at least. Walt Rostow invited Evron to dinner and told him, "Wait until the end of next week before you decide to act."

Evron said nothing.

At 1:00 A.M. the Cabinet meeting at Eshkol's house recommended the government "go to war."

•

BEN-GURION GIVES HIS BLESSING

THE SUN WAS shining brightly in Cairo on the morning of June 4 as tall, athletic, red-haired Richard Parker, a high official of the U.S. embassy, went to the banks of the Nile. Ever since the crisis had begun three weeks before, the personnel at the embassy had been working day and night, even on weekends, without a break, but now they could finally be sure that the situation had improved. The next week Mohieddin would leave for Washington. The word was being passed in diplomatic circles that there would be no war. Parker could at last resume his Sunday pastime of sailing on the Nile.

It would have been hard to find a diplomat in Cairo who was not taking a holiday. Some went picnicking with their families; others played tennis or rode horseback. Even Cairo residents sauntered through the streets without looking anxiously at the posters about bomb defense or at the antiaircraft guns placed all around the capital.

Nasser also thought he had won his poker game. That day he received an important delegation from Iraq, headed by Prime Minister Taher Yahia. The two men signed a mutual-defense agreement, similar to the one between Egypt and Jordan that had been signed the previous week. In his speech after the ceremony, the Egyptian President said: "Egypt will not recognize any declaration of the maritime powers in respect to freedom of navigation in the gulf of 'Aqaba. It will regard such a declaration as an act of aggression against the sovereignty of Egypt and the first step toward an act of war."

190

Since he had assumed power, Nasser had never felt so powerful. The Soviet bloc, the neutral countries, and France were all with him. The West regarded him with anxious astonishment. The entire Arab world was behind him: Iraq, Kuwait, Jordan, Libya, Sudan, Algeria, Aden, and Yemen. King Hassan II of Morocco had sent a special envoy to promise assistance; President Habib Bourguiba had promised that an Algerian army could pass through Tunisian territory on its way to fight the Zionists. Even Nasser's worst enemy, King Faisal of Saudi Arabia, had declared: "Every Arab who does not participate in this conflict will seal his fate. He will not be worthy of being called an Arab."

Shukairy broadcast his plan for the next stage: The Mandelbaum Gate between Jordanian and Israeli Jerusalem would be closed, and no Israeli convoys would be allowed to go to the enclave on Mount Scopus. "The Mandelbaum Gate will be another Tiran," he declared, "and the Hebrew University on Mount Scopus another Elat."

An Iraqi motorized brigade entered Jordan. The Arabs had never been so sure of their strength and their triumph. No one paid any attention to King Hussein's warning in a press conference in Amman: "Israel can attack within forty-eight hours. It is in the habit of doing things by surprise."

Foreign correspondents lined up at the ticket windows at the Lydda airport for passage home.

At 8:00 A.M. the Israeli government met in Jerusalem. Harman delivered his report on the situation in the United States. Dayan proposed that the government "give full powers to the Prime Minister and to the Defense Minister to put the Israeli army into action if necessary." Everyone knew what that meant. A little later the government met again. The Defense Minister's proposal was restated in the same terms. This time all the ministers accepted it, except for the two members of the Mapam who asked permission to consult their party. A few hours later they returned with positive answers.

Despite the oblique language in which the governmental

decision was phrased, its meaning was clear: Israel would go to war.

Ever since morning the Defense Ministry had been bustling with activity. Workmen and employees were carrying furniture, safes, storage cabinets, and files from the Red House to the huge Defense Ministry. Dayan's office was being transferred to that building, which also housed the General Staff headquarters. Dayan had decided on the transfer at the last minute. Eshkol wanted to keep his office in the Red House, and when Dayan learned of this decision he made up his mind to leave it. There could be but one boss in the Ministry, and he wanted to be near the General Staff, with whom he would direct the war.

At 3:30 P.M. a helicopter deposited Dayan in Tel Aviv, and he went directly to the operations room. Precise instructions had been sent to the forces on the Jordanian and Syrian fronts: "Do not attack, but consolidate your positions, and defend yourselves. Only in the event of a general offensive by the enemy would it be advisable to advance and seize key positions in enemy territory near the frontier in order to gain strategic superiority."

Dayan gave the General Staff the confidence and positive direction that had been wanting since the crisis began. He also made it known who was boss. When a heated argument started over a point of strategy, Dayan shouted, "If you want a democracy, fellows, that's O.K. with me, but not here and not now." He flew to the north to inspect the Syrian frontier.

The wife of a reservist wrote to the editor of *Ma'ariv:*

> My husband is a reservist. The night before he was called up, he went to see *Doctor Zhivago* at the Ramat Gan movie theater and told me that it is an excellent movie. I haven't been able to see it, because it's so hard to get a baby-sitter.
>
> Therefore, I demand that the army get this war over with and win a great victory very soon, while *Doctor Zhivago* is still being shown at the Ramat Gan movie theater and I can get to see it.

The papers also announced the great excitement in the Arab capitals since France's recent decisions. The Movement for World Peace had decided to back the Arabs and to condemn Israel as a "bridgehead of imperialism." Abie Nathan, the peace pilot, could not make up his mind as he sat beside his plane in Nicosia whether or not to fly on the following day to Cairo to make peace with Nasser.

In Washington even the diehard optimists admitted on June 4 that the multinational project had collapsed. Only four other nations had agreed to sign the international declaration: Great Britain, the Netherlands, Australia, and New Zealand. And Australia was the only other one that had agreed to send ships through the strait.

President Johnson had truly believed in the international force and had done everything he could to bring it off, but he had failed. But the State Department had never taken the possibility very seriously. Washington analysts were publishing statistics proving that very few Israeli ships ordinarily used the strait.

In the atmosphere of worldwide relief, few people paid attention to a statement that the Israeli government issued that afternoon: "The government is distressed at the slowness of progress on the part of the powers in the matter of opening the strait."

In New York talks went on all day in the corridors of the U.N. building in an effort to find a solution acceptable to the Security Council. Goldberg had dropped the idea of proposing an end to the "state of belligerence." It was clear that even if that "solution" received a majority vote in the Council, the Soviets would veto it. Nevertheless, toward evening Goldberg succeeded in lining up nine votes in favor of it. Even though it could not be put into effect, it would represent an important consolidation of international opinion.

At 6:30 P.M. Goldberg ended his official consultation with Hans Tabor, President of the Security Council, in the headquarters of the Danish mission. Feeling somewhat revived in spirit, he started walking with his assistant, Max Finger, toward American mission headquarters on First Avenue. About 7:00 P.M. they dropped into a small bar for a drink and to hear the latest news broadcast, which said that tension had decreased in Israel and that soldiers on leave were tanning themselves on the beaches. Goldberg screwed up his face. "I don't like those stories about Israeli soldiers on leave. If I know the Israelis, that means that they'll go to war tomorrow."

That night Cairo was deserted. Newspapers and signboards announced that "the crucial moment is at hand." Armed guards patrolled radio and television stations and foreign embassies.

At Inchas airfield, pilots were giving a party under the patronage of Marshal Mahmoud, Chief of the Air Force. It lasted until dawn, and the best belly dancers in Cairo had been imported to entertain the young eagles.

In Damascus, cabarets, discotheques, and officers' clubs were full and swinging despite the state of emergency.

At 11:00 P.M. Eshkol's Cabinet met in Tel Aviv for the last time. Dayan slept that night in the operations room.

Before going to sleep he asked one of his assistants to stop by Ben-Gurion's house to inform him of the government's decision. "Tell him," Dayan said, "that the government has approved my recommendation. I think the Egyptian concentrations are lined in an offensive formation."

Despite the total blackout in Tel Aviv, the emissary arrived at Ben-Gurion's house on Keren Kayemet Avenue. As Paula Ben-Gurion was already asleep, the old lion himself came to the door in his pajamas. The visitor followed him back to his bedroom, where the former leader sat down on the bed, with his famous white hair sticking up all over his head.

After hearing Dayan's message, Ben-Gurion thought for a moment. Then he asked, "Is Moshe sure of himself?"

"Yes."

"In that event, give him my blessing."

PART THREE

·

The War

•

THE FIRST SHOT

AT DAYBREAK ON June 5 a sentinel woke Captain Guy Jacobson, and a few minutes later the entire company was stirring. Then the order to march was given, and the company set out for the frontier. Jacobson still did not believe that he was going to war. Several times during the previous weeks he had received orders to advance by night in the direction of the Egyptian frontier, but after a few hours, counterorders had always brought him back to his starting point.

At the same time, Amos Katz's company started toward the village of Kerem Shalom, noticing on their way a second and then a third column of tanks moving across the flat desert. Half an hour later, Katz was in the middle of a veritable sea of tanks, waves of steel stretching to the horizon. Seeing that mighty power all around him, he said to himself, "No one could ever stop this army."

At the Egyptian air bases, pilots were awakened and sent running to their MIGs, which were on the runways, ready to take off. For weeks their superior officers had been telling them again and again that the Israelis would begin their offensive with an aerial attack on the airfields in the first light of dawn. The next few minutes were critical ones.

From the head of his unit Jacobson surveyed with astonishment the battalions, companies, and brigades of armored vehicles that were ploughing up the Negev wherever he looked. Companies crossed in front of one another; giant bulldozers

197

intersected lines of armored trucks; battalions of motorized infantry drove furiously toward the frontier. It was like the traffic on the Champs Élysées.

Then Guy noticed a weird and impressive scene: a white figure standing near a command half-track in the middle of the desert. It was a soldier in a talith—the ritual white garment of orthodox Jews—chanting the prayer of departure, his face turned toward the east. Guy was not a practicing Jew, but he was a believer, and he was deeply moved by the picture of that solitary praying figure who seemed to be asking heaven's blessing on the army swirling about him.

General Gavish, commanding the southern front, awoke at 5:00 A.M. He had spent the previous evening writing in his private diary his impressions of the three weeks of waiting. At 10:00 he had gone to bed, and he had slept soundly. In the morning he kissed his wife and said good-bye.

By the time the sun rose, everyone was awake. Soldiers were folding their blankets, and General Staff officers were taking their operation plans out of hiding. The Israeli radio had not yet begun to broadcast for the day, but the Arab stations were playing war songs and monotonous marches in which the words "Allah! Allah!" and "Nasser!" occurred frequently.

When Katz and Jacobson reached their respective destinations, the former hurried to his brigade commander, Colonel Raful of the paratroopers. Jacobson parked his tanks under some barren shrubs and sat in their shade to write a letter to Ruth.

At 6:07 A.M. the first news bulletins came over the Voice of Israel: "Neo-Nazis win in Lower Saxony elections. Fuel prices up in Israel." Nothing extraordinary.

What was extraordinary was the arrival of the generals and the Defense Minister in the operations room of the air force. At 7:10 General Hod, air force commander, picked up his microphone and uttered the words that had been on the tip of his tongue ever since the strait had been closed: *"Moked Go."**

---

* For a description of the hour of takeoff, see Julien Besançon's *Bazak: La guerre d'Israël* (Paris: 1967).

The army spokesman told reporters that the Israeli army was on the counteroffensive against the "threatening movements" of the Egyptian army.

Dozens of planes—Vautours, Mirages, Super-Mystères, Ouragans—took off from the airfields and formed into groups of four. The jets took off on a carefully plotted schedule so that all would reach their targets at exactly the same second. Those targets—Nasser's big airfields—were scattered over Egypt and the Sinai.

H-hour had been shrewdly chosen; when the planes reached their objectives, it would be 8:45 A.M. in Egypt, as there was an hour's time difference between Cairo and Tel Aviv. The Egyptians, who had expected the Israeli attack at dawn, would therefore be off guard. Visibility was excellent, for the sun had dispelled the early-morning mists. Most of the Egyptian air-force commanders were on their way to their offices, to their camps, or to appointments in the city. It was a perfect time for an air attack.*

The morning alert on the Egyptian airfields had just ended, and the MIG pilots had switched off their engines and gone to mess for coffee. One heavy plane took off from Cairo West carrying Amer toward the Sinai peninsula; he had decided to inspect the desert bases that day. The commanders of the various air bases in the peninsula were awaiting him at Bîr el Thamâda airfield. His flight was closely guarded.

Meanwhile Israeli planes were coming closer to their targets. Some of the fighter planes had started north, then, flying high over the Mediterranean, had veered west and headed straight for Egypt at low altitudes—only a few yards above the water— in order to avoid radar detection. When they were over the Nile delta, they turned sharply south along the route that commercial planes usually take, a route along which enemy planes were least expected.

Squadrons heading for airfields in the Sinai peninsula flew through mountain gorges in order to escape radar detection by the Egyptians. But they threw the technicians at Jordan's Ajlun

* See Randolph Churchill, and Winston Churchill, *The Six Day War* (London: 1967).

radar station into a panic, as flocks of airplanes heading south suddenly and incomprehensibly appeared on their screens.

At 7:45 A.M. every airplane was over its target. At the same moment all the jets dived toward the runways, and a hailstorm of rockets and bombs struck the grounded Egyptian planes. Heavy bombs dug yawning craters in the runways as the airfields burst into flame.

At once all networks of radio communication among the Israeli planes, hitherto silent, broke the dead stillness of the operations room with the triumphant shouts of the pilots: "Everything's on fire!" "I hit three Tupolevs!" "Inchas is burning!"

"They made it," Hod said calmly.

A general beside him called Gavish on the direct line: "Go! Good luck!"

The commander of the southern front called the three division leaders back: "Red Sheet!" he shouted, making no attempt to conceal his excitement. "Red Sheet!" It was the code command for the immediate establishment of the armored corps radio transmission networks, which had not been in use during the weeks of waiting. It meant that the ground war was going to start at any moment. The shouts of joy and relief that broke from the tents when "Red Sheet" was heard released all the suppressed anger that had been building up during those long three weeks of humiliating inactivity.

Katz was on the way to his tank when he heard it. Jacobson had just drunk a cup of hot tea and was returning to his group to finish his letter to his wife. When he heard "Red Sheet!" he jumped into his tank.

Arie Ben Or called his pilots together at their base. He was calmer and more reserved than usual. "Here it is, fellows," he said. "As I've been telling you, this is war." The Fougas took off at once.

In the operations room at air force headquarters, someone opened a bottle of whiskey. Dayan and Rabin joined Hod, as army chaplain General Shlomo Goren handed everyone present a tiny leaflet on which was printed the prayer of departure.

Katz called his men together. "The people of Israel are going to war," he said. "Anyone who doesn't know what to do, follow my tank. I look forward to seeing you all safe and sound this evening." The company prepared to move.

At 7:55 A.M. the air-raid sirens started screaming, but no one knew what was up. Men kept right on walking along the streets to their jobs, and no cars slowed down. At 8:10 the Voice of Israel interrupted its regular broadcast with an announcement: "Here is a statement from the official spokesman of the army. Since early morning violent fighting has been in progress on the southern front between the Egyptian air and ground forces, which began an action against Israel, and our forces, which joined action to repel them."

General Gavish grabbed the microphone in the radio station. "Forward! Forward! Good luck!"

The tanks rushed into battle. The Six-Day War had begun.

Seven crack Egyptian divisions were tucked into the sands of the Sinai desert waiting for the Zionists. Two divisions occupied the northern sector on the Mediterranean coast; the 20th Division, called the "Palestinian" because it was largely composed of refugees from the Gaza Strip, and the 7th Division were entrenched in the heavily fortified positions of Rafah, Sheikh Zued, Giradeh, and El 'Arîsh blocking the northern road of the Sinai peninsula, which followed the coastline to the Suez canal.

The central axis, which extended from Nizzana into the Israeli Negev on the east and passed through Gebel Libni and Bîr Gifgâfa to the canal, was blocked by the 2nd Division, which completely encircled the road junction at Abu 'Aweighîla. The guns of Abu 'Aweighîla guarded the road to Ismailia and also the road connecting with the parallel highway along the coast.

These two fortified spots were the keys to the two main roads in the peninsula. They relied for defense on the 3rd Division, which was extended from Bîr Lahfân on the north to Bîr Hasana on the south.

Much farther south, near the Israeli frontier, entrenched units at El Kuntilla blocked the third east-west road across the peninsula. There the 6th Division waited in ambush. At first the Egyptians did not want to believe that Israel would try to pierce the front in this zone, but they observed startling tank movements around Elat and hastened to send the 6th Division to that sector. They were unaware that the tanks they saw were dummies—made of wood and canvas and cardboard— and that the clouds of dust rising from the desert were produced by a kind of free-for-all indulged in by Israeli trucks, tractors, and other vehicles for no other purpose than to deceive the enemy. The trick worked perfectly. As a matter of fact, there were very few Israeli soldiers in that zone.*

Between the central and southern roads in the Kuraya valley, an Egyptian armored division waited to strike at the right moment. It was General Shazli's mailed fist. For two weeks he had been changing his position in the desert, first to the north, then to the south, in order to keep his men active. But he had finally pitched his tents in this valley, where he was awaiting orders to drive toward Israel, cut off the Negev, isolate Elat, and rendezvous with the Jordanian army from the other side of the desert. He would thus make Nasser's dream of recovering Elat for the Arabs come true.

Far to the rear behind those six entrenched divisions, which were armed to the teeth, was the jewel in Nasser's crown, the 4th Armored Division, which had taken a position south of Bîr Gifgâfa about forty miles east of the Suez canal. At Sharm el Sheikh, the gateway to the strait of Tiran, there was a brigade of paratroopers.

Altogether there were seven divisions, 100,000 soldiers, 1,000 cannon, thousands of antitank guns, hundreds of miles of trenches protected by concrete, stone, barbed wire, mine fields, sharpshooters, machine-gun nests—and a sea of hatred.

Nasser was waiting for Rabin.

At 2:50 A.M. in New York (8:50 A.M. in Israel), Rafael's telephone rang. It was Tekoa at the Foreign Ministry. "Get a pencil, Gideon," he said, "and write this down."

* *Ibid.*, and Besançon, *op. cit.*

A few minutes later, Rafael telephoned Security Council President Tabor and requested an emergency meeting of the Council. He was twenty minutes ahead of his sworn enemy, Egyptian representative El Kony, in asking for it.

In Cairo, Nolte and Parker, elegantly dressed in blue suits, white shirts, and well-polished shoes, had just reached the embassy. In an hour they were due at Koubba Palace, where Nolte was to present his credentials to President Nasser. The official car of the Moroccan Ambassador had just passed en route to a conference with Nasser. Soon it would be the Americans' turn.

Parker telephoned a high Egyptian official who lived in Heliopolis in order to inquire about some details of the ceremony. An excited voice greeted him: "Haven't you heard the news? The Israelis have attacked. The ceremony has been canceled."

The streets filled with people. Excited mobs jammed the squares, waving flags and shouting war slogans, weeping, kissing, dancing, screaming with joy. "At last war has started. Let them have it! We'll destroy them once and for all."

Queen Mother Zein of Jordan had been in Lausanne while tensions were mounting. When on May 31 she had learned that her son Hussein had signed a pact with Nasser, she had been terribly worried. "There will be war," she told a friend. "Hussein must be snatched out of Nasser's claws. I'm going to Amman." The Queen Mother arrived in Amman one hour after the outbreak of hostilities.

At Damascus airport, Syrian Foreign Minister Makhous was welcoming his counterpart from Kuwait. Suddenly the United Press correspondent dashed up to tell him that war had broken out. Makhous rushed back to his Ministry, where he found his advisers already waiting. "We must cable instructions to our representatives all over the world," he said. "Emphasize that thanks to constant pressure from Syria, Egypt has at last decided to open hostilities against Israel."

General Murtaghi, commander of the Sinai front, was driving at top speed along the desert roads toward his command post. The Israeli attack had surprised him at Ismailia, where he had been spending a long weekend with his wife. Amer's plane could not land at Bîr el Thamâda, for that airfield, like the other Egyptian bases, was a molten furnace. Flying blind, the heavy plane circled Egypt for an hour and a half and finally landed at Cairo international airport. Amer left at once for the main fighting headquarters in the Sinai peninsula, in order to find out what was going on.

At 2:38 A.M. the first bulletin appeared on the teletype in the situation room at the White House. The officer in charge, Ray Wettering, immediately called Walt Rostow. "Check that information," Rostow said, "and call me back." Ray also called Harold Saunders, Rostow's assistant on Middle Eastern affairs. Saunders dressed and left at once for the White House. By that time other information had been received, and Wettering called Rostow again. "It's war," he said.

Dayan went to war with a firm and hard-headed policy. He indulged in no dreams of conquering Gaza, and he did not want to go near the Suez canal. He was afraid to capture Gaza because of the 250,000 refugees living there, who would be a problem to feed and to control. Besides, he thought the Gaza Strip would fall of its own accord after the Sinai peninsula had been taken.

Dayan's hesitation about the canal was due to the powers having forced Israel to withdraw from it in 1956. He thought it wiser not to seize the canal, which would provoke world censure of Israel.* "The Gaza strip," he told a friend, "is a bees' nest. The canal is a hornets' nest. We'd better stay away from both."

Dayan hoped to keep the Jordanian front quiet, if possible. He told General Narkiss, commander of the central zone: "Don't harass the General Staff with demands for reinforcements. Grit your teeth, and say nothing." As soon as the first shot had been fired, Eban had sent through General Odd

---

* Dayan expounded this thesis at a press conference on June 7, 1967.

Bull, chief U.N. observer in the Middle East, an urgent message to King Hussein, asking him in Eshkol's name not to intervene in the war, in exchange for Israel's assurance that it would make no move against Jordan.

Dayan was worried about the northern front, for he knew how friendly with Moscow Syria was. Observers had advised him that, if Israel embarked upon a widespread campaign against Syria and invaded its territory, the Russians were very likely to intervene on the side of their protégé. The Foreign Ministry specialists, however, did not share that opinion. Tekoa, who had formerly been Ambassador to Moscow, stated categorically that the Russians would yell and threaten and go right to the brink of war but would not intervene.

The Egyptian air force was in flames. Israel had let fly at the ten best-equipped of Nasser's air bases: Abu Sueir, Kabrit, Inchas, Cairo West, Beni Suef, and Gardaka in Egypt, and El 'Arîsh, Gebel Libni, Bîr Gifgâfa, and Bîr el Thamâda in the Sinai peninsula. For eighteen years, the Israeli Air Force had been getting ready for "Moked," but now it was astonished to find that its success had far exceeded its hopes.

At 10:15 A.M., three hours after the first plane had taken off, there was no more Egyptian air force. The war was up to the ground forces, and the Egyptian ground forces could not be taken by surprise or attacked from the rear. There was no alternative to hitting them head-on as they fully expected to be attacked; they had aimed their big guns in the direction from which the Jews would have to come.

The Israeli strategy was the simplest possible and the most logical. The two key points guarding the way to the Sinai peninsula on the north and in the center had to be taken; the fortified positions of Rafah, Giradeh, and El 'Arîsh had to be reduced; the entrenchments at Abu 'Aweighîla had to be overrun in order to open the two roads across the peninsula and thus the road south. Then the Israelis could swarm into the interior of the peninsula, strike the Egyptian army, and destroy it.

Opening the roads was the first step, and Israel would have to fight a decisive battle to pierce the lines of fortifications and reach the paved road to the canal. This engagement was to be known as the "battle of Rafah." "It will decide the outcome of the war," General Tal said, "and from beginning to end it will be a matter of life and death." He attacked Rafah that morning of June 5.

In his youth Colonel Shmuel had been a student at an ultraorthodox academy. Now he was in command of Tal's crack brigade, which first crossed the frontier and opened fire. Its tanks crushed the positions at Khan Yunis, which were held by a Palestinian brigade, and then drove toward Rafah, where it engaged in a duel with the troops holding that well-known fortress.

A second column of tanks and half-tracks carrying para-troopers approached Rafah from the south in a flanking attack. The tanks were to pierce the lines and destroy the enemy tanks and cannon, but mopping-up operations were to be handled by the paratroopers and the mechanized infantry while the tanks continued to move forward.

The second tank in the battalion was that of Amos Katz. At first, he thought he was taking part in simple training maneu-vers, for after he had crossed the frontier he had proceeded for two and a half hours without encountering the enemy. Over his radio he heard a company commander declare that he had de-stroyed seven T-34s. "He's in luck," Katz exclaimed enviously. But he told his men, "Don't worry; there'll be plenty left for us."

Suddenly mortar fire descended on the tanks. Katz ordered his driver to scale a nearby hill so that they could locate the Egyptian position. When they saw the tanks coming, the Egyp-tians clambered into seven trucks and fled. "Fire!" Katz ordered. One after another the seven trucks disintegrated. That was how the war began for Amos Katz.

His tanks continued toward their objective until they en-countered two batteries of artillery backed up by three tanks. His men rushed them. In an instant, the Egyptian tanks were

on fire and the Egyptians in flight. Katz's company broke into
the camp, smashed its heavy guns, and proceeded on its way.

The next objective was Kafr Shan, to all appearances so poor
and innocuous a village that the paratroopers refused to follow
patiently behind the tanks but passed them and drove into the
hamlet first. They did not know that more than twenty Egyptian tanks were waiting in ambush behind the crumbling
houses.

Katz followed a half-track full of paratroopers commanded
by Lieutenant Giora Eytan down one of the dusty streets.
Suddenly, about thirty yards to his left, he saw a tank waiting
at a corner. In the same split second his cannon and the paratroopers' bazooka fired on the tank and blew it up. Then
Lieutenant Eytan signaled to Katz that another Egyptian tank
was waiting on the right. Katz did not have time to swing his
cannon around before the Egyptians fired. The first shell exploded in the paratroopers' half-track and killed all but one of
them.

Katz fired on the T-34 at the same moment that it fired on
him. His Patton burst into flames, which caught his hair, his
face, his hands, and his pants. He fired once more, and then an
Egyptian shell struck his tank again. A living torch, Amos
shouted to his men to jump, and then threw himself from the
turret into a clump of cactus, where he rolled in the sharp
thorns, trying vainly to extinguish the flames that were con-
suming his body. He did not even know that he had sprained
his ankle in the jump.

Some of the men saw their commander rolling in flames in
the cactus patch. "That does it!" they said. "They got the
captain!"

But the captain was not going to let himself be "gotten" so
easily. Freeing himself from the cactus, he burrowed into the
sand and finally put the fire out. He cut off his smoking trousers
and sleeves. What remained of his uniform, were shorts and a
sleeveless shirt, that made him look like a bathing-suit model
from around 1900. Then he climbed into a half-track, grabbed
a field telephone, and called the battalion commander. All hell

had broken out around him, as the battle raged between his and the Egyptian tanks. "My tank burned up," Katz told Colonel Uri, "and I got some burns, but I am still in command of the company."

The half-track was caught in the middle of the village. Disgusted, Amos climbed down and crossed the street under a rain of bullets. Two of his men, seeing him limping, scorched, and wounded, said again, "They got the captain." But the captain jumped onto another tank and resumed command. In a few minutes he had organized his company again and had destroyed twelve T-34s. The battle was almost over when Uri made his appearance. "Leave everything where it is," he ordered, "and go on to the Rafah junction. Destroy everything you see on the way."

A glance behind him showed Katz that he had only ten tanks left. Several of the company's vehicles had vanished, among them his own jeep and chauffeur. He set out for Rafah. Hundreds of Egyptian soldiers in light khaki uniforms were retreating in disorder all along the roadside. Katz and his men destroyed an artillery brigade that was entrenched beside the road. Cleverly camouflaged Egyptian tanks were lying in wait behind the sand dunes, but, as if by instinct, Katz spotted one after another and hit seven T-34s from a distance of thirteen hundred yards.

Four Egyptian tanks came at him from the direction of Rafah. One of Katz's lieutenants charged them and destroyed three; the fourth wheeled and fled. Katz's radio began to sputter; it was his friend Dani, also a company commander, reporting himself in trouble and surrounded by huge Stalin tanks. Katz rushed to his aid, destroyed three of the Stalins, and set seven others afire.

Through clouds of smoke and flame Katz led his men to the Rafah junction, which they reached at 5:00 P.M. He had eight tanks left. The junction was deserted, for Colonel Shmuel's armor had pushed beyond it, smashed the defenses at Sheikh Zued, and passed through the strongly fortified positions at Giradeh en route to El 'Arîsh, the capital of the Sinai area and headquarters of the front-line Egyptian troops.

Colonel Shmuel recalled that at the last conference in Tal's operations room he had told his colleagues, "In case of war, I'll be at El 'Arîsh by evening of the first day." The other officers had shrugged their shoulders at this boast. "I was wrong," admitted Shmuel now. "I said 'in the evening,' and here we are in El 'Arîsh at 4:00 in the afternoon."

A little after 3:00 A.M. Washington time, Rusk reached the State Department and climbed the stairs to the room nick-named the "hot shop" on the ninth floor of the huge building. That room kept in constant contact with its counterpart in the Pentagon and with the situation room in the White House. Rusk undid his necktie, unbuttoned his collar, and, gulping cups of steaming coffee, began to study the cables from the Middle East. Work teams, each consisting of ten men, were organized to alternate every six hours. The "hot shop" was being deluged with information from the C.I.A., press services, the Pentagon, and the White House.

From the situation room at the White House, Walt Rostow kept in constant touch with Rusk and McNamara. At 4:30 A.M. they decided to awaken the President. Rostow phoned him: "War has broken out in the Middle East." He added some details about the air attack on the Egyptian airfields.

The President was calm and restrained. His first questions were: "How did it start? Who fired first?"

"We're not quite sure right now," Rostow said. Then he turned to Saunders. "Find out at once how it started? I want to know who began the fighting."

Rusk called Johnson to suggest cabling Gromyko. Johnson agreed. The substance of the restrained message was that the American Secretary of State was sorry that hostilities had been opened in the Middle East. He emphasized that the United States would continue to hold firmly to the principle of terri-torial integrity and independence for every nation in that area of the world and expressed hope that the fighting would end as soon as possible. The United States, Rusk added, wanted an immediate cease-fire and would intercede with the govern-ments involved, as well as through the framework of the

United Nations. Rusk expressed his hope that the Soviet Union
would take a similar position.

At 5:00 A.M. an aide made an entry in the daybook of the
situation room: "All hell has broken loose."

When General de Gaulle learned that war had broken out,
he reacted with icy rage and deep concern. He was angry
because no one had listened to his advice. "They have not
listened to France," he complained to Pompidou, whom he had
summoned to the Élysée Palace. He was worried because he
feared an escalation of the struggle. "The Israelis are stronger,"
he said to one of his advisers. "There is no doubt that they will
win an overwhelming victory in these first few days. Then
what? Their advance will be slowed down and end by getting
stuck in the Arab sea that surrounds them on all sides. The
Arabs will make a counterattack and push the Israelis back into
their own territory, perhaps even penetrate it. The United
States will be obliged to intervene to defend the Israelis, and
that will cause the Soviets to intervene on the side of the Arabs.
That will bring a confrontation between the two great powers
and may even lead to a third world war."

De Gaulle's opinion was that France should do everything
possible to stop the fighting or at least keep it from spreading.
That morning he issued an official communiqué, announcing an
embargo on all French arms shipments to the Middle East,
thus making public the secret embargo that France had
slapped on Israel two days earlier.

On the other hand, large numbers of Frenchmen demonstrated in the streets, organized solidarity committees, signed
petitions, volunteered to fight for Israel, and proclaimed that
more than ever before they were friends of the Jewish state.

The teletypes in the White House situation room crackled
with bulletins from the Middle East. "Cairo announces the
destruction of seventy Israeli planes. What do you make of
that?" one officer asked at 6:43 A.M.

"Nonsense," answered the C.I.A. representative. "Divide the

number by ten, and you'll get the right answer. That's the way to do it."

The various branches of the American intelligence system collaborated on an emergency report to President Johnson. The master spies were certain that Israel would win within four or five days and estimated that it would take Israel no longer than twenty-four hours to destroy all Egyptian aviation equipment on the ground.

At 7:00 A.M. White House Press Secretary Christian issued a statement expressing the President's concern that hostilities had commenced and calling for an immediate cease-fire. Urgent cables were shipped off to military attachés and other American diplomats in Cairo and Tel Aviv, requesting immediate answers to the question who had fired first.

About 8:00 A.M. Saunders stopped trying to find out which cannon had lobbed the first shell. The question, his superiors told him, no longer mattered.

Johnson telephoned to Goldberg at the United Nations and to McNamara. He instructed Goldberg to propose an immediate cease-fire to the Security Council. He told McNamara to place all American units in the Middle East on emergency alert. Johnson had not had a chance to get up and dress; at that critical moment he was directing American policy from his bedside telephone.

At 7:30 he was still in bed scanning cables that had just arrived; Walt Rostow telephoned. The President got up and went into his bathroom, where he shaved quickly, dressed, and returned to speak with Christian, who was sitting in his bedroom. "I've got to go down to the situation room," Johnson said. "We've had a call from Kosygin on the hot line."

The politburo, the most important body in Soviet political life, had been in session since morning, considering only one topic, the war in the Middle East. The information that reached Moscow was confused and fragmentary, and the Soviets did not know who had opened fire, where the front was, or who was winning.

At 11:00 A.M. in Tel Aviv, Tekoa summoned Chuvakin and handed him a letter addressed to Kosygin and signed by Eshkol. Chuvakin was pale, for until two days earlier he had been assuring his government that war would not break out for another two weeks. "Where is the fighting?" he asked.

Tekoa put on a cloak of secrecy. "I can't tell you," he said. "The fighting is somewhere in the south."

"But where? I absolutely must know."

"Just look at the disaster you have created," Tekoa replied. "We warned you, we begged you to reason with Nasser. We told you danger was coming, but you would not listen to us. Now you've got a war on your hands."

Podyedyeev's information was as scanty and confused as was that sent by Chuvakin. The Soviet Ambassador in Cairo first cabled that a massive Israeli offensive with heavy bombings had opened the war and later that the Arab armies had won some important victories. He repeated official announcements that dozens of Israeli planes and hundreds of Israeli tanks had been destroyed.

In the midst of Soviet confusion the cable from Rusk arrived for Gromyko. Kosygin, leader of the conservatives in the government, offered to reply to the United States over the hot line.

The hot line actually consists of four teletype machines, two in the Kremlin and two in the Pentagon. Each of the two capitals thus has a double line of communication with the other. One of each pair of teletypes is equipped with the Cyrillic alphabet, the other with Latin letters. By means of these machines the heads of the U.S.S.R. and the United States can confer with each other at any moment to prevent a world crisis from turning into a catastrophe. Since its installation on August 30, 1963, the hot line had never been used except for periodic checks on its efficiency, during which the Americans transmitted baseball scores to Moscow and received passages from Ivan Turgenev's *The Hunter's Sketches* in return.

But that morning the situation was serious enough for the Pentagon apparatus to come to life: "Premier Kosygin wishes to know whether or not President Johnson is available." The automatic key stopped for a moment, as if to catch its breath, and then resumed, without waiting for an answer to the first question: "Please transmit the following message to President Johnson. . . ."

Johnson ordered black coffee and hot rolls from the White House kitchen, then concentrated on the message, in which Kosygin acknowledged receipt of Rusk's cable and declared that the Soviet Union was strongly opposed to war and aggression. Kosygin put all the blame for starting the war on Israel and asked the United States to bring all its influence to bear on the Israeli government, warning of the disastrous results that could easily follow the Israeli action. The Soviet Union, Kosygin added, was on the side of the Arab people, who wanted peace. In the event that the United States took Israel's side in the conflict, the Soviet government would immediately order its armed forces to give military assistance to the Arab states to stop such imperialistic aggression.

It was a polite way of saying to the Americans: "We don't want war. It's better that both of us stay out of it."

At 8:17 Johnson met with the celebrated "Tuesday lunch" team of Rusk, McNamara, Walt Rostow, and Christian. They had also invited Undersecretary of State M. William Macomber, who handled State Department relations with Congress. After a brief discussion Rusk and Rostow drafted the President's reply to the Soviet message. Its substance was that Johnson sincerely regretted that war had broken out. The United States and the Soviet Union had to keep calm in the crisis and carefully study the situation. He asked that Moscow and Washington work together to obtain an immediate cease-fire and to restore peace. The United States and the Soviet Union should not intervene but should take action to end the hostilities as soon as possible. The two powers should propose a cease-fire to the Security Council and put heavy pressure on the warring nations to accept it. At 8:47 that message was sent to Moscow over the hot line.

The American leaders devoted the next half-hour to the

situation in the Middle East. Anxiety over world peace figured
in everything that was said, but the statesmen were actually
relieved, for the beginning of hostilities had rescued the United
States from an impossible dilemma and had freed it from its
commitments to Israel. The United States' plans for a diplomatic solution of the crisis had been going nowhere. Another
reason for relief was Kosygin's message, which showed that the
Soviet Union was not going to intervene.

At the breakfast meeting two decisions were reached: to
see to it that the nature and extent of the conflict were
confined to their present status and to make every effort on
the diplomatic level and through American-Israeli contacts to
end the fighting and find a mutually satisfactory solution to the
Arab-Israeli problem.

The President asked Walt Rostow to call "some of our
experts" over to the White House, specifically George Ball,
Clark Clifford, McGeorge Bundy, and Dean Acheson.

Ball, a former Undersecretary of State, was not at his home
in Chicago, and Rostow could not reach him, but he found
Clifford in his Washington office and summoned Bundy, who
had been John F. Kennedy's adviser on national security, from
his Ford Foundation office in New York. Acheson also received
an urgent summons. The war had only just begun when the
White House organized its team to prepare a peace program.

Johnson's message reached Kosygin at 3:47 P.M. Moscow
time and was received with appreciation. It reinforced Kosygin's position in his struggle with the Soviet military leaders.
From the beginning Kosygin had not favored creating another
tension area in the Middle East, as had the secret service and
the hard core of the party. (According to some sources, Party
Secretary Leonid Brezhnev had been one of the promoters of
that project and had involved Kosygin in the scheme of dis-
seminating false information in May 1967.) The "hawk" bloc
had thought the Vietnam war had paralyzed the United States
and would prevent it from taking an active role in the Middle
East. The much more cautious Kosygin wanted the Soviet

Union to avoid at whatever cost slipping into armed conflict. The Americans' moderate policy on June 5 was similar to Kosygin's own, and strengthened his position.

But the fighting was increasing in momentum. At noon Hod recognized that he would have to shout *Moked* again, this time against Iraq, Syria, and Jordan. In fact, Syrian MIGs, Jordanian Hunters, and Iraqi Tupolevs had appeared in Israeli skies and had bombed various towns and villages but without taking many lives. As soon as Hod gave the order, several Israeli squadrons took off in the direction of the Syrian, Iraqi, and Jordanian airfields and destroyed the enemy aviation.

Dayan also had to alter his orders to his troops and extend his fronts. The armored columns that he had thrown into the Sinai peninsula had not attacked the Gaza Strip, but the batteries of the Palestinian division there had begun a heavy bombardment of the nearby Israeli kibbutzim. Dayan had no choice but to order his forces to take the Gaza Strip.

At 11:00 A.M. the Jordanians began to rain shells on the Israeli sector of Jerusalem. Narkiss made a quick estimate of the scope of that attack and telephoned Mayor Kollek, "Get ready to be Mayor of a united Jerusalem." Rabin, from whom Narkiss had requested permission to launch a counterattack, refused it categorically. Consequently, Narkiss spent the whole morning on the telephone. At 12:30 P.M., he called the Deputy Chief of Staff for authorization to initiate a restricted attack in order to take some strategic objectives. "Nyet!" said Bar Lev.

Eventually, however, the situation changed. In the early afternoon, units of the Arab Legion attacked Government House, the Jerusalem headquarters of the U.N. observers. Then Narkiss received permission to counterattack, led the Jerusalem brigade to Government House, and after a brief skirmish recaptured it.

Nevertheless, Israel would have preferred not to extend its action against Jordan. But the Jordanians gave them no choice. Early in the afternoon Jordanian batteries shelled the air base of Ramat David in Galilee. To silence them the Israelis attacked Jordanian positions near the town of Jenin. A little later Jordan's Long Tom guns in Kalkilya shelled Tel Aviv, and the government authorized the use of planes against the Jordanian batteries and the capture of Kalkilya.

In Cairo the muffled rumble of the antiaircraft defense continued without interruption, but the people were not alarmed. June 5 was a fine, warm, sunny day. Not until 9:50 A.M. did the Cairo radio broadcast the first news of the fighting with its own peculiar brand of accuracy. At 10:30 an announcer who seemed beside himself with excitement shouted into the microphone: "Dear brothers, the first news of our victory! An official military source has just informed us that twenty-three enemy planes have been shot down."

A great wave of enthusiasm swept over Cairo. In buses, on the streets, and in factories, people kissed, threw their arms around one another, and chanted war slogans. Hysterical crowds ran through the streets, shouting: "Nasser! Nasser! On to Tel Aviv!" Men and boys snake-danced through the squares and down the center strips of the boulevards. Even the dignified members of the National Assembly abandoned their reserve and climbed up on their leather seats to shout and dance. Women screamed with joy on the rooftops and street corners.

The rejoicing lasted for hours; no one paid any attention to broadcast references to "the treacherous aggression of the enemy, which has attacked the U.A.R. from the air and on land and has bombed its airfields." All anyone heard was the number of planes shot down, which the radio numbered forty-two at 11:10, forty-four at 11:30, and seventy at 1:43 P.M.

The rumor spread that an Israeli plane had been shot down near the Nile. Gangs of young fanatics swarmed over Cairo looking for the flaming Jewish plane, but it was not to be found. One Israeli plane had indeed been hit, but over a little village in the delta. The inhabitants hacked to pieces the pilot, who had parachuted to earth.

Special police details made a clean sweep of the Jews in Cairo and Alexandria, arresting them in their homes, their shops, and in the streets. Two thousand Jews were living in

Egypt, of whom 350 were arrested and jailed within a few hours. Most were tortured.

In all other Arab capitals, mobs invaded the Jewish quarters in the ageless tradition of pogroms. In Aden, Tunis, Tripoli, and Rabat, Jews were beaten, their synagogues set afire, and their stores looted.

Nasser spent the entire morning in his office, poring over maps and studying military reports. The telephone kept him in touch with developments, but gave him no bad news, lest it depress him. Toward the end of the morning he wired King Hussein, "The Egyptian offensive expanded into Israeli territory after the Israeli attack was repulsed."

During the afternoon the joy of the mobs continued to increase. Israel had lost eighty-six planes, the radio reported, against only two Egyptian planes. It was not until 4:00 P.M. that an air force officer entered Nasser's office. "I have come to tell you," he said slowly, "that we no longer have an air force."

At 4:30 P.M. Kosygin received a message from De Gaulle over the "green line" connecting Moscow and Paris, the French counterpart of the hot line. De Gaulle expressed his great anxiety over world peace as a result of events in the Middle East. He restated his former proposal: an immediate conference among the four great powers to find a solution for the problems of that region and to force the warring parties to accept a cease-fire and to retire behind their frontiers.

A little later, while the politburo was still in session, Kosygin was informed that the Ambassador from the U.A.R. was asking to see him at once. Kosygin left the conference room to receive the Egyptian diplomat. In great excitement Mohamed Gourad Ghaleb sketched the military situation: the large number of Egyptian planes destroyed by Israel's surprise attack and overrunning of the Sinai front at several spots by armored columns that had penetrated deep into the desert. The government of the U.A.R. was asking the U.S.S.R. for help.

Kosygin replied that the U.S.S.R. was and always would be on the side of the Arabs. It would supply them with arms to replace those that had been lost and would do everything in its power to stop the fighting and to compel Israel to quit the territory it had seized. Nevertheless, the Soviet Premier gave Ghaleb to understand that the Soviet Union would not intervene militarily in the conflict.

It should be mentioned that Russia had never promised the Arabs any direct military assistance. In all the diplomatic conferences and exchanges of letters between Moscow and Cairo, the Russians had always let it be understood that they would undertake only to keep the United States neutral in the event of war and also to prevent it from intervening. Furthermore, the Egyptians had never asked for anything more.

On the evening of June 5, however, the Egyptian Ambassador left in a state of bitterness. He cabled to his government, "These people can think of nothing but saving their own skins."

When the politburo heard the bad news from Kosygin, it succumbed to the influence of the extremists and decided at once to issue a statement charging Israel with aggression and demanding that its army stop fighting and withdraw behind its own frontier. Even more serious was the Soviet leaders' decision to use the hot line to Washington once more to transmit a forcible note calling upon the Americans to force Israel to withdraw.

It was almost 7:00 P.M. in Moscow—noon in Washington— when the hot line began to hum for the second time that day with another message from Kosygin.* This time the message was less a letter than an ultimatum. Its text brought to mind the well-known messages that the Soviet Union had sent to Great Britain, France, and Israel during the Suez affair of November 5, 1956. The Soviet Union possessed the means of causing terrible destruction, said the message. If the Israeli forces did not withdraw to their side of the frontier, the Soviet armed forces would use appropriate means to put an end to Israeli aggression. The Soviet Union would not remain indifferent to such criminal aggression as it saw progressing with its own eyes.

* Information gathered at the White House.

This time the Soviet message caused considerable excitement and true anxiety in the White House. Once again the world was being threatened with a nuclear war that might break out at any moment. President Johnson kept calm, and with Walt Rostow, worked out a plan of action on two levels. First he acknowledged receipt of Kosygin's message, then he ordered all the units of the 6th Fleet to move toward the fighting zone.

Within a few minutes dozens of American warships and aircraft carriers were heading under full steam for the Sinai coast. It was a magnificent display of strength, and it had a solemn significance. The outlines of the flotilla showed clearly on the radar screens of the Soviet ships patrolling the Mediterranean, causing the commanders of the Soviet fleet to cable Moscow at once every detail of the menacing activity of the American ships.

That was just what the President of the United States wanted. In his own handwriting he drafted, with Rostow's help, a message to the Soviet Premier, reminding him of the commitments of the American government to safeguard the integrity and the independence of Israel. The Americans were determined to honor their obligations, he wrote, and they wished the Soviet Union to do the same. The two powers should take a cautious, sober stand and should act in a constructive fashion to put an end to the fighting in that part of the world. Johnson's message reached the Kremlin within moments after the wave of cables from all sources of military information reporting on the 6th Fleet's progress toward the combat zone.

The Soviet Union understood. Any military action on its part would bring an immediate reaction from the 6th Fleet—and a confrontation between the two supreme powers.

Never since the Cuban crisis had the world come so close to nuclear war.

President Johnson refused to risk nuclear war simply to please Israel. All through the morning the White House had been swamped with cables reporting the astonishing triumphs of the Israeli army and making it clear that the Arabs would ask for help from their chief ally, the Kremlin. Johnson knew that if he could keep the Soviet Union neutral and prevent it from intervening in the war, the Israeli defeat of the Arabs would appear, in the eyes of the world, a terrible defeat of the U.S.S.R., even more humiliating than the one that had resulted from the Cuban crisis of 1962. The whole world would take note that the same Russians who had been encouraging the Arabs all along had turned tail as soon as the guns had started to bark. The Arab world, having lost the war, would believe that it had been grossly deceived by Moscow. In the last analysis the big losers in the Arab-Israeli war would be the Russians. Johnson had every reason to hope for an Israeli victory.

At the same moment when those dramatic messages were flying between the Kremlin and the White House, a "technical" accident occurred in the State Department, the seriousness of which could not be gauged until after the ultrasecret messages were published. At 12:30 State Department's press officer Robert McCloskey held a press conference on the Middle East. "What is the United States' attitude toward that conflict?" asked one reporter.

After a moment's thought, McCloskey answered, "We are neutral in word, thought, and deed."

There was a story behind that statement. When the first reports of the Israeli successes had reached the State Department very early that morning, several officials had whooped with joy. "Gentlemen, gentlemen," Eugene Rostow had cautioned with a broad smile, "do not forget that we are neutral in word, thought, and deed." McCloskey remembered and repeated that remark, with no idea that he had dropped a bombshell.

Immediately angry phone calls and tens of thousands of protest telegrams from American Jewish and non-Jewish leaders descended on the White House. McCloskey's statement had been interpreted not only as a declaration of neutrality but also as a confession of indifference and isolationism as far as the Middle East was concerned.

When Johnson heard of it, he flew into one of his terrible rages, for McCloskey's statement had been published just as the Russians were threatening to intervene against Israel. They could deduce from it that the United States was indifferent to the conflict and could pull the trigger in the belief that the United States would take no action. Johnson decided to issue a statement on the subject at once.

Christian ran to collect the reporters. "McCloskey," he explained, "did not mean that the United States is neutral and indifferent, simply not a belligerent." But that disclaimer did not satisfy Johnson. He gave Rusk the responsibility for reiterating the denial to the press. Rusk explained that the word "neutrality"—a great concept of international law—is not an expression of indifference. "Indeed," he said, "indifference is not permitted." The incident was closed.

After eight hours of debate, the meeting of the politburo ended. The strong reaction of the United States to Kosygin's message had put an end to any thought of Soviet military intervention in the future. The conservatives had won the day. At the close of the session two decisions were taken. The first was that the Soviet Union would vote in the United Nations for no cease-fire resolution that did not include an appeal to the belligerents to withdraw their troops from occupied territories. Such an injunction would, of course, affect only Israel, whose army had penetrated into Egyptian territory. The second decision—to break off diplomatic relations with Israel if that country pursued its policy of aggression—was not made public.

Disruption of diplomatic relations must be a spectacular move, and to make it effective all the countries of the Communist bloc would have to subscribe to it. The leaders of the Soviet Union were not sure that the peoples' democracies would all abide by such a decision from the Kremlin. For a long time Romania had been following its own policy, and Poland was timidly imitating it. In order to be certain that all states of the socialist bloc would follow Moscow's directives, it was decided to summon their leaders to a top-secret emergency meeting in the Soviet capital.

Goldberg proposed a simple cease-fire in the Security Council, but after a few minutes the delegate from India burst into President Tabor's office, sent by the Arabs. "The Arabs," he said, "will not accept a cease-fire resolution that does not include a demand for immediate withdrawal of troops."

Goldberg objected: "A return to the positions previous to those of June 4 means acknowledgement of the blockade of 'Aqaba. If a return to the *status quo ante* is desired, then the situation must be restored to what it was before the crisis began—namely, freedom of navigation in the gulf of 'Aqaba and the restoration of the U.N. Emergency Force in the Sinai peninsula."

"No," said the Arabs. "We demand a cease-fire and the withdrawal of the Israelis."

Fedorenko was helpless. He did not know the true situation in the Middle East. His government had sent him strict orders to support the Arab position, and the Arabs were being obstinate. About 5:00 P.M. an Israeli diplomat, Bar Romi, telephoned Finger to say, "We are continuing to advance, and this time we're picking up more Egyptian shoes than in 1956."

The Arabs adopted the desperate expedient of spreading rumors in the corridors of the U.N. building that the Egyptians had advanced deep into Israeli territory in the southern part of the Negev and were about to effect a junction with the Jordanians from the other side of the Israeli desert. Elat was as good as cut off, the Arabs said. Their strategy was plain: Egypt wanted the world to believe that its army too had conquered some enemy territory, so that everyone would be satisfied with the plan for the withdrawal of troops, believing that the Israelis would evacuate the Sinai peninsula and the Egyptians the Negev.

Fedorenko, ill at ease, finally proposed that the Council postpone the end of its deliberations until the next day. The Americans were astonished. Fedorenko had just made a serious mistake. Had he been a little less rigid, he could have worked out with them a program to resolve the issue, and the Council could have voted on it that evening. But he preferred to wait, unaware that every passing minute added to the successes of the Israelis and the losses of the Arabs.

Fedorenko, it appeared, did not know the meaning of the expression "lightning war."

Night had already fallen on the Rafah crossroads. Amos Katz tried to climb down from his tank but felt that he could not make it. His sprained ankle caused him frightful pain every time he put his foot down. He did climb out of the turret to lie down on the still-hot steel—and rolled off onto the road. Using an antenna as a cane, he limped toward his men. It was 9:00 at night. The fighting was still going on all around. Suddenly his jeep, which had been missing since morning, stopped close to him. Katz opened his eyes wide. "Where did you come from?" he asked the driver. "How did you find me?"

The driver lost no time in telling what had happened to him. All day long he had been evacuating dead and wounded under enemy fire, and as soon as he had finished he had started to look for his captain. "Captain," he said, "in five minutes I'll have tea ready."

Katz called to the battalion commander. "Will you take tea with me?" The Colonel looked at Amos as if he had lost his mind. Tea? Here? Then? But five minutes later the two officers and the driver were sitting in the middle of the road, sipping strong, sweet tea.

Katz lay down by the caterpillar tread of his tank. Fifteen yards away, twenty Egyptian soldiers were hiding in a camou-flaged bunker that no one had noticed. They could have crept out during the night and cut the throat of everyone around. But they did not.

Meanwhile, the mechanized infantry and the tanks under Colonel Shmuel's command had completely captured and cleaned out the road to El ʿArîsh. Beyond El ʿArîsh the road led straight to the Suez canal.

That same night Sharon's division attacked Abu ʿAweighîla

in the most sophisticated operation of the Six-Day War. Abu 'Aweighîla was taken by a combination of artillery, tanks, an infantry assault on the flank, and paratroop commandos in the rear.

The road junctions of Rafah and Abu 'Aweighîla were open to traffic. The locks on the doors to the Sinai peninsula had been blown up. The first phase of the operational plan had been accomplished.

Guy Jacobson spent the night near the Egyptian trenches at Bîr Lahfân, which he had reached with Yoffe's division. The tanks had crossed dunes considered impassable and were preparing to attack.

All day long Arie Ben Or's squadron had been bombing radar stations, artillery positions, and Egyptian convoys in the Sinai desert.

That first day had been one of doubt and distress for the entire nation of Israel. The radio had broadcast only Arab announcements of victories; the Voice of Israel had preserved an ominous silence. It was not until 1:00 A.M. on June 6 that Rabin and Hod reported the results of the fighting: 400 enemy planes destroyed in Egypt, Syria, Jordan, and Iraq and 19 Israeli planes lost. Rabin announced that the ground army had taken Khan Yunis, Rafah, Shiekh Zued, and El 'Arîsh.

At 3:00 A.M. Eban left on a Herald for Athens with his secretary, planning to go from there to New York, in order to take part in the Security Council debates. The Israeli war cabinet met. The Jordanians were continuing to attack. It was decided that the Israeli army should mount an offensive against Jordan and conquer all the western part of that country.

On the Egyptian front the next step in the offensive was coming up: the capture of Sharm el Sheikh and the total destruction of the Egyptian army in the Sinai peninsula.

•

"TOP SECRET MECCA"

THE TANKS UNDER the command of Tal, Yoffe, and Sharon charged westward into the vast, flat, empty spaces of the Sinai desert, to engage, on that huge battlefield, the bulk of the Egyptian tanks. To break through, they had to pierce the fortified defense lines behind the positions they had taken on June 5—the dug-in Egyptian 3rd Division, which was strung out between Bîr Lahfân on the north and Gebel Libni on the south.

At daybreak Tal's division, which had reached El 'Arîsh, split into two columns. One took the coast road toward the Suez canal; the other, Shmuel's armored brigade, moved south toward Bîr Lahfân. Yoffe's division was already at the Bîr Lahfân crossroads, but it had to attack and destroy the enemy tanks positioned in the surrounding area.

A faint rosy light was nibbling at the black sky when Jacobson looked at his watch. It was 3:30 A.M. He clambered into his tank and drove it to the crest of a little hill to survey the area. He had not closed his eyes all night. His battalion had set up a barrage at the Bîr Lahfân junction, in order to stop Egyptian reinforcements from reaching El 'Arîsh or Abu 'Aweighîla, where Tal and Sharon were fighting. All night long the battalion had been fighting off a column of Egyptian tanks, which had attacked the roadblock.

From the top of the hill Jacobson looked down into a bare,

225

uninviting valley still partially veiled by handfuls of mist, through which he could see sixty stationary Egyptian tanks in hiding. They saw him as well, and their first shell hit his tank, though without causing great damage. Jacobson returned to alert his company. His baptism by fire was beginning.

Thirty-three Israeli Centurion tanks hurled themselves on the sixty Egyptian tanks. Jacobson remembered what Colonel Iska, his brigade commander, had said: "The Egyptian leaders have roused their soldiers to the level of hysteria. If we can smash them right at the start, their morale will collapse. The very first blow will decide the issue." Before the skirmish was over Jacobson had destroyed six enemy tanks. The company as a whole had hit twenty-four. The other thirty fled.

But the Israelis had no time to rest on their laurels, for right away they received orders to dash into the attack on Gebel Libni. Jacobson led them down the road to the infantry trenches, which they demolished. Then eighteen Egyptian tanks began a counterattack. It was a short battle, however, for all the enemy tanks were destroyed; Jacobson himself disposed of three.

At 7:37 A.M. June 6, the Cairo radio broadcast a special bulletin:

> Fellow citizens!
> The Supreme Command of the armed forces announces that it has definite proof that the American and British air forces are participating in Israel's aggression.
>
> We have proof that several British and American aircraft carriers are conducting wide scale operations off the coast of Israel.
>
> On the Egyptian front British and American planes are providing air coverage for the Israeli ground forces.
>
> On the Jordanian front those planes are engaged in direct attacks, as the radar stations have proved.

That bulletin was the result of feverish consultations between Cairo and Amman, which had begun the day before when the radar station at Ajlun in Jordan had picked up waves of Israeli airplanes leaving to attack the Egyptian airfields. The number of planes, as well as the frequency of the raids, had convinced the Jordanians that hundreds of foreign planes were fighting alongside the Israelis.

On the evening of June 5, that information had been transmitted to Cairo. Either Nasser actually did believe it, or he saw in it a plausible explanation for the losses he had suffered. During the night rumors had spread in Cairo and Amman that British and American planes were helping the Zionist aggressors. At midnight Ambassador Nolte cabled Washington, "You should take immediate action to stop these false reports."

But it was too late to halt the spread of the misinformation. At 4:30 A.M. Israeli engineers intercepted a wireless conversation between Cairo and Amman, which had been initiated by Nasser, who was speaking directly to Hussein in person.

"Shall we say that the United States is fighting on Israel's side?" Nasser asked. "Shall we say the United States and England or only the United States?"

"The United States and England," Hussein replied.

"All our troops are in action," Nasser went on, "and the fighting continues on all fronts. We have suffered some losses, but it does not matter. Allah is with us. . . . I am going to issue a statement, and so are you. We will do what is necessary to get the Syrians also to announce that British and American planes from carrier bases are attacking us. We are going to emphasize that point."

"That's all right," said Hussein.

Since morning, the Egyptian, Syrian, and Jordanian radio stations had been transmitting broadsides of abuse against the United States and Great Britain for their "participation" in Israel's aggression.

In Washington and London official spokesmen emphatically denied the charges, but in the Cairo streets a furious mob went after every American it could find. In Alexandria a mob set fire to the American consulate and to the new cultural center; the American Consul and his staff were locked in a stinking cellar. From one end of the Arab world to the other, violent

demonstrations were directed against England and the United
States; and detachments of the police and soldiers were hard
put to control mobs determined to wreck havoc on the diplomatic and cultural establishments of the two nations.

Egypt, Syria, Algeria, Yemen, Iraq, and Sudan severed diplomatic relations with the United States. The Arab countries
announced the end of oil sales to the West because of the
"shameful aggression of the Anglo-Saxons."

In Moscow the eleven members of the politburo met again in
a long, dreary session. They were no longer under any illusions.
The air forces of the Arab states had been annihilated, their
airfields destroyed, and the Egyptian and Jordanian frontiers
overrun.

The conference table was hidden under piles of cables from
the United Nations. The Soviet mission to the "big glass box"
was exasperated by the Arabs' refusal to consent to a cease-fire
unaccompanied by the withdrawal of Israeli troops. Time was
working against them, and every passing hour was increasing
their losses and those of their Soviet protectors.

About noon, the Egyptian, Syrian, and Jordanian ambassadors in Moscow appeared at the Foreign Ministry, with messages from their governments denouncing the participation of
Great Britain and the United States in the fighting.

A surprise was awaiting them. The Soviets reacted vigorously to their accusations. "We know," the ambassadors were
told, "that there is no American or British participation in the
fighting. The Soviet Union will not permit itself to be drawn
into a conflict with the United States on charges that have
absolutely no basis in truth."

The Arab ambassadors called a press conference and repeated their charges against London and Washington to the
correspondents, but Tass received orders from on high not to
publish the story.

Egyptian Ambassador Ghaleb was received once more by
Kosygin, whose position had not changed--the U.S.S.R. would
furnish arms to the Arab countries on an emergency basis and

would lend assistance in the diplomatic arena; the Arabs and the Soviet Union should work together in the United Nations for a cease-fire.

Kosygin sent another message to Washington, proposing that Johnson support a resolution in the Security Council for a cease-fire and a withdrawal of troops. Johnson telephoned Goldberg and then cabled Moscow his agreement, provided that the resolution also included freedom of navigation in the strait of Tiran and restoration of the U.N. Emergency Force to its previous stations.

At almost the same moment another cable from Fedorenko reached the Kremlin, reporting that the Arabs were fiercely opposed to any resolution of that sort and were still demanding unconditional withdrawal.

All through the previous day, Jordanian shells had been falling on Jerusalem. By nightfall the paratroopers had arrived to conquer the Old City and thus to reunite Jerusalem. At 2:00 A.M. they launched an assault on the fortified Jordanian positions in the Sheikh Jarrah quarter, on Ammunition hill, and at the Police Training School.

A paratrooper burst into the Magen David Adom station (the Israeli equivalent of the Red Cross) with an urgent request for an ambulance. "We have a lot of wounded," he explained.

"I'll go," said Esther Arditi.

Esther, who had left her children in the care of a friend and gone to work at the station, drove an ambulance into the section of Jerusalem that was being shelled; there she gave injections of morphine, applied tourniquets, and bandaged wounds while bullets whistled and shells fell all around her. The paratroop surgeon, Dr. Jacob, told her to leave: "This is no place for a woman." But, once he had seen how efficient the tiny nurse was, he changed his mind. "You've come to me like an angel from heaven," he said, not knowing that he had just coined a term that would be engraved forever in the memory of the wounded: "the white angel of the paratroopers."

Meanwhile, violent fighting was going on on Ammunition hill, in the northern sector of the city. Esther climbed into a half-track that was heading for that battlefield and arrived breathless at the Rockefeller Museum, where the Israeli flag had just been hoisted.

Dayan had spent the entire morning in the operations room at General Staff headquarters. The fighting on the Egyptian front was progressing more or less as expected, but the battle with the Jordanians was an unplanned campaign dependent upon the considerable inventiveness of the Israeli army, which was fighting more and more on Jordanian soil in response to provocation.

That morning Dayan had ordered the occupation of all western Jordan: the territory between the eastern border of Israel and the Jordan river. On the other hand, despite the recommendations of some ministers, he had refused to launch an assault on the Old City. His objections were based on political considerations; he wanted to avoid destruction of the holy places so as not to arouse world criticism; there were also military considerations: He wanted to keep losses small. An assault on the Old City might falter before heavy fire from the Arab Legion positions, which dominated the entire area. The perfect solution would be for the Old City to surrender without a struggle.

Dayan went to Mount Scopus as soon as the road that linked it with Israeli territory had been captured. To Narkiss and the other officers with him, he said: "We must encircle the Old City and take all the positions surrounding it, so that it will fall without a blow being struck. Put that into immediate execution!"

That morning the Fougas were no longer operating on the Egyptian front in Sinai: they were attacking on the newly opened front against Jordan. There was heavy fighting all around Jerusalem, for the Arab Legion was dispatching reinforcements of tanks, half-tracks, ammunition convoys, and infantry into western Jordan. Ben Or led a Fouga formation in an attack on a convoy near Jericho. The Jordanian antiaircraft defense went after the subsonic Fougas, which were diving tirelessly on the tanks; many tanks were damaged. But finally the Fouga pilots ran out of ammunition, and Ben Or told them to return to their base. "I will stay on here," he said, "to direct the formations that are coming to join us."

He kept circling over the enemy convoy, even though he was out of ammunition and exposed to the antiaircraft fire that hit him occasionally but did no serious damage. Three new formations arrived one after the other, and Ben Or, still in the air, gave them precise instructions on the tactics to follow in their attacks on the convoy.

The operation was a complete success, and Ben Or later received the highest military decoration of the Israeli army for his direction of the battle of Jericho.

That day Gaza fell. Amos Katz and his tanks, along with the paratroopers, had made a rash attack on the very center of the town and had then fanned out all through it. Katz had also been in the fighting at Rafah and Khan Yunis, where pockets of resistance had had to be reduced. His tank had been hit twice during these skirmishes and had been blown up. Each time, however, he had managed to jump out at the last minute and to clamber into another. Each time his men had said, "They got the captain."

After the fighting was over, the Israeli soldiers could grin at the enormous signboard over the Gaza motion-picture theater, advertising a coming film significantly entitled *Help!*

At dawn a mechanized brigade attacked western Jordan and took several villages around Jerusalem; in the afternoon it conquered Ramallah, the "white city."

Passengers in the KLM plane over the Atlantic en route to New York lined up to shake Eban's hand. Radio messages for the Israeli Minister kept coming in. At 3:30 P.M. there was one from Rafael, Israeli representative in the United Nations: "This very evening you are to address the Security Council."

The Dutch stewardesses invited Eban to use the tiny dressing room where they usually changed their uniforms and makeup and took their meals. He sat down at the table there and buried himself in his papers, drafting in that airborne boudoir high above the Atlantic the speech he would make that evening, one of the best of his career.

At 4:00 P.M. Kosygin exchanged messages with De Gaulle. The French President had repeated his eternal proposal for a conference among the four great powers and had reasserted his support of a resolution in the Security Council calling for an immediate cease-fire and withdrawal of troops.

But by the end of the afternoon, the U.S.S.R. was facing facts. It could no longer support demands for a continuation of the war from the side that was suffering increasingly severe defeats. The Kremlin decided on an about-face. Kosygin sent a message to the White House, declaring that the Soviet Union would vote for an unconditional cease-fire.

The message caused considerable astonishment in Washington. It was reminiscent of Nikita Khrushchev's capitulation in the Cuban crisis. It was also typical of Soviet policy, which ventures to the very brink of the abyss and then backtracks. The Soviet Union's acceptance of the original American proposal came to the attention of the United States government even before Fedorenko learned of it. In a telephone call the White House informed Goldberg that the Soviets would endorse an unconditional cease-fire.

At 7:10 P.M. New York time—2:10 A.M. Moscow time—the Security Council unanimously approved one of the shortest resolutions in its history:

> The Security Council, noting the oral report of the Secretary General in this situation, having heard the statements made in the Council, concerned at the outbreak of fighting and with the menacing situation in the Near East,
>
> 1. Calls upon the governments concerned as a first step to take forthwith all measures for an immediate cease-fire and for a cessation of all military activities in the area;

2. Requests the Secretary General to keep the Council promptly and currently informed on the situation.

In his speech Eban praised the vote and declared that Israel would comply on condition that the other side also complied. When the roll was called, the Arab representatives, however, declared that they would not accept the resolution.

The war continued.

It was dusk when the armored columns of Tal and Yoffe reached Gebel Libni. There too the fighting ended in the same final tableau: dozens of Egyptian tanks burning on the sands and throngs of dazed soldiers running barefoot over the dunes and along the roads toward the canal.

Tal decided to give Colonel Shmuel's brigade a little rest, for it had fought continuously since the beginning of the war. But just then a helicopter landed nearby, and the commander of the southern front emerged. Gavish rushed up to Tal. "The Egyptian high command," he said, "has just ordered its troops to fall back to the second line of defense. We've got to go after them at once."

The chase started up again. Shmuel turned west toward the canal; Iska's brigade headed south toward the enormous camps at Bîr Hasana and Bîr el Thamâda. Sharon had already mopped up the territory south of Abu 'Aweighîla. The Israeli army's shock troops had broken Egyptian resistance in the eastern part of the Sinai peninsula and had destroyed the armored units intended to stop them.

On the next day would come the great drive into the vast expanses of the desert, the largest battlefield in the Middle East.

In Washington, preparations were already being made for the postwar settlement. That afternoon Walt Rostow called Evron. "You're winning," he said, "but you ought to know that now the greatest danger for Israel could be the overweening pride in your victory. You ought to begin to give serious thought to the refugee problem, if you want peace in the Middle East."

At the White House, Bundy had organized a little team of specialists to prepare reports that would be helpful in arranging a peace settlement and also policy suggestions for the United States to consider in dealing with the Middle East after the war.

Another team had been organized in the Pentagon to prepare at once a detailed report on the same area and to suggest solutions for the Arab-Israeli problem. The task was assigned to a two-star general whose vast knowledge of the Middle East was summed up in a vague notion that somewhere in that part of the world there is a city called Mecca that is holy to the Muslims. He therefore decided to call his report "Top Secret Mecca."

Fortunately, his experts were better acquainted with geography. They split into small working groups, each of which studied one of the many problems: refugees, water, disputes between the Israeli and Arab governments, composition and policy of the various governments, major political problems, and influences and interests of foreign powers.

The experts were given only forty-eight hours in which to produce their reports. "Look at the speed of those damn Jews," the General growled. "Forty-eight hours is plenty of time."

•

"JERUSALEM THE GOLDEN"

AT 8:30 A.M. on June 7, Israeli fighter planes dove on the last armed position still in the hands of the Jordanians—Augusta Victoria, on the eastern heights dominating the city of Jerusalem. Two battalions of paratroopers took it in one attack; then in the same drive they hit the Old City on all sides, penetrating the walls through St. Stephen's Gate. Leading them was brigade commander Colonel Mordechai ("Motta") Gur in an open half-track.

At 10:00 the first paratroopers reached the Wailing Wall. After two thousand years the Jewish people had recovered the City of David, their eternal capital.

Esther Arditi was in one of the half-tracks that were hauling the paratroopers into the Old City. Her clothes were so torn and dirty and covered with blood that she could hardly be recognized. Reaching the heart of the Old City with the first of the soldiers, she had her first sight of the Wall. She was not a practicing Jew, not even a believer, but she pressed her entire body against the huge cold stones of the Wall and wept like a child.

A few moments after the Old City had been captured, marine torpedo-boats and paratroopers captured Sharm el Sheikh and hoisted the blue-and-white flag above the dirty, neglected little fortress over which the people of Israel had gone to war.

Naomi Shemer, author of the song, "Jerusalem the Golden," was then at El 'Arîsh to sing for the soldiers. When she heard a radio report of the capture of the Old City, she changed the words of the song; when she stepped up on the platform to face the sea of soldiers, she sang a new stanza, which cheers and applause almost drowned out:

> *We have come back to the deep wells*
> *To the market place again.*
> *The trumpet sounds on the Mount of the Temple*
> *In the Old City.*
> *In the caverns of the cliff*
> *Glitter a thousand suns.*
> *We shall go down to the Dead Sea again*
> *By the road to Jericho.*

"Jerusalem the Golden" became the anthem of the Six-Day War.

The third day of the war was to be marked by a wild tank ride into the Sinai peninsula. The tanks had two objectives: to wipe out the Egyptian tanks concentrated there and to block the Egyptian escape to the other side of the canal, thus turning Sinai into a gigantic trap for Nasser's generals.

Shmuel's tanks rolled toward the west, sweeping over Bîr Hamma and winning a big battle near Bîr Gifgâfa airfield. Sharon's division went south toward Nakhl, where the remains of General Shazli's armored division and the 6th Division were regrouping. Yoffe's division also moved south in the direction of Bîr Hasana and Bîr el Thamâda.

Jacobson's company was approaching the enormous Bîr el Thamâda base, located in a hill-rimmed hollow, where the Egyptians had built a jet airfield, infantry bases, and a tank school. The Israeli Centurions attacked once more.

As soon as the fighting ended, the deputy divisional commander brought his helicopter down near Colonel Abraham, Jacobson's commander. "Take your tanks," he said, "and proceed forward with all speed toward Mitla pass. The Egyptians are in flight. We must block their way."

Abraham gathered a dozen tanks, two jeeps, and two groups of mechanized infantry, and headed for the Mitla pass. Guy and some of his company's tanks went with them.

Egyptian soldiers with rifles slung across their backs were walking on both sides of the road, looking at the Israeli tanks with complete indifference. Later the little Israeli unit encountered a long Egyptian column composed of all kinds of vehicles, trucks, half-tracks, tanks, and jeeps. The convoy was also proceeding toward the Mitla pass but did not react to the passage of the Israeli tanks. Presently the Israelis were installed in a frightful traffic jam, surrounded by hundreds of vehicles and thousands of soldiers—a defeated and demoralized army fleeing toward Egypt. "It would take only one officer, even a noncom," thought Jacobson, "to rally those men and attack us—if he had the guts. There are enough of them to wipe us out."

But the Egyptians had had enough of fighting. Even when engine trouble halted Jacobson's own tank, no Egyptian made any attempt to capture him. He hitched his Centurion to another, which towed it through the huge Egyptian convoy.

Beside the road lay the hulks of tanks and trucks. Israeli planes had passed over there.

That evening nine Israeli tanks reached the Mitla pass on their last drops of gasoline. The pass, a narrow gully between high hills and cave-ridden cliffs, was swarming with Egyptian soldiers, for it was the only route by which the Egyptians could reach the Suez canal and safety.

The Israeli tanks set fire to two Egyptian trucks that were blocking the way. The flames leaped into the sky, followed by terrific booms, for one of the trucks had been loaded with explosives. All around Egyptian soldiers were hidden in the caves shouting curses at the Jews. Some Egyptian tanks tried to cross the barrage and were hit. The nine Israeli tanks had halted the whole enormous convoy and closed the Mitla pass.

In the midst of the monstrous traffic jam, Lieutenant

Ovadia's tank stopped because of engine trouble. From time to time the men in it fired on little bands of Egyptians who attacked them. Then a tall man limped up to the tank. "I want to surrender," he said in excellent English.

"Who are you?" asked the astonished lieutenant.

"General Salah Yakut, commander in chief of the Egyptian artillery."

At the end of that afternoon of June 7, Nasser summonded the Soviet Ambassador in Cairo. Podyedyeev saw before him a desperate man. "Please ask your government," Nasser said, "to take immediate steps to stop the fighting in the Sinai peninsula. The Israeli pressure on our troops is enormous, and we cannot hold out much longer."

Podyedyeev cabled Nasser's request to Moscow. Kosygin made contact with Johnson over the hot line at once. There was no time for diplomatic protocol or evasions. Kosygin laid his cards on the table; he quoted Nasser's appeal word for word. "You must stop the Israelis," Kosygin said. "The cease-fire must be put into effect at once." Johnson's answer reached him quickly. The President of the United States declared that he had no absolute power over the Israelis but that the United States was ready to support a resolution in the Security Council setting an exact time for the application of the cease-fire in the whole Sinai region.

In the big glass box in New York, Fedorenko hurried to Tabor's office and demanded an emergency session of the Security Council. Once it had convened, he excitedly demanded an immediate vote on the cease-fire. Goldberg could not resist teasing his Russian colleague, reminding him that two weeks earlier, when other nations had asked for an emergency session of the Council to discuss the Middle Eastern situation, Fedorenko had opposed it on the grounds that there was no hurry.

Finally, the Security Council unanimously approved the Soviet resolution, which demanded that both sides cease firing at 8:00 P.M. Greenwich time. Then, to the utter astonishment and consternation of the Soviet delegation, the delegate from

Egypt declared that his country would not heed the demand for a cease-fire.

In Tel Aviv Ambassador Chuvakin handed Tekoa an urgent message from the Soviet government. The Soviet Union, it said, would sever diplomatic relations with Israel if the Israeli army did not end the fighting at once. The Israeli government's response to that threat was an ironic sigh of relief, for the U.S.S.R. had as much as said that it would not intervene militarily in the Middle East.

A bizarre situation was developing in the middle of the Mediterranean. For several days the Soviet ships there had been clinging like leeches to the ships of the American 6th Fleet, which was cruising in open waters. At times some of the Russian destroyers had come within a few yards of the American aircraft carriers. As one American officer said, "It seemed as if all one had to do to touch a Russian ship was to stick out a finger." Russian officers equipped with long binoculars constantly scrutinized every movement on board the American vessels, and the enormous swaying antennae on some of the Soviet decks indicated that all ears were eavesdropping on conversations. It was the same with the Americans. This unpeaceful coexistence caused the United States some anxiety. There was fear of a local incident that might have endless repercussions. Strict orders were cabled to the Yankee captains: "Keep cool. Don't give them any provocation!"

But the patience of one of those captains came to an end at last. He had been cruising along the shores of Crete for five days when a Soviet missile-launching cruiser started to maneuver among the American ships. The officer sent a message to the Soviet captain:

> You are in a zone where our ships are performing maneuvers, and you are hindering our movements. You are therefore violating the terms of the international agreements on freedom of movement in open water. In thirty minutes my ships will be fanning out in various directions. If you are still in our zone then, you will be responsible for whatever serious consequences may ensue.

As soon as the cruiser received that message, it turned around and steamed off at full speed.

On the evening of June 7, the Israeli units completed their conquest of western Jordan and were in pursuit of the columns of the Arab Legion that had crossed the Jordan river. In Washington, panic-stricken officials deluged the Israeli diplomats with messages: "Are you out of your mind? Where are you going? To Amman? Are you going to dethrone Hussein?"

The Israeli army had no intention either of going to Amman or of depriving Hussein of his crown. The fighting was over. The Jordanian government announced that it would accept the cease-fire.

In the Sinai peninsula some of the greatest tank battles in history were going on. In the evening the Israeli vanguard reached its objectives. In the north the Israelis had reached Români on the coastal road about ten miles from the canal. In the center they held the road to the canal from Bîr Gifgâfa, about thirty miles from Ismailia. In the south they had blocked the Mitla pass. All exits from the peninsula were therefore sealed, and the Egyptians were caught.

In Tel Aviv, Dayan told a press conference: "Israel has attained its political and military objectives. The strait of Tiran has been opened to international navigation, and every country has a right to use it—including Egypt," he added as everyone laughed.

He recalled his position in respect to the Suez canal: "The Israeli army can reach the canal without any difficulty, but that is not our objective. What is important for us is Sharm el Sheikh. So why should we push on to Suez and get ourselves involved in international problems when it is of no interest to us?"

In Beirut, Lebanese Chief of Staff Émile Bustani was summoned about midnight to the house of Prime Minister Rashid Karame. "We ought to enter the war in order to reduce the pressure on the Syrian and the Egyptian fronts," Karame said.

Bustani refused. He had only 12,000 men in his army, and he knew he did not stand a chance against the Israelis. When Karame lost his temper and threatened Bustani with punishment, the Chief of Staff replied: "When you wear this uniform, then you will be free to decide on the suicide of the Lebanese army. So long as I wear it, I will not do that."

The argument grew into a fierce quarrel. Lebanon is the most advanced of the Middle Eastern countries, but it is also militarily the weakest. Bustani was convinced that war with Israel would be a national disaster, but that was not his only difference of opinion with Karame. The Chief of Staff was a Maronite Christian, whereas the Prime Minister was a Muslim who felt great loyalty toward other Muslim countries. Their relations were almost completely ruptured that night, and Bustani even threatened Karame with house arrest.

Early in the morning an appeal was made to President Charles Helou, also a Maronite Christian, who settled the quarrel in Bustani's favor. Half the Lebanese army was sent to the frontier to repel a possible attack from the Israelis; the other half was stationed in the nerve centers of the cities, in order to prevent any trouble from Muslims who were demanding an attack on Israel.

Radio Beirut decreed a "mobilization of spirits" against the Zionist aggressors, but the Lebanese army would not go to war.

•

JOHNSON: "IT'S WORLD WAR III"

THROUGH BROADCASTS FROM the Voice of Israel and the BBC, the crew of *Dolphin,* which had been forgotten at Massawa, learned of the capture of Sharm el Sheikh. The men were deeply disappointed. "If I'd known that would happen," complained one old salt, "I would have volunteered for some other kind of mission. Now we've missed all the fun."

But on the morning of June 8, the long-awaited orders finally arrived. *Dolphin* was to set out at once for Elat, passing through the strait of Tiran.

A news flash from Sinai was received in the operations room of Israeli General Staff headquarters: The first Israeli units had reached El Qantara, had destroyed the Egyptian tanks there, and had gone all the way to the banks of the canal. Dayan was annoyed. Just the day before he had told the press that he wanted no repetition of the mistake of 1956. Furthermore, he was afraid that the Israeli forces on the canal would suffer heavy losses, for they were exposed to enemy attacks from the west and the south. But when he learned that other Israeli armored units were advancing toward the canal over two other roads—from the Mitla pass and Bîr Gifgâfa—he relaxed and ordered the conquest of the entire peninsula, including the eastern bank of the canal.

At daybreak Amos Katz was ordered to drive toward the canal along the coastal road. He had only five tanks left; all the others had scattered in different directions during the last days' fighting. But, with his excellent organizational sense, he picked up some auxiliary tanks and added them to his company. At El 'Arîsh he "borrowed" two tanks from another company, and a little farther west he swiped a third. By the time he reached El Qantara that night he was leading eleven tanks of all the various types that the Israeli army possessed.

The knot of Israeli tanks in the Mitla pass had fought all night against superior numbers of Egyptians but had been able to prevent many Egyptian tanks from the center of the peninsula, as well as the reinforcements being rushed to the Egyptians from the western bank of the canal, from using the pass. Jacobson's men had had no sleep since the war had begun and were so exhausted that they reeled in their turrets like drunken men. The night had been terrifying, as sallies from the dark hills and the caves had kept them on tenterhooks; all around them were the shooting flames from burning tanks and trucks and the rumble and roar of artillery.

The first Israeli reinforcements arrived at dawn, after having passed through desolate territory littered with tanks and trucks that had tried to clamber over the sheer rock of the cliffs and hills in order to break the roadblock from the rear and had been trapped in the sand and stalled.

A fresh brigade from Yoffe's division passed near Jacobson's tanks, crossed the mouth of the Mitla pass, and proceeded toward the Suez canal. Jacobson was ordered back to Bîr el Thamâda. As far as he was concerned, the war was over. Once in Bîr el Thamâda he took a shower, put on a clean uniform, lay down near his tank, and finally finished the letter to his wife that he had begun seventy-two hours earlier.

Toward the end of fierce fighting in the center of the peninsula, a figure leaped out of an Egyptian trench and was dashing toward the Israeli lines, when it was riddled with a burst of machine-gun fire. The soldiers who stopped to examine the body thought it was just another Egyptian soldier, shrugged their shoulders, and moved on, totally unaware that the man had been one of Israel's best spies planted in Nasser's army. Not having had time to reveal his true identity to the Israeli soldiers, he had paid with his life for his services to the Hebrew State.

At 2:05 P.M. the U.S. communications ship *Liberty* was cruising in the Mediterranean exactly seventeen nautical miles from the minaret of El 'Arîsh. The American Navy's secret files listed the *Liberty* as an "elint," that is, an electronic-intelligence ship. It carried three big supersensitive antennae capable of receiving any wireless message transmitted within a radius of 100 miles, and its crew included plenty of translators, code experts, and hand-picked information officers, whose assignments were to monitor the Israeli and Egyptian radio messages and to decode them. The ship reported directly to the C.I.A. and was thus independent of the rest of the fleet.

Suddenly two Israeli Mirages zoomed over the ship, dived, and fired on it with bombs and guns. Then three torpedo boats from the Israeli navy approached, signaling to *Liberty* to declare its identity, but they received no answer. In fact, *Liberty* seemed a phantom ship from some old legend of the sea: Not a soul was visible on its decks, there was no flag on its mast, and it was absolutely motionless. After the torpedo boats opened fire on this suspicious vessel, a sailor appeared on deck, ran toward the heavy machine guns, and returned the fire.

The Israeli gunners immediately shot and killed this solitary enemy and a moment later fired two torpedoes at *Liberty*. One struck it squarely and opened a gaping hole in the hull. The ship listed dangerously, but heavy steel bulkheads were immediately lowered to seal the gash, and the ship did not sink.

Then an oversized American flag went up the main mast of *Liberty*, revealing to the Israelis their ghastly error in thinking it an Egyptian ship. They were utterly astonished to find that they had fired on a ship of the U.S. Navy, for that very morning the commander of the 6th Fleet had informed them that no American ship was cruising near the coast. Their only excuse was that *Liberty* had refused to identify itself. Not until later was the unusual nature of the ship and its mission, which had been cloaked in mystery, revealed to them.

Now the Israeli captain asked, "Do you need help?"

"Go to hell!" was the Americans' immediate response.

The Israelis could do nothing but humbly apologize for their blunder, which had cost the lives of thirty-four American seamen. But the most sensational aspect of the misadventure was already causing a crisis thousands of miles away at the White House, where a little after 9:00 A.M. a laconic message was received: "American ship attacked and damaged in the Mediterranean."

President Johnson was in the situation room with Christian and some of his other advisers, including McNamara and Rusk, when the cable hit like a bomb.

"That's it!" Johnson exclaimed. "We are in it!"

From the very start of the fighting, the American leaders had been extremely apprehensive of what would happen if a Soviet ship attacked a ship of the 6th Fleet. If any unit of one of the great powers attacked, even by mistake, a vessel belonging to one of the others, it would very likely spark an armed conflict and perhaps even nuclear war between the two greatest powers. And now that very thing had happened.

McNamara, Rusk, and Johnson were certain that the American ship had been hit by a Soviet submarine. According to one witness to the scene, it was the most terrible moment of that whole critical period in June. The Russians had just attacked the United States. Johnson sat down and, in a voice faint with despair, said: "Twice in its history, this country has been provoked into war because American ships have been attacked and sunk. First, the *Maine,* then the *Lusitania.* And now. Perhaps they've gone and done it. Perhaps we're on the verge of World War III!"

At the same moment bright dots appeared on Soviet radar screens in the Mediterranean, indicating that dozens of American planes were taking off to put a protective curtain around *Liberty* and to retaliate against its attackers. The excitement in the White House reached a new peak. The whole American army, as well as the Strategic Air Command and perhaps even the American missile bases, had to be placed on the alert. Could it really be war? The next few moments were a nightmare.

Then a second cable arrived directly from the Israeli government, informing the President that the Israelis had attacked an American ship from the air and on the sea by mistake and were profoundly sorry for the unfortunate incident.

The President was dumbfounded. The Russians, perhaps even the Egyptians, might well indeed have attacked *Liberty* —but not the *Israelis*. Nonetheless, he heaved a great sigh of relief. At least the Russians had not attacked, and war would not follow.

But there was still another danger. Soviet ships in the Mediterranean had alerted Moscow to the sudden take-off toward Sinai of several dozen American planes, and the Soviets also had to be reassured. For the first time the United States was to use the hot line on its own initiative. Walt Rostow and McNamara hastily drafted a message to Kosygin, informing him that the Israelis had attacked an American ship in the Mediterranean by mistake and that American planes had taken off to defend it. The mission was a purely defensive one, and there was no intention of any hostile move against Soviet ships at sea or of any aid to the fighting forces in the Sinai peninsula.

To convince the Russians, Johnson added the text of the Israeli cable to his own message; a little later the Kremlin acknowledged receipt of his communication and accepted his version of the incident.

Strange rumors were circulating in Washington on June 8. It was declared certain that the Egyptian General Staff was dangerously unsettled and that some generals were planning to overthrow Nasser. General Dessouki, Chief of the 9th Armored Division, and General Sobhi, a field officer, were mentioned as conspirators.

The atmosphere in Cairo had changed greatly overnight. There was no more dancing in the streets. The radio continued to broadcast marches and victory bulletins, but no one any longer believed that Haifa was burning, Beersheba destroyed, or Tel Aviv in ruins. Englishmen and Americans shut themselves up in their houses to escape the mobs, for some had been beaten in the street for having lit cigarettes during the black-out "in order to signal the Zionist bombardiers."

As a matter of fact, Cairo had not been bombed, and if official announcements were to be believed, the Jews did not have a bomber left. But the rattle of the antiaircraft guns had not stopped, and from time to time planes bearing the colors of Israel flew low over the capital. When the radio broadcast that Egyptian troops "had attacked a squad of Israeli soldiers who were preparing to attack the Gaza Strip," the shrewder Cairenes recognized that Gaza had fallen to the enemy. When it was announced that "Israeli troops had been surrounded at El 'Arîsh," they concluded that El 'Arîsh, too, had fallen. A bulletin that "the Egyptian troops at Sharm el Sheikh had made contact with the majority of our forces in Sinai" meant that the garrison there had fled before the Zionists. And, when it was finally announced that "our troops have fallen back in order to encounter the enemy on the second line of defense," it was clear that the Egyptian army in the desert had been routed.

On the evening of June 7, Egypt had declared that it would not accept the cease-fire and would continue the war. This morning strong pressure was being exerted on the government to accept the cease-fire, and the Soviets were using all their influence on Nasser to that end. In fact, the Kremlin was finally acknowledging that Nasser's army was only a paper tiger. Radio Moscow was broadcasting no more bulletins about Arab victories; instead it broadcast official announcements from the Israeli army. When they learned that the Israeli force was approaching the Suez canal, the Soviet leaders did not conceal their alarm that it would cross the canal and advance on Cairo. The Soviet Ambassador in Cairo, as well as the Egyptian Ambassador in Moscow, were urgently requested to transmit to the U.A.R. government an appeal that it accept the cease-fire. The message let it be clearly understood that the Soviet Union would not intervene.

Nasser yielded. His army had been annihilated in the Sinai peninsula, and he had practically no troops left for resistance

to the Israelis. In desperation he asked Riad to instruct El
Kony to announce Egypt's acceptance of the cease-fire. With
tears in his eyes El Kony read a brief statement: "I have the
honor to inform you that, according to instructions from my
government, the U.A.R. has decided to end the fighting in
accordance with the resolution of the Security Council, on the
condition that the other side does the same."

The cease-fire was not announced on the Egyptian radio
until 11:30 P.M., when almost everyone was asleep.

At Egyptian General Staff headquarters in Heliopolis, Marshal Amer tried to commit suicide, but friends prevented him.

In El Qantara Israeli tank units and paratroopers mounted
their last attack on Egyptian units. Night was falling when
Colonel Shmuel's armored vehicles reached the canal opposite
Ismailia. All along the way they had fought the famous tanks
of Nasser's 4th Armored Division and had left behind them the
blazing remains of 100 Egyptian tanks.

About midnight Yoffe's tanks reached two spots on the canal.
Sharon's division had destroyed the Egyptian tanks that had
regrouped at Nakhl.

Israelis had taken the entire Sinai peninsula.

That evening the pilots of Ben Or's squadron were almost
convinced that the war was over for them. The fighting on the
Jordanian front had ended, and the Egyptian army had been
destroyed in Sinai. The Fouga squadron had accomplished all
it had set out to do, and Rabin personally thanked Arie for his
unit's fine work. It was time to celebrate.

The squadron opened up its secret stores, where several
bottles of cognac and whiskey had been stashed away. The
base commander produced twenty bottles of champagne for
the pilots. At nightfall a victory ball began at the Hotel Neot
Midbar.

Syria was the one serious problem still confronting Israeli
statesmen. It had in a sense been responsible for the crisis and
had created tension by sending al-Fatah terrorists into Israeli

territory. Syria's hatred for Israel was greater than that of any other Arab state. For nineteen years Syria had been bombing defenseless kibbutzim on the plain below its fortified block-houses. It had suffered less than the other Arab states after the Israeli victory of 1948 and had emerged unharmed from the 1956 fighting. Should it be spared again?

Since the beginning of the fighting the previous Monday, the Syrians had been bombing kibbutzim in Galilee. A few companies of infantry and armored vehicles had made mild attacks on Kibbutz Dan but had fled as soon as the Israelis counter-attacked. Since then the Syrians had preferred to stay well entrenched behind their impregnable fortifications and to rain tons of shells on the unprotected villages in the valley.

More than anyone else, Allon sympathized with the kib-butzim in the north. In order to persuade the government to mount an offensive against Syria, he had even organized a delegation from the bombed villages to demand from Eshkol an attack on the Syrian heights to put an end, once and for all, to the batteries that sent death into their homes. "This war cannot end leaving the Syrians unharmed," Eshkol was told by the delegation leaders. "If the Syrians keep the heights after the war, we will leave our villages and seek peace elsewhere."

Eshkol and several other ministers believed that a broad military operation should be organized against Syria. The only person who opposed it was Dayan. Dayan had good reasons. Memories of 1956 haunted him, especially what had happened at Port Said when that city was conquered by the French and British. The Soviet Consul had come to see the prominent citizens of the city and had told them, "Don't surrender, and don't sign a cease-fire, even if you can't go on fighting."

Dayan did not yet know that Egypt had already accepted the cease-fire. "What will happen," he wondered, "if Egypt refuses to stop fighting in spite of our victory in Sinai? We would be obliged to keep a large army on the Egyptian front for perhaps a long time. Furthermore, we still do not have enough troops to open an offensive on the Syrian front. We would have to shift what troops may be available from fronts in the north where there is no trouble, but even if we did assemble enough reinforcements from those sources to be able to strike against Syria, what would happen then, if Syria and Egypt do not accept the cease-fire and our army is spread out on two fronts hundreds of miles distant from each other?"

Dayan was also afraid of Soviet action if such moves were made against Syria. Several experts had emphasized how dear Syria was to Moscow's heart, and the Soviets had many times promised to defend Syria against aggression from any source. The U.S.S.R. would intervene militarily to help the Syrians— and Israel had no assurance that Soviet intervention in a limited area and for an unspecified time would produce American help for Israel.

Such were the reasons for Dayan's categorical "no!"

Late that night the meeting of the war cabinet broke up. Syria was not to be attacked, and the indications were that it would escape the fate of Jordan and Egypt.

•

REVOLT IN THE EAST

DAYAN SPENT THURSDAY night on his cot in the operations room. At 6:00 A.M. June 9 he awoke and asked for the latest news. His aide brought him the most important cable of those that had arrived during the night: Egypt had accepted the cease-fire. Nasser's decision removed the specter of a long war that had so worried Dayan. He asked where Rabin was. The Chief of Staff was not there, and neither was General Weizmann.

"Get me Dado on the telephone," Dayan ordered. Dado, whose real name was David Elazar, was the general in command of the northern front. Before Dayan reached Elazar he received other reports, from which he gathered that the Syrians were increasing their bombing of the villages in Galilee.

"Dado," Dayan said, "you've got the green light. Take the Syrian plateau."

"The whole thing?"

"The whole thing."

Eshkol's secretary told him of Dayan's order, which required his immediate endorsement. Eshkol's first reaction was a burst of anger, for Dayan, who on the previous day had been unalterably opposed to an attack on Syria, had now changed his mind and ordered one without consulting the Premier. Eshkol had no choice but to confirm Dayan's order and finally, though with poor grace, informed Dayan that he agreed. "I'm not going to order the troops back," he muttered.

At 9:40 waves of Israeli planes dived on the Syrian plateau and pounded the fortified positions. At noon, tanks, infantry units, and paratroopers launched an attack on the heights under a rain of Syrian shells.

The Syrian plateau is like a big table towering above the entire surrounding region. On the north this table reaches to the slopes of Mount Hermon; on the south and the west it ends in steep slopes. The Israelis could approach only from the west, and it was on the west that the Syrians were waiting for them.

The Israeli tanks and commandos began their attack at five different points simultaneously. The terrain differed vastly from that of the Sinai peninsula; if the Egyptian fortifications had seemed impregnable, the Syrians' were much more so. The whole plateau seemed to be a single great fortress with underground bunkers of several stories, thick concrete barriers, endless trenches and blockhouses, mine fields, and artillery and tank positions. To the rear, in the town of El Quneitra, Russian artillery officers and instructors were stationed to direct the Syrian troops. Their instructions and orders could be clearly heard on the Israeli receiving sets.

At lunch Yonina Ben Or was reading *Combat Journal*, the daily paper issued by the air force during the battle, when she came upon a long interview buried in the middle pages with "Commander Arie of the Fouga Squadron":

> We feel that we are fighting on the soil of the land of our ancient inheritance. It is a very moving experience to be flying over Hebron and Jericho and Bethlehem. Three thousand years ago, Joshua captured Jericho. We are capturing it now for the second time. I admit that I am deeply moved. I didn't know how deep within me were the feelings about these places, the cradle of the Jewish people. I would like my children to visit all these places where the Jewish people have dwelt, and I myself would like to visit them once the war is over.

These words touched Yonina Ben Or. It was 1:30 P.M. At that very moment her husband was in his Fouga diving on a fortified Syrian artillery position in the center of the plateau. An antiaircraft shell struck him, and his plane crashed on the rocks below.

The countries of the Soviet bloc were officially supporting the Arab cause, but their leaders were worried. For the first time in many years the policy was encountering active opposition from their people in general, from intellectuals, and from parts of their armies. These groups openly sympathized with Israel in its struggle against the Arab states.

In Poland there were spontaneous demonstrations in favor of Israel, which Jews and non-Jews alike hoped would win. Quite a large number of high officials, even some Polish ministers, refused to consider Israel the aggressor. High army officers steadfastly refused to disseminate propaganda on the theme of "Israeli aggression" among their troops. General Mankiewicz, commander in chief of the air force; Brigadier General Dombakovski, Chief of Staff; and his assistant, Brigadier General Staniavski, refused to circulate propaganda material against Israel in the air bases.* Other highranking officers, especially in the air force and the armored divisions, did not hesitate to speak out in meetings of the party leaders, prophesying a "real revolt of the army."

In Czechoslovakia reporters and editorial writers refused to sign petitions condemning Israel or to publish articles against Israel in the daily papers. One of the best-known, Ladislas Mnaçko, even left Czechoslovakia for Israel in a gesture of protest against the attitude of the authorities against Israel's just war. In Hungary intellectuals and ordinary citizens proclaimed their solidarity with the Israelis, and the Israeli embassy in Budapest received many letters, most of them anonymous, from Hungarians who offered their best wishes for an Israeli victory. The Romanian government, unlike its "sister nations," openly refused to take an anti-Israel position. Serious crises shook the Communist parties in Western Europe, for many of their militant members were sympathetic to Israel.

---

* After the war they were relieved of their command because of that refusal.

Two days earlier the Soviet Union had threatened Israel with severing of diplomatic relations if its aggression continued. But the heads of the Communist nations in Europe were meeting in Moscow in the greatest secrecy, in order to work out a policy that they could all adopt toward Israel. All the big Communist leaders were there: Antonin Novotny, Zhivkov, Janos Kadar, Gomulka, Ceausescu, and their foreign ministers. For the first time in several years Yugoslavia was also represented in a meeting of this kind; Marshal Tito had come to Moscow, less from friendship with the Kremlin than from loyalty to his personal friend Nasser.

Tito acted as prosecuting attorney in the twelve-hour meeting, severely criticizing the Soviets for their refusal to aid the Arabs. After a long debate seven Communist countries issued a long statement in which they proclaimed their solidarity with the Arab cause and promised to help the Arab countries in the event that Israel continued its aggression. But the statement carefully avoided any allusion to the possible use of force against Israel. Only one country refused to sign the statement—Romania.

During the meeting one secret decision was taken: As soon as their governments had given formal approval, the socialist countries would sever diplomatic relations with Israel. Again Romania refused to join them.

"They did not listen to France!" De Gaulle thundered. The President of the French Republic did not conceal from his guest the anger he felt toward Israel. "I told Eban," he said, "that they should not be the first to fire. They did not listen to me!"

Before the fighting had begun, De Gaulle had been afraid that another Vietnam or even a nuclear war among the great powers would result. He had been sure that even if the Israelis won some victories they would eventually be defeated by the Arabs. But once Israel's victory was an established fact he had a new theory for his close friend. "During the crisis itself," he said, "Israel's survival was never threatened. But Israel is an imperialist country that dreams of conquest. It has been conducting an aggressive war, for it saw a chance to increase its territory and occupy vast stretches of land. When I received Ben-Gurion here in Paris, he strengthened my belief that Israel was aspiring to larger territory and greater population and that it would seize the first opportunity to start a war of conquest.*

"Israel must withdraw from the territory it has seized. Otherwise, there will be no chance whatever for a settlement of the disputes between Israel and the Arab countries. But if I were in the Israelis' shoes, I would not budge from those territories. They are now good securities.

"France must align itself with the Arabs. France is a Muslim power. It has vital interests with the tens of millions of Arabs. We must be sure of our supply of oil for a long time to come. Some day the West will thank me again for this policy of mine, for France will be now, and for a long time to come, the only Western power to have any influence with the Arab governments.

"The U.S.S.R. and France will now proceed to consolidate

* General de Gaulle's version of his conversation with Ben-Gurion is inaccurate to say the least. In my book, *Ben-Gurion: The Armed Prophet* (Prentice-Hall, Englewood Cliffs: 1968), p. 253, I reported the conference of June 13, 1960, between the two men as follows: "While having coffee outside under the trees, De Gaulle leaned towards Ben-Gurion and asked smilingly: '*Monsieur le Président,* tell me truthfully, what are your real ambitions for the frontiers of Israel? I promise I'll keep it secret.'

"'If you had asked me that question fifteen years ago,' Ben-Gurion replied, 'I should have answered—I want the State of Israel to include the whole of Jordan and to extend as far north as the river Litani, in the Lebanon. But as you've asked me today, I'll tell you quite frankly that I am more concerned with immigration, development and peace. We will be satisfied with our present frontiers in order to avoid exposing our young people to danger. We need very many immigrants, for Israel is the land of all Jewish people.'

"De Gaulle called to his Foreign Minister, Couve de Murville, and Michel Debré to come over. 'Imagine that!' he said to them, Prime Minister Ben-Gurion is not a bit satisfied with two million Jews. He wants to double that number at least. Men are more important to him than territory.'"

their positions in the Middle East. The real loser will be Great Britain. The closing of the Suez canal will have a serious effect on its economy. France will gain, for Great Britain's economic crisis will weaken the British position on the European scene and in the struggle between Great Britain and France in respect to the Common Market."

At 9:30 P.M. a soldier rapped on Yonina Ben Or's door and asked her to step outside for a moment. The garden was dark because of the blackout. Taking a flashlight from his pocket, an air force officer came up to Yonina and took her arm. "I am Dr. Baruch," he said bluntly, "and it is my painful duty to inform you that your husband has fallen in combat."

Yonina's whole body stiffened. Gently he pushed her forward and walked by her side in the darkness. After a long silence she asked: "Where did it happen? When?"

She did not weep, and she did not awaken her children. She only asked that Ben Or's parents not be told until the next day. "His mother," she said, "is doomed to long years of suffering. Arie was her only son. Let her get one last night of good sleep."

During the night Cairo had changed in appearance. Signboards calling for the total destruction of Israel had disappeared, and so had the street-corner effigies of Jews and Americans hanging from gallows. Armed soldiers were stationed in the center of the city and on the bridges over the Nile. Angry crowds thronged the streets and demonstrated before the Soviet embassy, shaking their fists and shouting, "Why did you desert us?"

In the Sinai peninsula the guns were silent. On the other side of the narrow ribbon of water known as the Suez canal, Jewish soldiers could be seen moving into positions that overlooked Ismailia, El Qantara, and the very heart of Egypt itself.

The Egyptian General Staff met in Heliopolis to utter some hard truths. The field officers hurled charges at one another. General Murtaghi, chief of the ground forces, blamed Marshal Mahmoud, chief of the air force. War Minister Badran received his share of the criticism also. The most honorable of all the officers was once again Marshal Amer, who shouldered the blame for the "waiting strategy." It was he who had directed the fighting during the first two days of the war. Nasser had had complete confidence in him and had entrusted him with planning all the military operations. Amer was the only one who did not try to shift the blame to someone else.

Nasser was present during part of the meeting. The rest of that morning he spent with a select committee of his advisers. The man who had been the idol of the Arab world until the day before was the picture of defeat, the laughingstock of the world, deserted even by his Soviet allies, who had not been willing to fight to save him. Worse yet, his military defeat threatened his personal power. Bitter crowds in the Cairo streets were shouting insults at him; ministers and army officers were openly accusing him of having brought about their ruin. His worst enemies had gone over to the extreme left wing of the single party, the Arab Socialist Union, whose leader was Ali Sabry. Some of the political and military leaders were blaming Nasser not only for the defeat but also for having accepted the cease-fire. They had favored fighting to the bitter end.

Nasser stood in need of all his shrewdness and every trick in his bag of political magic to keep himself in power. That evening he appeared on television, looking tired and depressed, to deliver a long speech on the fundamental reasons for the defeat, for which he took the entire responsibility. Then he uttered the words that astounded millions of watching Egyptians: "Nasser resigns!"

He designated as his successor his deputy Mohieddin.

Egypt was plunged into despair. By the hundreds of thousands, Egyptians ran out of their houses into the streets and swarmed over Cairo, weeping and shouting: "Nasser, Nasser, don't abandon us! Don't leave us!" Foreign correspondents still in the city were completely astonished by the sight of an entire nation stricken with sorrow and despair. Many demonstrations were not exactly spontaneous. Barely a few minutes after

Nasser had finished his speech, trucks full of workers, farmers, and young people appeared in the suburbs, waving banners inscribed with slogans. They were the people who had paraded to demand Nasser's return to power. It seems that a part of the "spontaneous" demonstrations had been staged and well rehearsed.

While Cairo was rumbling, the last act in the final battle for power was being played out. Mohieddin, the heir presumptive, had learned of Nasser's resignation only through the televised speech. In utter astonishment he had gone to Nasser's house to refuse the Presidency. As he threaded his way through the street crowds, he heard shouts of abuse. Presently, his colleague Mohammed Fayek also arrived at Nasser's house in Minshat al-Bakhari, his clothes torn by a mob that had mistaken him for Mohieddin and had almost lynched him.

Nasser's rivals had sought his resignation, but they had been caught unaware by his unexpected announcement and by the reaction of the people. Now they were attempting to stem the pro-Nasser tide sweeping over Cairo. Some officials telephoned the broadcasting station to say that Mohieddin would make a speech in a few hours. It was, of course, a bluff.

Other officials tried to stop the demonstrations that were strengthening Nasser's position. Suddenly the deafening scream of the air-raid sirens sounded in almost all parts of the city, and the antiaircraft guns began firing, to create the impression that the war was beginning again and that the Zionists were attacking Cairo.

The trick failed. The mobs did not disperse, and the demonstrations continued late into the night. Finally, three hours after he had resigned, Nasser declared that he would reconsider and would announce his final decision the following morning in a speech before the National Assembly. Half an hour later Amer and Badran announced their resignations. Nasser had found scapegoats for his defeat.

•

HOT-LINE ULTIMATUM

"THE BLACKS ARE running away!"

This was the message, in Russian, that Israel's radio receivers intercepted that morning on the Syrian front. It reflected the deep contempt the Soviet instructors had for the Syrian soldiers. It proved, moreover, that the Syrian front was beginning to collapse.

Israeli units were invading the Syrian plateau from all sides, and one brigade had planted the Israeli flag on the snowy slopes of Mount Hermon. One armored unit was advancing on El Quneitra. The Russian instructors were the first to scurry out of town; they were followed by Syrian soldiers fleeing in terror to Damascus. The previous day they had fought bravely in their trenches, but on June 10 they were running for their lives.

About noon Israeli leaders acknowledged that, as far as they were concerned, the last grains of sand were trickling through the diplomatic hourglass.

That week Walt Rostow had spent two nights in the White House on a cot that had been moved into his office. On Tuesday he had had to give up his tennis game. He had barely begun to play on this morning of June 10 when he received an emergency call from the situation room.

"We've just had a message over the hot line," he was told. Rostow ran to the basement of the White House.

259

The Israelis had penetrated deep into Syrian territory, and the U.S.S.R. was determined to rescue its Arabian Cuba. Kosygin had just sent word that if the Israelis did not stop their aggression against Syria at once, the Soviet Union would intervene in the fighting, as the Israeli army presently on the road to Damascus intended to overthrow the "democratic" regime of Syria. That the U.S.S.R. would not tolerate. Orders had been given to the Soviet armed forces, which would go into action immediately. The Soviet representative in the United Nations, Nikolai Fedorenko, had received instructions to inform the Security Council that, if Israel did not cease firing at once, his government would take "all necessary action to end the aggression and punish the aggressor."

The White House realized that Israel had to be stopped. Already the fighting on the Syrian front had caused much alarm in Washington. Rusk had telephoned Harman, and Walt Rostow had requested details on the military situation from Evron. There was no time to lose.

An emergency telephone call instructed Ambassador Barbour in Tel Aviv to intervene with the Israelis and to demand that they cease firing as quickly as possible. (Although only a few days earlier, State Department experts had been asking Israel every morning, "When are you going to attack Syria?"* If there was one regime that the United States would have liked to see toppled, it was the pro-Communist government in Damascus.) But everything had changed; the Russians were about to make their move.

Chairman of the Joint Chiefs of Staff General Wheeler was unmoved. "We have nothing to fear from Soviet action," he told one of his friends that morning. "The Soviets have no large mobile units to put into action at once in the Middle Eastern war. They have alerted their paratrooper divisions, but they know how dangerous it would be to put them into action."

Israeli Ambassador to the Soviet Union Katz made his usual appearance in the great synagogue of Moscow that morning.

* Interviews with several high officials of the State Department.

When he had last worshiped there, the previous Saturday, many Jews had come to shake his hand and to express anxiety and hope for Israel's future. But on June 10 no one came up to him, no one shook his hand, and no one spoke to him. The turned backs and the non-seeing eyes expressed the general feeling of fear.

No sooner had Katz returned to the embassy than his telephone rang, calling him to an emergency meeting at the Foreign Ministry, where Gromyko's deputy, Anatoly Kuznetzov, was expecting him. He and the Director of the Middle Eastern Department of the Foreign Ministry Chiburin, greeted Katz and asked him to sit down. Then Kuznetzov took up a paper and read aloud the text of the Soviet decision to sever diplomatic relations with Israel.

"What date have you set for our departure?" Katz asked.

"The earliest possible," replied Kuznetzov.

After a moment's pause the two men shook hands and parted.

When he returned to the embassy, Katz saw that a police cordon had been placed around the building and that a crowd was gathering outside. At a given signal the mob began to shout anti-Israel slogans and to brandish placards and banners. As if in an ecclesiastical ritual, three lines of policemen took their places at the door of the embassy. The crowd took their cue from this balletic procedure and surged gently against the policemen, who locked arms to restrain them. After an hour had passed one of the policemen looked at his watch and gave an order. The crowd moved peacefully away.

During the next few days other Communist countries—Bulgaria, Hungary, Czechoslovakia, Poland, and Yugoslavia—also broke relations with Israel.

During a special session of the Egyptian National Assembly, Nasser announced that, in response to the wishes of his people, he would stay in office. In the streets of Cairo there were demonstrations of tens of thousands of Cairenes, workers, and fellahin in white robes waving palms. The National Assembly granted Nasser special powers, of which he stood in great need, for in the space of a few hours he had succeeded in completely reversing the entire situation. Now his power in Egypt was greater than ever, but the hour had come for him to settle his score with the previous day's rebels against him.

Nasser ordered the high command to recall on an emergency basis some units of the crack troops in Yemen. He left Sabry and his friends in the government alone, for they were too strong for him. Instead he skillfully divided power between Mohieddin, the leader of the moderates, and Sabry, the extremist, in order to neutralize both. He placed under house arrest the group of officials who had taken part in the mini-conspiracy of the previous day and then requested the resignations of several generals, among whom were the chiefs of the air force and navy. The army, headed by Amer, was to pay the bill for the 10,000 corpses that littered the sands of Sinai.

A storm was brewing in the Security Council. Since 4:30 A.M. the delegates had been sitting in special session while Syrian delegate George Tomeh performed for his colleagues and millions of television viewers. Every five minutes one of his aides would burst into the hall and slip him a piece of paper, which he would read aloud in an emotional voice: "El Quneitra is in the hands of the Zionists! They are bombing our capital city! They are already in the suburbs of Damascus, the pearl of the East! The aggressors want to conquer our whole country!"

Fedorenko delivered an ill-tempered harangue against Israel, which he compared to Nazi Germany, and accused its leaders of crimes against humanity. Rafael retorted, "It was not we who signed a pact with Hitler."

Goldberg did his bit. As one member of the American delegation put it, "After Rafael had played the *Eroica Symphony* in the Security Council, Goldberg could hardly play a polka." Fedorenko and Goldberg traded verbal blows; the Soviet delegate called Goldberg a provincial lawyer, and the American returned the compliment with a sarcastic "My learned friend, Professor Fedorenko."

During that exchange Eshkol was conferring with Dayan in

Galilee near the advance command post of General Elazar,
who was directing the battle on the Syrian plateau. They knew
that every second counted. Dayan turned to one of his aides
and ordered, "Get in touch with General Bull and arrange a
meeting with him at once."

At 9:30 A.M. New York time, Goldberg asked Rafael to meet
with him outside the Council chamber. Goldberg had just
heard by telephone from the White House news of the Soviet
hot-line ultimatum.

"The situation is extremely serious," Goldberg told Rafael.
"In a few minutes the Soviet delegate is going to announce that
his government will intervene militarily in the Middle East if
you do not halt your advance. The United States cannot ignore
such a declaration. No matter what the cost, the war must now
end, even if the threat is not carried out. As everyone will think
that Israel and the United States capitulated in the face of the
Soviet ultimatum, you must immediately announce that your
country accepts the cease-fire."

"But I can't do that. I have no instructions to do so."

"Then do it on your own responsibility. Every second
counts."

Just then one of Rafael's aides came out of the Council
chamber and told him that Fedorenko had asked for the floor.
Then Rafael was called to the telephone. A high official of the
Foreign Ministry was calling from Tel Aviv to inform him that
at that very moment, Dayan had told General Bull of Israel's
willingness to cease firing. Bull had set the time for the cease-
fire at 6:30 P.M. (12:30 P.M. New York time).

Rafael ran to the Security Council, where he went up to
President Tabor and whispered to him: "I must have the floor. I
have a very important announcement to make."

According to the rules of the Security Council, a nonmember
country, as Israel was at that time, had no right to take the
floor until after the representatives of member countries had
spoken. Rafael would therefore have had to wait until after the
other delegates, including Fedorenko, had finished. Tabor decided to suspend the rule.

Slowly Rafael read the message from Israel. "Please forgive

me for being so slow," he said, "but I must translate from the Hebrew at sight. . . . We have just accepted the cease-fire and an agreement has been reached with General Bull."

The Soviets could not hide their disappointment at having the wind taken out of their sails. Fedorenko pouted in anger. Rafael commented, "I have the impression that the distinguished delegate of the Soviet Union is quite disappointed to learn that the war has come to an end."

At 6:30 P.M. paratroopers who had been transported into Syria by helicopters stopped firing. They had just captured the road junction of Butmiye on the Syrian plateau. El Quneitra had fallen during the afternoon without a battle. The Syrian plateau was in Israeli hands, and the Six-Day War was over.

Shukairy reached Beirut that evening after a long, hard, and sorrowful journey. The first shots of the war had taken him by surprise in Jerusalem, and on the same day he had fled to Amman. When the Jews had neared Jordan he had run to Damascus. As soon as the Israelis had approached Damascus, he had hightailed it to Lebanon.

In Jerusalem paratroop officers were searching for the "White Angel." No one knew her name, but tiny Esther Arditi had already become a legendary figure.

At Sharm el Sheikh, the soldiers were welcoming *Dolphin*, which had just passed through the strait of Tiran. It was the first Israeli ship to negotiate the strait since Nasser had closed it.

At the moment when the cease-fire became effective, Dayan was in the operations room of General Staff headquarters. "The war is not yet over," he said thoughtfully. "I am afraid that sooner or later the fighting will begin again."

About 700 Israeli soldiers had been killed on all three fronts. At the Suez canal Colonel Shmuel addressed his troops: "You have looked death in the face," he said, "and death has turned its eyes away." To a group of correspondents who came for information, Shmuel said: "Do you want to know what this victory cost me? Seventy of my boys, my best soldiers!"

"But, Colonel, you destroyed hundreds of tanks and killed thousands of Egyptian soldiers."

"Seventy boys!" repeated Shmuel. "Gone!"

At Kefar Menahem Mrs. Tikva Ben Horin was asked to come to the administration building. She knew that something bad must have happened. "I have two sons in the army," she said. "Tell me, which one is it?"

The secretary answered, "Both."

As night fell on the Suez canal, Amos Katz's driver lit a little alcohol stove, opened two boxes of rations, made dinner, and poured hot tea into the tin cups. Katz climbed out of his tank, and both men ate in silence, saddened by news of the deaths of several comrades. Katz did not know that at headquarters everyone thought he too had been killed. He had disappeared, his company had been scattered, and no one knew what had happened to him. Soldiers kept saying to one another, "They got Amos Katz."

In two weeks, Amos Katz celebrated his wedding to Jenny. It was she who got him in the end.

Deep in the desert near Bîr el Thamâda, a squad of kibbutz-born commandos were celebrating the end of the war around a wood fire. Twenty boys were sitting in a circle while one cooked huge omelets over a little stove. A coffeepot was sizzling in the middle of the fire. Guy Jacobson was one of the commandos' guests. Together they sang the songs of the pioneers and of the War of Independence, songs that they had almost forgotten over the years.

A cold wind swept over the desert as Jacobson spoke of Jerusalem. "The reunification of Jerusalem," he said, "is the greatest achievement of this war, which has been crowned by

the capture of the Old City. Jerusalem gives our war an historical dimension, a sublime character, a taste of eternity."

In the government printing office in Cairo, the presses were
turning out a new Egyptian postage stamp. It had been designed only a week earlier, two days before the war had begun,
when victory had seemed in sight, luck favorable and Allah on
Nasser's side. The stamp showed Nasser smiling confidently
and bowing to a sea of cheering human beings; in one corner
Israel appeared in flames. The inscription on the stamp read,
"Arab unity for the defense of Palestine."

The stamp was ready, but it was too late—six days too
late.

CONCLUSION

AT THE END of the war, General Dayan said: "Now I expect a telephone call from the Arabs."

No such call ever came. The Arabs consistently refused to make peace with Israel, and all the evidence points to the probability that the Six-Day War will not be the last one. Others, perhaps even bloodier ones, will probably break out in the Middle East. Peace is not expected tomorrow.

The June 1967 war is an indication of the true state of the relations between the Israelis and the Arabs. Deep hatred of the Israeli nation motivates the latter, who still aim at conquering and obliterating the Jewish state. The Jewish state is the stronger. The last war proved, to the astonishment of the Israelis themselves, that the Arabs will not surpass them, at least militarily speaking.

Peace will come to the Middle East when the Arabs accept the existence of Israel. The Israelis do not ask the Arabs to begin to love them from one day to the next, or subscribe to the Zionist ideal; they simply ask them to understand the one simple fact that Israel is a reality than can neither be conquered nor wiped off the map. Friendship and mutual understanding cannot be achieved until much later, for the wounds of the Arabs will not heal for many long years.

The Arabs still refuse to acknowledge that Israel does, in fact, exist. They go on dreaming of a day of vengeance when they will expel or kill all Zionists.

The principal obstacle to the reconciliation of the Jews and the Arabs is the psychological barrier between the two nations. Several times, President Bourguiba has criticized the state of mind of the Arab people of the Middle East as a mixture of fantasy and reality, emotions and half-truths, and a lack of clear, simple logic. That disposition in particular still keeps the Arabs from acknowledging, as the rest of the world admits, that Israel is a strong nation which its neighbors cannot destroy either now or within several years. Already the Arab leaders in Amman, Bagdad, Cairo, and Damascus are promising their people a fourth round.

Because of that attitude, the main roads to peace are barred. To be sure, Israel will have to make some concessions if that peace is to be achieved, but we have not yet reached a point where that might be possible. To make concessions, there must be someone to talk to, and the Arabs refuse to talk. For the Arabs to recognize the existence of Israel, a long, slow, painful process is necessary. It is much to be feared that they will undertake other wars before making the simple admission that Israel is here in their midst, and they cannot destroy it, and so should find a way to coexist with it.

Those who advise the peoples of the Middle East to live in peace frequently refer to the reconciliation of the French and the Germans—which took several wars to achieve. Forgotten is the fact that the Germans and the French are two peoples of Western Europe who have a common civilization and a common cultural and historical heritage, who are at the same level of development, and who can understand each other. Jews and Arabs are perhaps of the same origin, but they represent two entirely different worlds: on the one hand is a small, westernized, homogenous nation at a high level of technical development; on the other hand are peoples largely underdeveloped and of an utterly different civilization.

If these two worlds still cannot understand each other, it can be sensibly assumed that at least they can learn to coexist. Unfortunately for their neighbor, and especially for themselves, the Arab states of the Middle East do not act sensibly but emotionally. The clearest proof of that fact is the Six-Day War itself, which broke out for no sound reason after a ridiculous sequence of events.

The Israelis have no illusions about the future. They want to live in peace with their neighbors. To achieve such peace, they want to bargain, and bargain they must. They must make some vital concessions. The great majority of Israelis are ready to do so in order to achieve peace with the Arabs, but the Arabs are still dreaming of destroying Israel. Until they recognize that Israel will not just disappear like some modern Crusaders' Kingdom of Jerusalem, they will keep fomenting new wars.

Israel knows that for long years to come it will be paying for its survival with its blood. But even at such a price, the Israelis would not exchange their little piece of earth for all the paradises of the world.

THE SIX-DAY War has produced a great deal of literature, some of which is listed in this bibliography. I have also examined and used articles on the war published in Israeli, French, British, and American newspapers and magazines. I have pored through massive documentation: official papers, maps, and transcripts of speeches.

I have, however, relied most heavily on information supplied by more than 200 people whom I interviewed in Israel, Europe, and the United States and on confidential papers that they supplied to me. In many cases I was sworn to secrecy about the identities of the officials whom I interviewed—especially in France, Great Britain, and the United States—and I can therefore, give only very incomplete identifications here. I thank everyone, whether mentioned or not, who helped me prepare this book.

INTERVIEWS

Israel
Ministers and high officials of the Israeli government; Israeli ambassadors and diplomats in Europe and the United States; generals and officers of the Israeli army, both active and reserve; officials of the public-information office of the Israeli army; reporters, editorial writers, and commentators.

Esther Arditi   Guy Jacobson
Yonina Ben Or   Amos Katz

France

High officials interviewed November 9–30, 1967.

Great Britain

High officials interviewed January 15–30, 1968.

United States

Lucius D. Battle, Assistant Secretary of State for Middle Eastern and South Asian Affairs

Daniel Brown, State Department, Middle East Division

George Christian, White House Press Secretary

Messrs. Day and Smith, State Department, U.N. Division

Eli Eyal, Washington correspondent of *Ha'aretz* (Tel Aviv)

Philippe Ben, New York correspondent of *Le Monde* (Paris)

Miss Kay Folger, State Department

Max Finger, Arthur Goldberg's deputy in the United Nations

Dan Henkin, Assistant Undersecretary of Defense attached to the Pentagon

Roderick MacLeish, Westinghouse Broadcasting Company

Robert McCloskey, official State Dept. spokesman

Richard H. Nolte, former U.S. Ambassador to Egypt

Gideon Rafael, Israeli Ambassador to the United Nations

Eugene Rostow, Undersecretary of State (interviewed with his assistant, Robert Gray)

Walter W. Rostow, President Johnson's adviser on national security

Bernard Reich

Harold Saunders, Walt Rostow's assistant at the White House

William Stricker, Foreign Correspondents Center, New York

Senator Stuart Symington

Shlomo Shafir, Washington correspondent of the *Davar* (Tel Aviv)

Leon Volkov, *Newsweek* specialist on Soviet problems

Charles Yost, special State Department emissary to Cairo during May 1967 crisis

Officials of the State Department, the Pentagon, and the White House, whose names I cannot mention; officials of the U.N. Secretariat in New York; and Israeli diplomats in the United States, all interviewed October 20–November 8, 1967.

REFERENCES

Allô Tel-Aviv, Allô Le Caïre, Ici Europe No. 1. Paris: Laffont, 1967.

Associated Press. *Lightning Out of Israel.* Englewood Cliffs, N.J.: Prentice-Hall, Inc., 1967

Besançon, Julien. *Bazak: la guerre d'Israël.* Paris: Seuil, 1967.

Churchill, Randolph, and Winston Churchill. *The Six Day War.* London: Heinemann, 1967.

Dayan, Yaël. *Israel Journal: June, 1967.* New York: McGraw-Hill, 1967.

Donovan, Robert. *Israel's Fight for Survival.* New York: New American Library, 1967.

Herzog, H. *Israel's Finest Hour.* Tel Aviv: Ma'ariv, 1967.

Hewat, Tim. *War File.* London: Panther, 1967.

Holy War, The. London: *The Sunday Times,* 1967.

MacLeish, Roderick. *The Sun Stood Still.* New York: Atheneum, 1967.

Marshall, S. L. A. *Swift Sword.* New York: U.P.I., 1967.

Rouleau, Eric, Jean-Francis Held, Jean Lacouture, and Simone Lacouture. *Israël et les Arabes, le Troisième Combat.* Paris: Seuil, 1967.

Schiff, Zeev, and Eliahu Ben Elissar. *La guerre israélo-arabe.* Paris: Julliard, 1967.

Seguev, Samuel. *La Guerre de Six Jours.* Paris: Calmann-Lévy, 1967.

Stevenson, William. *Strike, Zion.* New York: Bantam, 1967.

Trost, Ernest. *David et Goliath.* Paris: Buchet Chastel, 1967.

Victory, The. Tel Aviv: Levin-Epstein, 1967.

War, The. Tel Aviv: Ma'ariv, 1967.

Works in Hebrew

Nakdimon, S. *H-Hour.* Tel Aviv: Ramador, 1968.

Six-Day War, The. Tel Aviv: Israeli Army, 1967.

Tevet, S. *Hassufim Batzariach.* Tel Aviv: Schocken, 1968.

INDEX

DATE DUE